# THE DEATH OF CLASS

Jan Pakulski and Malcolm Waters

D1333845

## SAGE Publications

London • Thousand Oaks • New Delhi

SAGE Publications Ltd
6 Bonhill Street
London EC2A 4PU

SAGE Publications Inc
2455 Teller Road
Thousand Oaks, California 91320

SAGE Publications India Pvt Ltd
32, M-Block Market
Greater Kailash – I
New Delhi 110 048

**British Library Cataloguing in Publication data**

A catalogue record for this book is
available from the British Library

ISBN 0 8039 7838 3
ISBN 0 8039 7839 1 (pbk)

**Library of Congress catalog card number 95–071985**

Typeset by M Rules
Printed in Great Britain by The Cromwell Press Ltd,
Broughton Gifford, Melksham, Wiltshire

# Contents

# Preface

This book is an admission of hypocrisy. We have written a book about class while being committed to the view that books about class should no longer be written. We might defend it on the grounds that class is a historically relevant concept and that we have written a history of the life and death of class. However, we also intend it to be a pronouncement of the last rites on the demise of a faithful theoretical and conceptual servant. We believe not that class theory and analysis were a waste of intellectual effort but rather that their season and purpose have come to an end.

We have not arrived at our funereal position easily. We are in the middle of careers in sociology that until now have maintained a deep if increasingly uncertain commitment to the salience of class that is grounded at least as much in our own early biographical experiences, within differing cultural contexts, as in our training. As late as 1993 Pakulski published a paper in *International Sociology* that could still find some room for class analysis. Waters published a text on how to analyse class in 1990 and his most cited paper on the topic, published in *Theory and Society* in 1991, affirms a happy convergence between various theories of class. The key turning point for each of us was the collaborative effort we made with Stephen Crook in writing our book *Postmodernization* published by Sage in 1992. In that book we addressed directly the issue of whether 'new times' were on the way and first seriously considered whether an era of class relevance was finally coming to an end. This book is an expansion and elaboration of many of the themes that were engaged in Chapters 4, 5 and 6 of that book.

Our respective conversions were also driven by an increasing awareness of changing academic and public agendas. Since 1958 many brave souls have had the nerve to ask about the emperor's clothes, old and new. As a consequence very many vigorous debates are prosecuted in the learned journals. We have drawn support from them, but in taking up an 'anti-class' position we continue to insist on a respect for our opponents, many of whom are far more accomplished social scientists than ourselves. However, the world is changing. The social context is now very different from that in which sociology was formed and in which our generation was socialized. It is simply, for us, an obvious truth that class can no longer give us purchase on the big social, political and cultural issues of the age. For Pakulski, in particular, the decomposition of the major political bloc that was committed to the class paradigm represents an auspicious confirmation of the possibilities of a social science without class.

The reviews of *Postmodernization*, which were more generous than we could have hoped for, occasionally accused us of an unrealistic utopianism in relation to class and we suppose that we must brace ourselves for similar assaults on the basis of this altogether more explicitly entitled volume. As we say from time to time in the text, we insist on pleading 'not guilty' and believe that a careful reading of what we have to say will acquit us. Once more for the record, we take the view that advanced societies are riven by unacceptable divisions of inequality, conflict and domination that are often marked by coercive or exploitative practices. However, they can no longer be sheeted home to class and any insistence in sociology that class should be our primary focus will divert attention from these conditions and thus hinder our understanding of contemporary social processes.

The book is a joint effort and each of us fully supports all of its claims. In these days of research performativity, however, some will want the details of who did what. Pakulski drafted most of the Introduction and Chapter 2, the 'debate' section of Chapter 1, all of Chapters 3 and 7, minority contributions to Chapters 5 and 6, and the first section of Chapter 8. Waters drafted the rest and redrafted all of the text for stylistic consistency.

We have rehearsed our arguments in front of our colleagues at the University of Tasmania so often that they must be thoroughly sick of them. Their patient understanding and occasional opposition cannot be underestimated. Many of the arguments have also been presented by Pakulski at the meeting of the Social Movements Research Committee of the ISA in Paris and at the Central European University in Prague, and by Waters at the World Congress of Sociology in Bielefeld, at the Flinders University of South Australia and in the Research School of Social Sciences, Australian National University. We received many comments, some of which were helpful, some decidedly awkward, but all intelligent, interested and useful.

Stephen Hill, who reviewed the proposal and the manuscript for Sage, gave us a supportive appraisal and a number of useful corrective comments. Although our publisher appears to us to have a high staff turnover, it also appears to us to have an unerring eye for the appointment of committed, knowledgeable and highly professional staff. Among them Stephen Barr, Karen Phillips and Robert Rojek have had the largest involvement in the editorial production of this particular book.

Our families will be relieved to see that the *Death of Class* is at last coming to life. Zofia, Peter and Magda and Judith, Penny and Tom have forborne and understood our absences and have been there for us when we needed them.

Jan Pakulski
Malcolm Waters
*Hobart*

# Introduction

'Class' has always been a contentious concept. In its most famous Marxian version, it is an explanatory term linking the economic sphere of production with the political and ideological superstructure. Here it is also a label for collective social actors, especially for that new historical subject, the proletariat, whose destiny was to transform social consciousness and to turn class society into a classless one. This mixture of sociology and eschatology proved exceptionally potent in propelling the concept to celebrity status. Class became a master term for both sociology and political analysis. With the formation of class parties of the left, the concept was further implicated within the global and national, political and ideological confrontations that became particularly acute during the hot and cold wars of the first three-quarters of the twentieth century. This was especially true in Europe where class became an ideological icon, a battle standard for the left and a bogey for the right. The intellectual left became preoccupied in identifying class divisions and condemning class inequalities, providing the central dogma of radicalized social science throughout the 1960s and 1970s. By contrast, denying the centrality of class became the hallmark of 'bourgeois' sociology. Even if the term was used in an ideologically neutral context, the semantic-ideological halo it acquired made it inherently contentious and prone to political appropriation.

The degree of political appropriation has reduced in recent years. With the declining commitment to Marxism, the collapse of Soviet communism and the waning appeal of socialist ideologies in the West, class is losing its ideological significance and its political centrality. Both the right and the left are abandoning their preoccupation with class issues. The right is turning its attention to morality and ethnicity while the critical left is becoming increasingly concerned about issues of gender, ecology, citizenship and human rights. This rearrangement of political concerns coincides with a shift in intellectual fashion and a growing scepticism about the compatibility of class models with contemporary social reality. Class divisions are losing their self-evident and pervasive character. Class identities are challenged by 'new associations' and new social movements. Class radicalism is no longer the flavour of the month in the intellectual salons and on university campuses. Like beads and Che Guevara berets, class is *passé*, especially among advocates of the post-modernist avant-garde and practitioners of the new gender-, eco- and ethno-centred politics.

Naturally, these shifts in public attention and intellectual fashion cannot be decisive in debates about the objective significance of class. However, they are important because they create an auspicious climate for reaching conclusions on its relevance. For the first time in over half a century, such a debate can be conducted outside the trenches of the Cold War and in a spirit of impartiality and mutual respect. In this new climate, arguments about the declining salience of class can no longer be dismissed as symptoms of ideological bias, intellectual weakness or moral corruption. More importantly, such arguments are receiving an increasing measure of empirical support from scholars both in 'advanced' Western societies and in post-communist Eastern Europe.

The main task of this book is to confront this empirical evidence within the context of theoretical argument. It involves three steps: clarifying the notoriously vague and tenuously stretched concepts of class, class society and class analysis; assessing critically the theoretical and empirical arguments in the class debate; and constructing a theoretical framework that fits the fragmentary but convincing evidence of the emergence of a new form of stratification in advanced societies.

The debate about classes combines issues of semantics and substance. Although our focus is firmly on the latter we must also pay some attention to the former. This is quite natural in a situation where a concept has been so stretched that it can be used to mean almost any identifiable collectivity ranging from occupational position to political association, and any theoretical object from structural location to collective actor. It is impossible simultaneously to give justice to this semantic diversity and to present a consistent argument against the class paradigm. We therefore focus on analytic usages of 'class' rather than the confused and vague applications of the term in popular discourse. In the context of the latter, 'class' is bound to remain a routinized and vague classificatory term because it is a useful shorthand for a wide range of social entities and divisions. We respect this popular usage but refuse to accept it as evidence of, or an argument for, the relevance of class. We will also avoid defining class in such a restrictive way that it becomes a straw person, on one hand, or can be used to designate any structured inequality or conflict, on the other. The latter strategy transforms the class thesis into a virtual tautology because no known society is egalitarian and free of conflict. However, we do admit that there is a range of legitimate meanings of the term, each of which can be examined independently in terms of its theoretical utility and empirical relevance.

In the analytic vocabulary of contemporary sociology, 'class' refers to a specific social location and causality, a specific pattern of groupness, and a specific form of identification. In the hands of some authors, as in classical Marxism, these aspects are combined, while for others, mainly those who subscribe to Weberian and action approaches, they are separated. However, we subscribe to the broad consensus that class is primarily about *economic-productive* location and determination; that is, it is based on property and/or market relations. People participate in class as producers rather than, say, as consumers, members of gender categories or organizational position-holders, although the impact of class may extend far beyond production roles. When stripped of this economic connotation and detached from its classical Marxist and Weberian roots, 'class' loses most of its explanatory power.

It is equally untenable to treat class as a mere substructure or as a statistical category, without at least drawing some implications for social relationships, social distance, patterns of interaction and patterns of association. Class is sociologically important as a social entity, as *social* class, and as such must transpire in detectable patterns of exploitation, struggle, domination and subordination, or closure. The number of classes, the extent of polarization, the clarity of class boundaries and the extent of conflict between classes may vary because they are not definitional elements. However, a minimum level of detectable clustering or groupness is essential if we are to say that classes exist. A society in which such economically caused social clustering occurs, and where these clusters are the backbone of the social structure, is a *class society*.

Lastly, a fully formed class involves a measure of self-recognition and self-identification on the part of participants, although this identification need not involve explicit class terminology or imply a consciousness of antagonism and struggle. Minimally, the members of a class have to be aware of their commonality and employ some recognized terms for collective self-description. A sense of difference between 'them' and 'us' is a necessary condition for the formation of *class actors* that marks the most developed examples of class articulation.

All of this implies that the articulation of class is a matter of degree. Its strength, and the extent to which it structures society, can vary from a minimal level, where economically based social clustering is weak but still predominant, to an advanced level. Here classes are well articulated in the social, cultural, and political-ideological domains, class identifications predominate, class consciousness is acute, and politics is dominated by struggles between class-based groups and organizations. Few historical instances of whole societies approximate a fully fledged class configuration. More typically only a degree of 'classness' can be observed. Moreover, the strength and the pattern of classness can vary historically and between contemporaneous societies.

The issue of the degree of classness of a society is linked to the issue of the relevance of 'class analysis', a type of social analysis that seeks to identify classes and to trace their social, cultural and political-ideological consequences. Class analysis makes sense only when applied to a class society. Its utility is proportional to the degree of classness. At one extreme, in a fully fledged class society, class analysis can be a legitimate substitute for social analysis. However, if classes are dissolving, a form of analysis that privileges class as an explanatory category has to give way to a more open-ended social analysis.

Historically there have been numerous examples of non-class societies. We embrace the convention that societies based on slave labour, such as ancient Rome and Greece, the estate societies of feudal Europe and modern state-socialist societies are non-class societies. In none of these societies are property and market relations the skeleton of the social structure or the predominant grid of social power. They are all unequal, stratified and conflictual but not made so predominantly by class. Class and class society are, in our vocabulary, distinctly modern phenomena inseparably linked to the market and its institutionalization within the early and mature forms of industrial capitalism.

This leads us to the central argument of this book, that classes are dissolving and that the most advanced societies are no longer class societies. The most important aspect is an attenuation of the class identities, class ideologies, and class organizations that framed West European corporatist politics in the middle of this century. Equally, the communal aspects of class, class subcultures and milieux, have long since disappeared. The issue of the decomposition of economic class mechanisms is more controversial. The book confirms the following developments: a wide redistribution of property; the proliferation of indirect and small ownership; the credentialization of skills and the professionalization of occupations; the multiple segmentation and globalization of markets; and an increasing role for consumption as a status and lifestyle generator.

We must stress the book's concentration on the advanced societies of the capitalist West and, to a lesser extent, on the 'newly industrializing countries' (NICs) of East and South East Asia and the rapidly democratizing and marketizing societies of Russia and Eastern Europe. Quite clearly, class remains salient in the 'less developed countries' (LDCs) of Asia, Africa and Latin America that have not reached an advanced social, political and economic stage. In so far as such societies are structured by productive industrial property they clearly remain class societies.

The historical side of the argument charts the process of class decomposition in the industrialized West over the last century and a half. We argue that class societies are specific historical entities. They were born with industrial capitalism, changed their form under the impact of organized or corporate capitalism, and are disappearing in the face of post-industrialization and postmodernization. The early forms of class were chronicled in England by generations of social observers from Engels (1892) to Thompson (1980). They arose in parallel with a gradual decline of such pre-industrial collectivities as village communities and estates and the strengthening of nation-states. From the early twentieth century onward the fate of classes, nation-states and parties became intimately linked. While localized communities of fate were gradually marginalized, politically organized national classes were gradually institutionalized mainly as class parties and trade unions. These national classes were quite different from their predecessors. They were politically generated rather than spontaneous, occupationally heterogeneous, and reconstructed as imagined communities on a national level. Participation in these national classes involved little by way of interaction and communication. Their constitutive common interests were abstract political constructs developed by elites. What such classes lacked in social bonding and cultural cohesion, they compensated for in political organization and strategic coherence. It was these politically organized national classes, the power of which peaked with the establishment of corporatist structures, that became the most powerful social actors and agents of social transformation of the twentieth century.

The decomposition of these national classes that we affirm does *not* imply a decline in social inequality. Post-class societies will remain internally differentiated in terms of access to economic resources, political power and prestige. Indeed it is possible to argue that class societies in their late corporatist forms achieved a historically unique degree of egalitarianism. Nor does the dissolution of class imply the end of social division and conflict. Non-class social divisions and non-class conflicts have always been resilient, even if overshadowed by class under conditions of industrial capitalism. The new cleavages that are emerging in post-class society may prove even more crippling and destabilizing than the old ones. Unlike many post-industrial visions of social change, then, this argument does not imply progressive equalization and social harmony.

As this clearly suggests, we find most of the old 'class decomposition' arguments to be unsatisfactory. They are either too timid in refusing to make a decisive break with class orthodoxy and to make a paradigmatic switch to a non-class interpretation of social reality, or are too utopian in charting optimistic visions of a classless future. A more radical and sober argument about change is required in order to make sense of current social developments.

However, despite its radicalism, our argument on the dissolution of class follows some established paths. It treads in the footsteps of an entire generation of critical social scientists, whose contributions are acknowledged in Chapters 1, 2 and 3. Some of these theoretical paths are rehearsed in *Postmodernization* (Crook et al. 1992) which outlines an overall theoretical framework for the analysis of contemporary social change. The empirical evidence is, by and large, not the product of our own primary research either. Nor, typically, was it produced with the intention of debunking class visions. In deploying it in support of this argument, we therefore risk offending many of our colleagues. To minimize this risk, we stress that while the glory of discovery is theirs, any ignominy that might arise from interpretative error rests squarely on our shoulders.

The overall plan of the book follows the logic of our argument. Chapter 1 identifies two types of class perspective: *class theory* that specifies class as the fundamental explanatory concept; and *class analysis* that takes class to be a privileged explanatory variable. In each case, we seek to show that the concept of 'class' has been seriously stretched in order to accommodate emergent social developments as well as to preserve ideological convictions. Here we also identify the state of the contemporary debate on class and elaborate our position within it. Chapters 2 and 3 review the classical arguments on the decomposition or recomposition of class. They isolate the key dimensions of the death of class: the economic-industrial, the state-political, the communal and domestic, and the cultural-ideological. Chapter 2 concentrates on structural arguments and Chapter 3 focuses on class formation.

The remainder of the book charts our argument on the dissolution of class. Chapter 4 reviews the economic dimension of this process. It addresses the issue of property and power and comments on the separation of corporate ownership and control, the proliferation of property ownership, the widening distribution of personal domestic and productive property and, generally, the occlusion between owning and non-owning categories. The chapter also examines changes in the labour market and the occupational structure in the context of debates on the 'managerial revolution', the rise of the new middle class, the embourgeoisement of manual labour, and processes of market segmentation, globalization and stratificational fragmentation. Chapter 5 examines the domestic context, including patterns of patriarchy and the status of female labour. While in the past gendered domesticity was a key site for the reproduction of class society, more recently an increasingly interventionist state has gradually reconstructed patriarchal relations and facilitated the induction of women into the labour market. In this way, gender has become an important principle of stratification in the public arena. The domestic reproduction of class relations gives way to educational reproduction. The pattern of community engagement follows a similar path. The original class communities have been absorbed into a national state (a societal quasi-community) in which citizenship is the central mode of participation. With subsequent globalization, these national communities are giving way to wider but more ephemeral configurations in which identity focuses on lifestyles or value commitments.

Chapter 6 shifts the analysis even more firmly into the cultural realm. It initially examines the decline of class cultures and traditions, especially of working-class subcultures, and then examines the shift from a high–low cultural configuration to an elite–mass one. It discusses the impact of the state and the culture industry, and the emergence of a 'postculture' characterized by diversity, stylization and choice in the context of these processes. The chapter concludes with a brief comment on popular ideologies that legitimize economic inequality. Chapter 7 focuses on the critical role of the state and political parties in reconstituting class into politically organized entities. This institutionalization and political organization of classes transforms them into powerful political actors and key agents of social transformation but also makes them vulnerable to political decomposition. We discuss this decomposition within the context of the 'shrinking state', the erosion of corporatist politics, including class and party dealignment, the decline of political partisanship, the changing idiom of political appeals, the erosion of the left–right polarity, and the decomposition of ideological-political packages. The articulation of new political agendas and new political actors known as 'new politics' and attempts at the construction of a 'new political order' mark the final stage in the decomposition process. Chapter 8 takes on a more synthetic character in pulling together the arguments developed in Chapters 4–7 within a theoretical framework that specifies the emergence of a *status-conventional* society to displace class society.

*

If we can be permitted a somewhat iconoclastic summary of our view, it is that sociology dwells with a peculiar bedfellow. Like spouses in a marriage gone bad enough to be just about bearable, sociology and class cohabit in a relationship orchestrated by both hatred and passion. All sociologists find class inequality so unacceptable that, if they think it is there, they connive in its departure, and if they think it is not, they are glad to be rid of it. But many have become so dependent upon it that they lean on its centenarian frame and insist that its limbs are as sturdy as they ever were. This book confirms the good news that class has collapsed and is decomposing, leaving only the merest traces of its effects. If it ever was real and salient, and we are certainly prepared to admit that class was a sturdy historical reality, it is no longer. This means that sociologists cannot go on relating and reducing every social phenomenon, from feminine subordination to taste in music, to class. We must begin the search for a new theoretical *terra firma*.

# 1
# The Sociologist's Chimera

Class has always been desperately difficult to pin down. On reading the claims made for it by one of its most iconic evangelists, the English historian E.P. Thompson, an observer might be forgiven for doubting that it ever existed. Indeed Thompson's own anti-sociological declamation is entirely explicit on that point:

> By class I understand a historical phenomenon, unifying a number of disparate and seemingly unconnected events, both in the raw material of experience and in consciousness. I emphasise that it is a *historical* phenomenon. I do not see class as a 'structure', nor even as a 'category', but as something which in fact happens (and can be shown to have happened) in human relationships . . .
>
> [I]t is a fluency which evades analysis if we attempt to stop it dead at any given moment and anatomize its structure. The finest-meshed sociological net cannot give us a pure specimen of class, any more than it can give us one of deference or love . . . class happens when some men, as a result of common experiences . . . feel and articulate the identity of their interests as between themselves, and as against other men whose interests are different from . . . theirs. (1980: 8–9, original italics)

If we leave aside for the moment Thompson's unfortunate tendency to omit one half of humanity, we can concentrate on the Heisenbergian character of class, its tendency to disappear when one tries to observe it. This leads him to an odd conclusion. Even though class is a 'phenomenon' and something that happens 'in fact', it apparently has no existence: '"It" does not exist, either to have an ideal consciousness, or to lie as a patient on the Adjustor's table' (1980: 10). This leaves Thompson contradicting himself on whether class is primarily an objective or a subjective phenomenon. At one point he is a historical materialist: 'The class experience is largely *determined* by the productive relations into which men are born – or enter *involuntarily*' (1980: 9, italics added). But just over the page we find that he is a social constructionist: 'Class is defined by men as they live out their own history, and, in the end, this is its *only* definition' (1980: 10, italics added).

We introduce our argument with Thompson not so much to defend sociology from his confused attack but because his contradictions nicely express the sociological predicament. On his argument, class cannot be an object of social-scientific analysis but only the subject of historical or philosophical interpretation. It exists almost by virtue of the observation that it exists made by the ideological experts who are committed to its existence. Many who insist on the continued salience of class are indeed the victims of this conceit, but the sociological community can take pride in the fact that its members also frequently view class as a demonstrable set of arrangements and make honest and important attempts to subject their theories of class to intersubjective argument and their empirical descriptions to validation.

The difficulties of theory and research on class are captured in a widespread formulation that distinguishes between, on the one hand, an abstracted structure of positions or places that can be regarded as objective or given and, on the other, a formation, an actual process of social arrangements that is apparent to observers, a pattern of stratification that is close to the experience of participants. Poulantzas makes this distinction explicit:

> [I]f we confine ourselves to modes of production alone, examining them in a pure and abstract fashion we find that each of them involves two classes – the exploiting class, which is ideologically and politically dominant, and the exploited class, which is politically and ideologically dominated . . . bourgeois and workers in the capitalist mode of production. But a concrete society (a social formation) *involves more than two classes*, insofar as it is composed of various forms and modes of production. No social formation involves only two classes: but the two fundamental classes in any social formation are those of the dominant mode of production in that formation. (1982: 106)

This formulation is, of course, derived from Marx's specification of an abstract model of two historic classes (bourgeoisie and proletariat) and his simultaneous statement that capitalism accommodates a trinity of classes (capitalists, landowners and wage labourers) and that even between these the lines of demarcation are obliterated by middle and intermediate strata (1977: 506). But Weber (1978) is no stranger to the device either. For him the structure has two dimensions, the property and commercial classes, and the formation consists typically of four 'social classes'. The most influential contemporary neo-Weberian class theorist, Goldthorpe (1987), follows this tradition by distinguishing between class schemas and patterns of 'demographic class formation'.[1]

The difficulty for sociologists of class is always to reconcile the formation with the structure because the apparent events and experiences of social life and the trajectories of societal development simply do not match up with the theoretical proposal. Holmwood and Stewart (1991: 42–4) show that such a reconciliation can only be accomplished by employing one of two types of fallacy. Under the horizontal fallacy different individuals are argued to have radically different types of experience. Here a class sociologist might claim, for example, that proletarians are experiencing class exploitation while employed professionals are engaging in status competition. The alternative vertical fallacy preserves the theory of class by suggesting that individual experience is false and that all employees experience alienation, whether they are subjectively aware of it or not. For many years these fallacies have pervaded the sociology of class and kept it alive. This book tries to show that the alleged class formation is now so far out of kilter with any structure theorized that we must at last attempt to address our fallacies by revising the assumptions that underlie the class paradigm.

In making our claim we must clearly distinguish between 'class theory' and 'class analysis'. The former, of which Marxist class theory is the best known example, embraces all four of the following propositions:

- The proposition of *economism*. It views class as a fundamentally economic phenomenon. Class refers principally to differences in the ownership of property, especially of productive or capital property with an accumulation potential. It can also refer to differential market capacity, especially labour-market capacity. Such economic phenomena as property or markets are held to be fundamental structuring or organizing principles in societal arrangements.
- The proposition of *groupness*. Classes are held to be more than statistical aggregates or taxonomic categories. They are real features of social structure having quite clear boundaries that set up the main lines of cleavage in society. Classes are socially distant from one another and social relationships and associations tend to be exclusive. So deep and fundamental are these cleavages that they are the enduring bases for conflict, struggle, and distributional contestation.
- The proposition of *behavioural and cultural linkage*. Class membership is also claimed causally to be connected to consciousness, identity and action outside the arena of economic production. It determines political preferences, lifestyle choices, child-rearing practices, opportunities for physical and mental health, access to educational opportunity, patterns of marriage, occupational inheritance, income, and so on. This proposition legitimizes the continuing salience of class analysis.
- The proposition of *transformational capacity* based on objective interests. Classes are (at least potential) collective actors in the economic and political fields. They have latent access to resources that can hold entire societies in thrall. In so far as they consciously struggle against other classes, classes can transform the general set of social arrangements of which they are a part. Class therefore offers the dynamic thrust that energizes society: classes are collective actors that can make history.

Figure 1.1 summarizes these propositions in a slightly different way. It draws two distinctions from the ways in which sociologists use the concept of class: first, between class as a generative (determining) factor in social life and class as a set of categories for simply describing social divisions and ranks; and second, between class as an objective condition of human existence and class as a subjective component of experience and consciousness. Intersecting these distinctions gives us the four aspects of class that centre sociological debates. Sociologists variously identify class as an abstract structure of positions, as a set of economic categories, as communities of common interest and culture, and as collective political actors. The four propositions given above establish theoretical linkages between these aspects of class: economism specifies that the main divisions in society are economic; groupness specifies that these economic categories will develop shared cultures; behavioural linkage specifies that cultural milieux will determine political behaviour; and

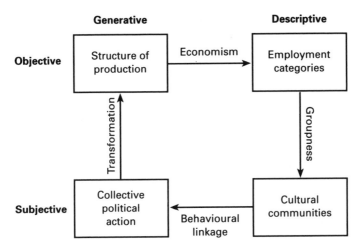

Figure 1.1   *Aspects of the sociology of class*

transformation argues that class-based political action will lead to reform of the fundamental underlying structure.

As we have said, 'class theory' embraces the entire diagram. However, it tends to concentrate on the proposition of economism, examining the ways in which structure generates categories, groups and collective actors. We want to stress that many supporters of class sociology reject this 'hard' version of class theory. For example, Goldthorpe and Marshall (1992) and Hout, Brooks and Manza (1993) distance themselves from the proposition of transformative capacity and concentrate on the propositions of group formation and behavioural linkage. Class analysis, according to them, 'has as its central concern the study of relationships among class structures, class mobility, class-based inequalities, and class-based action' (Goldthorpe and Marshall 1992: 382). Although in Chapters 2 and 3 we discuss critically the most influential and indeed the best contemporary examples of 'hard' versions of class theory that embrace all four propositions, our prime target is the more common 'soft' or *gesellschaftlich* versions of class analysis.

In developing our argument, we are mindful of what Marshall, Newby, Rose and Vogler call 'dualistic thinking', or what we would call 'retrospective projection'. This refers to the practice in which an allegedly 'communitarian and solidaristic proletariat of some bygone heyday of class antagonism is set against the atomised and consumer-oriented working class of today' (1988: 206), although we might take exception to the contradiction involved in describing the working class as 'atomised'. Because the presuppositions of class theory include all of those underlying class analysis, if we can show that this less ambitious class analysis is inadequate then class theory also fails.

**Class theory**

Class theory began with Marx whose original statements about the class system that emerges from the social relations of production are primarily political and persuasive in character. In the *Communist Manifesto*, he and Engels outline what has come to be known as the abstract model of class, a progressive tendency for society to divide into two great classes, the *bourgeoisie* and the *proletariat*. However, the colourful invective disappeared as the optimistic and youthful Marx tried to come to terms with the realities of capitalist society. A major disappointment was the failure of the European revolutions of 1848. This disjunction of theory and experience was explained by Marx (1962) as the consequence of the immaturity of capitalism and the development of alliances between the emerging industrial bourgeoisie and the residual and conservative feudal classes, that is, the landed aristocracy, the petty bourgeoisie, and, above all, the peasantry. Already, then, the originator of class theory was being forced to recognize not only the persistence of the intermediate classes but also the fractionalization of the historically significant classes.

Among contemporary neo-Marxist theorists, Poulantzas is possibly the most determined to stick to Marx's abstract model. However he is also obliged by the facts of historical experience to make certain reformulations of Marx's main theoretical categories, 'ownership of the means of production' and 'labour process'. Ownership is respecified as possession, the capacity to put the means of production into operation (1982: 102). In capitalist societies the exploiting classes are constituted not by the shareholders of large companies but by the controlling managers of those companies; in state-socialist societies, the owners of the means of production are not the citizens but senior party officials and bureaucrats (1982: 103).[2] Because Poulantzas is unwilling to amend Marx's definition of the proletariat and therefore wants to exclude non-manual workers from the working class, he must also abandon pure economism: 'purely economic criteria are not sufficient to determine and locate social classes . . . it becomes absolutely necessary to refer to positions within the political and ideological relations of the social division of labor' (1982: 107). The new and growing intermediate strata can be found within these political and ideological relations.

Classes therefore 'exist only in the class struggle' (Poulantzas 1974: 14) but this is an economic *and* a political and ideological struggle:

> It may be thus said that a social class is defined by its place in the ensemble of social practices, i.e. by its place in the social division of labour as a whole . . . [It] is a concept which denotes the effects of the structure within the social division of labour . . . This place thus corresponds to what I shall refer to as the structural determination of class, i.e. to the existence within class practices of determination by the structure – by the relations of production, and by the places of political and ideological domination/subordination. (1974: 14)

While 'class places' in the social division of labour are structurally determined by struggle, Poulantzas holds that class positions, that is the location of classes in historically specific political-ideological configurations, are 'conjectural', that is false or imaginary. Thus, for example, the pro-bourgeois position of artisans does not reflect its 'real' class place. Moreover, Poulantzas follows Marx's modifications of the dichotomous class scheme ( in *The 18th Brumaire,* 1962) in expanding the class map to include sub-classes, strata, fractions, sections, residual classes, etc. This allows Poulantzas to 'explain away' the emergence of the new middle class, in his terms the 'new petty bourgeoisie', as a conjectural formation.

There is much in this theoretical outline that is in principle acceptable because we can only identify structures by using abstract theoretical constructs. However, in Poulantzas there is a widening gap between the postulated structure and the observed social and political configuration. The latter, it seems, can acquire a life of its own that has only tenuous links to the 'determinant' structural fault. Poulantzas assures us that this structural fault is productive-economic but when he comments on politics the class structure appears superfluous. We are invited to 'see through' the appearances of observable social and political configurations but little justification is given for this effort. We gain nothing by postulating the hidden determinations of the class structure, except perhaps a sense of remaining faithful to the original Marxian class project.

In contemporary sociology, the main influence of Marx and Poulantzas is felt through the work of Wright and his associates (Wright 1978; 1985; 1989; Baxter et al. 1991; Marshall et al. 1988). In an early formulation Wright (1978) takes his main cues from Poulantzas but finds him to be inadequate in specifying boundaries between the classes, in particular in terms of the non-economic accommodation of the intermediate classes. In differentiating between the criteria for class membership (that is, economic, political, and ideological criteria), Wright finds that it is possible to be dominant on one or more criteria while being subordinate on others. These possible situations are called 'contradictory class locations'. He maps a class structure with three consistent class locations, two of which are defined within the capitalist mode of production in its pure form, the familiar bourgeoisie and proletariat, with the third being identified by simple commodity production, the petty bourgeoisie. Between these three are contradictory class locations: small employers, managers and semi-autonomous wage earners (employed professionals).

Three factors appear to have changed Wright's mind about the contradictory locations argument. First, the contradictory class locations can be shown to be stable and consistent at the level of experience. The term 'contradiction' implies that conditions of work do not fit each other, but in the contradictory locations they clearly do (see Holmwood and Stewart 1983). Second, on reflection Wright notices that he has been sliding in an ideologically unacceptable Weberian direction, that he has in fact defined classes in terms of domination and subordination when he should have been defining them as relations of exploitation (1985: 56–7). Third, Wright's empirical work on the changing shape of the American class structure produced notably negative results. The majority of the labour force was in the contradictory rather than the historic locations and the trend was not helping his cause. He finds 'a substantial, negative overall change in the working class', and that 'The critical expectations for the various components of the middle class . . . are equally unsupported by the results' (Wright and Martin 1987: 15–16). Wright is forced to admit that the results 'ran . . . consistently counter to our theoretical expectations' (1987: 16). Indeed he goes so far as to embrace an opposing thesis consistent with the one advanced in this book: 'the detailed patterning of these class and sector effects is much more consistent with the essential thrust of postindustrial theory than with conventional Marxian analyses of transformations of the class structure' (1987: 19).

In Marx and Poulantzas the production of commodities forms the basis of exploitation under capitalism, and exploitative relations define the classes. In seeking to develop a new theory of class that retains this Marxist principle, Wright (1985) adopts Roemer's theory of exploitation that extends the concept of class to a range of 'principal assets' that operate in parallel with the means of production. Two such assets are important within contemporary capitalism: organizational assets and credentialized skills. The notion of organizational assets is based on the idea that it is possible to control productive resources without actually owning them. Senior managers, entrepreneurs and owners possess the means of production and the major portion of organization assets although some of these are also distributed further down bureaucratic hierarchies, even in non-capitalist organizations. Credentialized skills also offer the possibility for exploitation by rendering certain forms of labour scarce and allowing workers to appropriate surplus through monopolistic control.

Wright's second map of the class structure, known as 'the principal assets model' (1985: 88), therefore cross-classifies property ownership (owner/ non-owner) with credentialized skills (positive/neutral/negative) and organizational assets (positive/neutral/negative). This produces a scheme of twelve class locations. The fundamental division is still between owners and non-owners of the means of production. However owners are internally differentiated according to the extent to which they exploit the labour of others, into large employers, small employers and the petty bourgeoisie. Non-owners are also internally differentiated on the basis of organizational assets and credentialized skills, so that there are nine classes of non-owner, eight of which are non-proletarian, 'intermediate' classes.

Several aspects of the new Wright model can be applauded. He accepts that the social relations of commodity production are not the only bases for the formation of classes. He also accepts that property is not the only dimension on which critical forms of domination and subordination are possible. The theoretical move is also accompanied by a retreat from the notion that relations between classes are unidirectionally exploitative. He also accepts the existence of stable, middle classes. This means that the historical significance of the ownership and working classes may well be in decline, as may the possibility of a class-based politics.

The weakness of the scheme lies in a continuing insistence on the reality of class structure and the dependent, if not epiphenomenal, status of class experience. Historical experience is accommodated by the theoretical construction of social classes. However, the more history escapes from the nineteenth-century model of a class structure posited by Marx, the more tenuous becomes the theoretical connection between structure, formation and experience. This is because the class structure does not determine the actual class formation, especially the formation of class actors, but 'rather it determines the underlying probabilities of different kinds of class formations' (Wright 1989: 29). The weakness of class theory can therefore be inspected, first, in Wright's tendency to multiply the number of classes each time he revises his scheme, and second, in the shrivelling of the historic classes. The 'proletariat' and 'bourgeoisie' now contain fewer than half the members of the employed labour force of any advanced capitalist society, and thus a very small minority of the adult population. While this class multiplication may allow Wright to seek to explain non-polarization by reference to theories of globalization and post-industrialization, the cogency of these theories ought to lead him to call into question the entire enterprise of class theory.

## Class analysis

As we have indicated, class analysis follows a similar epistemological strategy to class theory, by specifying a structure and then indicating variation in actual class formation. However, class analysis is always more agnostic than class theory, in so far as it accepts multidimensional bases for stratification. For a class analyst, class does not determine the entire topography of society and classes are not the makers of history. Class analysis grants autonomous causal capacity to gender, religion, ethnicity, political arrangements, and even individual preferences. It simply seeks to establish the impact of class on these and other arenas. However, in order to distinguish itself from sociological analysis in general, it nevertheless must privilege economically defined class over these other social dimensions and presuppose highly effective causal linkages.

Class analysis draws its inspiration from Weber whose multidimensional model of class, status and party remains an iconic if problematic paradigm in stratification analysis. The underlying structure of class places entails differential life chances for their incumbents. These places are differentiated on the basis of the ownership of property or opportunity for income where such ownership is 'represented' within markets for capital, commodities and labour. Because Weber concentrates on life chances, access to scarce goods and services, his is a consumption theory of class rather than a production theory. A class situation is one in which there is a shared typical probability of procuring goods, gaining a position in life, and finding inner satisfaction (1982: 69). Note that the market, rather than production, is the crucial concept. The potential for class membership is not real until the determining factor is used in a market to secure access to privilege: 'the kind of chance in the *market* is the decisive moment which presents a common condition for the individual's fate. Class situation is, in this sense, market situation. The effect of naked possession *per se* . . . is only a fore-runner of real "class"' (1982: 62). The class structure intersects with the individual at the point of the market to provide for the emergence of *social classes*, 'the totality of those class situations within which individual and generational mobility is easy and typical' (1982: 69).

Although claiming descent from both Marx and Weber, Goldthorpe's class schemas (1980; 1987; Erikson and Goldthorpe 1992) are clearly associated with this Weberian model especially in so far as they stress the effects of the market. Goldthorpe begins with the employment relationship, specifying three possibilities: employer, self-employed and employee. However, because contemporary society is composed mainly of corporate rather than individual employers he discards this distinction in the final schema: apart from small owners, we are all employees now. Employees are primarily divided into those who exercise 'delegated authority or specialized knowledge and expertise' (Erikson and Goldthorpe 1992: 42), those who do not, and those who are in between. This authority factor is the one most likely to give rise to differences in working conditions and market capacity. Further subdivisions are made by skill level and by whether the sectoral location is industrial or agricultural. Taken together these yield a schema of eleven classes that can be collapsed into seven-, five- and even three-class schemas.[3] The schemas represent the class structure.

Goldthorpe (1987) then moves on to the traditional second formation stage to try to discover what actual classes have demographically been formed in each class position.[4] Here he employs the recognizably Weberian criterion of whether mobility within each class position is 'easy and typical'. He reaches two conclusions. First, there is a marked level of intergenerational solidity at the peak of the class structure. There is only a small chance that professional, managerial and senior administrative origins will lead to dissimilar destinations. The further down the hierarchy one goes the less likely it becomes that a person will move up to class I. Second, while this high solidity declines as one moves down the hierarchy, it does so in an irregular way. In particular, the proprietorial petty-bourgeois class also exhibits a high level of solidity. So property continues to be effective in structuring class. Third, while there is a historical increase in working-class mobility, it is limited in its range, so that there is a significant barrier between white-collar and blue-collar occupations.[5]

An uncharitable observer might suggest that, like Wright, Goldthorpe changes the number and the position of various occupational categories according to theoretical purpose or methodological convenience. More importantly, if we take demographic class formation as an indicator of the centrality and pervasiveness of the class structure it can only be regarded as weak and uncertain. Assuming a correct methodology, only the petty bourgeoisie, the mature working class and the emerging service class are truly formed. That great mass of people in the inchoate and unformed classes III (routine white-collar employees) and V (lower technicians and supervisors) are, on this argument, not members of classes at all and their behaviour is therefore not subject to class determination. Lastly, we might suggest that because Goldthorpe allocates individuals to classes on the basis of their occupations we might just as well employ occupational status as the main predictor of so-called class effects. Indeed, there is a considerable body of evidence suggesting that the predictions will improve if one does (see e.g. Halaby and Weakliem 1993; Prandy 1990).

## The shimmering mirage

We can now turn from descriptions of class schemes to focus on more fundamental debates about the continuing salience of class theory and analysis. As has often been the case, these debates began in the USA, provoked lively responses in Western Europe (mainly in Britain, home of the most committed defenders of class), and arrived at incommensurable conclusions ranging from the fideistic through the agnostic to the atheistic.

The 'death of class' debate begins with Nisbet's (1959) seminal paper, 'The Decline and Fall of Social Class'.[6] It stimulated vigorous responses from Heberle (1959), Barber (1959) and Duncan (1959), and set an agenda for the debate summarized in Westergaard's (1972) well-known essay, 'Sociology: The Myth of Classlessness'.[7] 'The term social class', wrote Nisbet, 'is by now useful in historical sociology, in comparative or folk sociology, but it is nearly valueless for the clarification of the data on wealth, power, and social status in contemporary United States and much of Western society in general' (1959: 11). While in the past classes were more tangible entities that were crystallized in the economic, social, cultural and political realms, that were relatively uniform, stable, conscious and solidary, in modern industrial democracy they are decomposing:

> National democracy, economic and social pluralism, ethical individualism and an ever-widening educational front joined to create new patterns of social power and status and to make class obsolete in constantly widening sectors of Western society . . . When economic power derives no longer exclusively from the process of capital accumulation, or even management, when it is a reflection of positions in the economy which arise from and are sustained by labour and government, the relationship between property and class becomes more and more tenuous. (1959: 14–15)

The shift in employment from manufacturing to the service sector, combined with increasing levels of education and massive social mobility, serve to destroy stable hierarchies in all but 'backwater areas'. Similarly, the 'disengagement of economic and political power' undermines class politics and consciousness. Class divisions are replaced by multidimensional, fluid and continuous status inequalities: 'But social status is at once too continuous within each of the numerous scales of status to make possible any identification of classes that have more than the most restricted or specialised acceptance.' (1959: 16). 'The proof of existence of a social class worthy of the sociological name', he concludes, 'should not have to depend upon multi-variate analysis, with correlations generally reaching no higher than 0.5' (1959: 11). Presumably Nisbet would be even more firm in his view under current circumstances in which the correlations are seldom as high as 0.2.

Heberle's (1959) response is equally 'classical' in the sense of setting an agenda for contemporary protagonists of class. Class theory, according to him, is still the most effective framework for making sense of contemporary social divisions and conflicts that separate capital from labour. The empirical utility of the Marxist concept of class, he argues, is best demonstrated in political sociology. Prefiguring Lipset's famous argument (1960), Heberle claims that class theory is the one best able to 'explain the complexity of political movements and parties' (1959: 23).

Westergaard (1972) offers a much more elaborate defence. Its critical edge is directed against the embourgeoisement and decomposition theses that propose an end of the industrial classes, the amelioration of social inequality, and the end of class ideology and thus of class conflict. The persistence of class divisions and conflicts is confirmed for Westergaard by: the failure of egalitarian reforms to eliminate inequalities of income and property; the persisting *relative* inequalities of opportunity between broadly defined classes; the 'clustering of power' in the hands of a 'small, homogeneous elite of wealth and private corporate property' (1972: 140); and the rise of organized labour. He also reiterates a Sombartian point on American exceptionalism to explain the absence of 'class consciousness' and class organization in the USA.[8] These became the central themes in contemporary defences of class. Except for the strength of organized labour which is most at odds with current developments, Westergaard's agenda still dominates class fideism.

Westergaard also shifts the defence of class from purely theoretical to empirical grounds by addressing the vexed question of class formation. He regards the evidence of declining inequalities and increasing universalism as inconclusive. Although he acknowledges the cultural dissolution of (working-) class communities and the corporatization of capital, he nevertheless concludes that because of persistent inequalities there remains a large potential for class conflict in Western Europe. In the 1972 Postscript he claims to provide new evidence of class division and conflict: the rediscovery of poverty; persisting substantial inequality of opportunity; 'the escalation of war in Vietnam; the assertion of civil rights and black power in America; industrial conflict in Britain and elsewhere; widespread student militancy; and the recurrence of sporadic "direct action" outside the limits of conventional politics' (1972: 153–8). Class consciousness and class discontent, according to him, are firmly embedded in workers' world views, in spite of an absence of revolutionary ideology and an apparent fragmentation of class conflict. The 'decline of class' thesis, he concludes, is mere right-wing opinion and ideology.

Three elements in this defence are worth noting. First, it generalizes the issue of class to all inequality and conflict rather than confining it to a specific pattern of inequality and conflict centred on the capital–labour division. This device allows Westergaard to muster an impressive posse of proofs of class persistence so that, by implication, only an unlikely egalitarian and harmonious society can be considered classless. Class is easy to confirm on such an argument that all conflicts and inequalities are class generated. Second, he tries to turn the tables by demanding 'convincing and clear' evidence from critics of the class paradigm as to its non-existence, but without making it clear just what would constitute such convincing evidence. Westergaard, in fact, dismisses many of the data on income and wealth equalization, increasing mobility, the fragmentation of stratification, and changing lines of conflict as 'unconvincing' or 'incomplete' without specifying what measure of evidence would convince. Third, Westergaard simply assumes, rather than examines critically, the vital class-theoretical proposition of behavioural linkage. Almost any form of action, from civil rights movements in the USA to student protests in Europe, become relevant pieces of evidence in his view. The links between class structure (in production and ownership relations), forms of consciousness and identity, and types of action are regarded as unproblematic. These three flaws have also been inherited by more recent supporters of class, along with the overall class-fideistic agenda.

Provocative articles by Pahl (1989) and Clark and Lipset (1991) concerning current class analyses in Britain, Western Europe and North America,[9] have rekindled the debate, mainly in the pages of *The International Journal of Urban and Regional Research*, *Sociology* and *International Sociology*. Pahl's argument begins in a seemingly orthodox fashion. He agrees that capitalist society is fundamentally class divided. However, this theoretical axiom, useful in global historical comparisons, is of little value, he argues, for sociologists studying smaller-scale social processes, especially contemporary urban divisions and conflicts. In such analyses class theory is at best superfluous because it adds nothing to contextualized explanations, or is at worst misleading. Its weakness lies in its assumption of correspondence between structure, consciousness and action (the SCA model in Pahl's parlance). He finds this assumption to be particularly problematic in studies of urban protest that seek to explain social dissent by reference to the structural-economic location of the disadvantaged:

> [Firstly] the links in the SCA chain are inadequately theorized and there is little empirical indication that the [class] model has much relevance in practice. Secondly, as a classificatory device class does little to help us understand the lifestyles of the privileged and adds nothing to the brute facts of poverty when considering the other end of the social structure. Finally, it is apparently well-nigh impossible to operationalize the concept in order to make international comparisons. (1989: 715)

The declining utility of 'class' can be attributed, Pahl argues, to a decline in manufacturing industries that generated the classic industrial class divisions and to a reduction in the regulative power of the state that once was an effective tool for social reconstruction in the organized class struggle. In a service-based economy that responds to global market forces, schemes based on an industrial class model of interests and strategies are becoming increasingly anachronistic. Moreover they blind social researchers to such new and important developments as the emergence of credit dependence and its associated consumption-based social divisions, the emergence of conflicts related to the residential environment, and the decomposition of collective consciousness. The politically active groupings that are emerging in the new social environment are 'issue-oriented and territorially based' (1989: 719). By sticking to 'class mantras' sociologists risk missing an appreciation of a changing world.

Pahl's paper stimulated responses from Crompton (1991) and Marshall (1991). Crompton restates the fideistic position, if in a rather cautious manner: classes are still salient and class schemes are worth preserving, though they need adjusting, especially to accommodate women. It must also be remembered that their utility may vary from problem to problem and time to time. While Marxist class theory may be obsolete, an updated version of class analysis is relevant and useful. By contrast, Marshall's response has a much sharper edge. Pahl's arguments, according to him, are either 'marvellously inconsistent' and 'impenetrably vague' or plainly inaccurate. Class, according to Marshall, has been well theorized in terms of the contemporary occupational structure (e.g. Goldthorpe 1987), the model of the functions of capital and labour (Carchedi 1975) and the principal assets model (Wright 1985). There is overwhelming evidence that 'life chances are massively associated with class', that 'social class remains the single most important variable in British psephology', and that some important correlates of poverty are class related (Marshall 1991: 115). In conclusion, Marshall, not for the last time, affirms his unwavering faith in the reality and utility of class: 'Class voting actually exists, and class as a meaningful category of everyday culture and discourse is both understood by the vast majority of people in [Britain], and demonstrably shapes some important aspects of their lives' (1991: 116). While he seeks to avoid a 'blanket defence of class theory', he nevertheless declares that colleagues endorsing the 'death of class' thesis are the victims of the ideology of the new right (1991: 117). The similarity between this defensive strategy and that of Westergaard is noteworthy. Not only are the core 'proofs of class' basically the same but so also are the accusations of ideological bias. This is in clear contrast to the arguments of class atheists who provide evidence of advancing processes of decomposition.

In this respect, the most crucial statement is doubtless the one that marks the conversion of Lipset, a leading class analyst, to a class-atheistic position (Clark and Lipset 1991; Clark et al. 1993). The shift[10] is somewhat akin to the Pope joining a society of free thinkers. The central thesis of the articles is that the decline of old hierarchies and the fragmentation of stratification are leading to a 'declining ability of class to explain social and especially political processes' (1993: 293). The stratification system in the industrialized West is becoming increasingly pluralistic, multidimensional and shaped by factors located outside the workplace. In the three major situses that Clark and Lipset examine – family, economic organization and politics – the old hierarchies and the old class divisions based on them are decomposing. This is due to the impact of the welfare state, occupational differentiation, rising affluence and consumption, changing political party dynamics as expressed in dealignment and the new politics, market fragmentation, and the rise of institution-based divisions. The net result is a declining importance of class cleavages, especially ideological ones between the left and right, and the growing salience of a politics that embraces non-class divisions and issues (1993: 313).

Lipset's articles stimulated two responses: Hout, Brooks and Manza's (1993) sharp disagreement and Pakulski's (1993b) agnostic but broadly sympathetic endorsement.[11] Hout, Brooks and Manza offer a vigorous defence of class along fideistic lines: 'Class is an indispensable concept for sociology because: (1) class is a key determinant of material interests; (2) structurally defined classes give rise to – or influence the formation of – collective actors seeking to bring about social change; and (3) class membership affects the life chances and behaviour of individuals' (1993: 261). Alas, however, the authors fail to specify criteria for four critical class effects: whether class is a central determinant of material interests relative to other determinants; how significant material interests are in the moulding of identities and the generation of behaviour relative to value commitments; how important class actors are in bringing about social change relative to non-class actors; and how much class membership structures life chances relative to, say, race, gender or ethnicity. The evidence mobilized in support of the continuing relevance of 'class' is the persisting concentration of 'wealth and power at the top and growing poverty and degradation at the bottom of the contemporary class structure' (1993: 263). This is another rehearsal of Westergaard's old argument that assumes all its flaws: class lives on because there are social inequalities and conflicts; class accounts for an impressive 17–20 per cent of income variation and 10–12 per cent of variations in voting behaviour; evidence of progressive dealignment is dismissed on the grounds that parties have only abandoned class appeals and not class representation; marketization has not seriously affected the distribution of power; and there is no evidence of egalitarian trends in family relations. In sum, Hout et al. argue, the class structure is changing but class divisions and conflicts are as vigorous as ever.

Pakulski (1993b) identifies a general semantic confusion in the debate and particular pitfalls in Hout, Brooks and Manza's defence. Class supporters, he argues, are vague as to what would constitute evidence of class decline. They uncritically identify classes with inequality in general, so that their key evidence is a persistent gap between wealth and poverty. For Pakulski, such an argument fails to engage Clark and Lipset on the fragmentation of stratification and the relative decline in the political significance of class divisions. Clark and Lipset, in turn, according to Pakulski, misdirect their attack. The real object of their criticism, according to him, is the *Marxist* concept of class and its theoretical residues, rather than a class analysis of the type suggested by Hout et al. A multidimensional Weberian approach that plays down the centrality of class and stresses the autonomy of politics might, he argues, provide a better framework for revamping the sociological analysis of politics, including studies of the impact of class on voting.

The recent exchanges in the pages of *Sociology* begin with the fideists rejoining the battle, freshly provisioned. Responding to their critics,[12] Goldthorpe and Marshall (1992) first distance themselves from orthodox ('hard' or *gemeinschaftlich*) class theory, especially of the Marxist type, and outline a programme for a 'class analysis' that 'does not entail a commitment to any particular theory of class but, rather, to a research programme . . . within which different, and indeed rival, theories may be formulated and then assessed in terms of their heuristic and explanatory performance' (1992: 382–3). They call for conceptual clarity in distinguishing class from non-class divisions and for analytical sophistication in examining causality. This class analysis entails 'no theory of history according to which class conflict serves as the engine of social change', 'no theory of class exploitation, according to which class relations must be necessarily and exclusively antagonistic', and 'no theory of class-based collective action'. It does not even entail an '*assumption* of the pre-eminence of class' (1992: 382, original italics):

> To the contrary, it is integral to the research programme [of class analysis] that specific consideration should be also given to the theories holding that class relations are in fact of diminishing importance for life-chances and social action or that other relations and attributes – defined, for example, by income or consumption, status or lifestyle, ethnicity or gender – are, or are becoming, of greater consequence. (1992: 382)

Such a programme expresses a refreshing humility that is open and undogmatic by comparison with the Marxian class paradigm. However it presents problems of a different nature. If Goldthorpe and Marshall do not privilege class – if, in other words, they propose to study racial, ethnic, gender and other divisions, as well as class, without assuming the primacy of the latter – then there is no need to insist on calling their approach *class* analysis. It could be called, say, 'social analysis' or a 'stratification study'. Few social analysts would deny the empirical importance of looking for 'class', in the sense of looking for the effects of socioeconomic or occupational inequality, but this does not make them 'class analysts', because they may discover that such effects are so weak that they call into question the assumption of class. More importantly Goldthorpe and Marshall fail to specify the empirical threshold at which they would abandon their claim for the privileged position of class. Clearly, a class analysis that could find no evidence of class would be misnamed.

Semantics apart, there is also a question of consistency. While declaring theoretical and conceptual openness, Goldthorpe and Marshall seldom follow this declaration in practice. They firmly focus their research on class divisions and class mobility so that non-class divisions are rarely considered. Moreover, when taken at face value, the Goldthorpe and Marshall manifesto inevitably raises the issue of theoretical relevance. Class, according to them, cannot be treated as a universal key to the mysteries of social divisions, popular consciousness, social conflict, collective action and historical dynamics. Class structure, they imply, does not necessarily reflect *the* basic division and the universal rift. If this is so, there is no good reason to place it at the centre of a research programme. The implications of such openness are even more profound for class theory. If class theory is stripped of its 'assumption of the pre-eminence of class', it either dissolves into a general theory of inequality or becomes a footnote, something not worth knowing outside a small circle of specialists.

Holton and Turner (1994) respond to Goldthorpe and Marshall by staking out an essentially agnostic position. They note 'the intellectual retreat from class analysis' but do not endorse its extinction. Instead, they suggest an overhaul in a Weberian spirit: restricting the scope of class analysis, widening its narrow occupational focus and loosening its scientistic pretensions. Such a cure, however, might kill the patient. '[W]hat is left for class analysis', they ask, 'once the "strong" class idiom is rejected?' (1994: 800). The answer must be clear: when stripped of metaphoric connotations and ideological overtones, the class concept adds little to the explanatory value of studies of occupational location, economic organization, the labour market, and other elements of the economic arena.

To sum up, supporters of 'class analysis' face three dilemmas. First, there is a dilemma of identity. The more successful is the adjustment between class schemes and social formations, the less distinguishable they become from their main competitors, especially neo-Weberian multidimensional stratification schemes, status-attainment models and human capital theory. In other words, class theory and analysis can only gain credibility by sacrificing their identities and by converging with non-class theories. At the end of this road lies a 'class theory' that imitates its competitors in all but name. Second, there is a dilemma of theoretical relevance. The more that the class paradigm adjusts its propositions to contemporary social conflict and change the less relevant it becomes. The *gesellschaftlich* version tells us little about the direction in which societies are heading by comparison with the original promise of the class paradigm and the potential of its current competitors. Third, there is a dilemma of ideological relevance. The more thorough and successful are the correctives proposed by class fideists, especially the supporters of the 'class analysis', the more routine and less ideologically exciting are the theoretical outcomes. Less and less is left of the ideological attractiveness and appeal of class theory and of its original seductive emancipatory promise. It would be an interesting exercise to mount a charge against the barricade, leading supporters deeply indoctrinated in Wright's twelve-class scheme and fired up by the catchy phrase, 'semi-autonomous employees of the world unite'. Those few remaining radical social critics, who in the past might have embraced class iconography for its fiery and prophetic qualities, can only find these 'updated' class schemes disenchanting and disappointing. Many must now turn for both moral consolation and ideological zeal to theoretical competitors, especially to 'post-Marxist' theories of civil society and 'post-materialist' theories of politics.

**A revisionist history of class**

The arguments in the previous section suggest that there is nothing new in the claim that classes have withered almost to the point of disappearance and that the continuation of the class paradigm merely obstructs the development of a robust sociological analysis. The claim has certainly been rehearsed very widely. The new proposal of this book is, rather, a statement of *how and why* it happened rather than that it happened. Class sociologists have tended to be seduced by ideological commitments into explaining history away, so that the characteristics of nineteenth-century societies have been imposed on twentieth-century ones. This section presents an alternative history in which class is shown to have gone through a series of critical transformations that ultimately bring it to a point of decomposition.[13]

This book proceeds according to the following premises:

- The possible bases of stratification are several.
- Weber has signalled, in the class-party-status triplet, the most significant possible stratification orders.
- Stratification orders exhibit patterns of competition, domination and succession over time.
- Class, in its hardest, property-based sense, was the dominant stratification order only under early Western capitalism.
- Since then we have witnessed the progressive subordination of class to other stratification orders.
- During the twentieth century the predominant stratification mechanism in advanced societies has shifted from private property and production to the state and organizational systems.
- under current circumstances, predominance is shifting away from the state and organizations to cultural items and processes, generating quasi-communities that focus on lifestyles and value commitments.

Therefore the notion of economic-class society should be restricted to particular historical configurations in which collective actors determined by production relations struggle within that arena for control of the system of property ownership. Employment relations or labour-market position may continue to have salience in determining social rewards outside this configuration. However, in many if not most instances, these will be determined by factors other than property ownership, including organizational position, skills and credentials and the social worth of value commitments. Under such an argument the history of industrial-capitalist societies might be conceived, not as the history of struggle between classes, but as a history in which there is competition and struggle between *orders* of stratification.

In summary, the stratification order of capitalist societies can be traced as a succession of three periods roughly demarcated by the nineteenth century, the first three-quarters of the twentieth century, and the contemporary period. In highly formalized and abstracted terms they are as follows.

*Economic-class society*   This is a society arranged into patterns of domination and struggle between interest groups that emerge from the economic realm. In the familiar terms of Marx, the classes will be property owners and sellers of labour power, but they can be conceptualized as employers and employees. The dominant class can control the state and maintain itself as a ruling class either by capturing its apparatuses, or by rendering them weak. In so far as the subordinate class undertakes collective action, it will be rebellious or revolutionary in character, aimed at dislodging this ruling class by the abolition of private property. Culture is divided to match class divisions, into dominant and subordinate ideologies and into high and low cultures.

*Organized-class society*   This type of society is dominated by a political or state sphere. The state is typically ruled by a single unified bloc, a political-bureaucratic elite, that exercises power over subordinated masses. The bloc may be factionalized horizontally into formally opposed parties. The elite will comprise either a party leadership or a corporatized leadership integrating party leaders with the leaders of other organized interest groups including economic and cultural ones. The elite uses the coercive power of the state to regulate economics and culture. The state can dominate the economy by redistribution or by the conversion of private into public property, although this need not be a complete accomplishment. Masses, in turn, reorganize themselves in national-political classes rather than in industrial terms by establishing links with milieu parties. Meanwhile, the cultural realm can be unified under the state umbrella or under the aegis of state-sponsored monopolies. It can thus be turned into an industrialized or mass culture.[14]

*Status-conventional society*   In this type of society stratification emerges from the cultural sphere. The strata are lifestyle- and/or value-based status configurations. They can form around differentiated patterns of value commitment, identity, belief, symbolic meaning, taste, opinion or consumption. Because of the ephemeral and fragile nature of these resources, a stratification system based on conventional status communities appears as a shifting mosaic which can destabilize the other two spheres. The state is weakened because it cannot rely on mass support, and the economy is weakened (in its capacity for social structuring) because of the critical importance of symbolic values. Each order is deconcentrated by a prevailing orientation to values and utilities that are established conventionally rather than by reference to collective interests.

In failing to recognize these developments the class paradigm has made two errors that have seriously damaged the capacity of sociology to generate public debate about social and economic inequality. First, it has offered continued credence and legitimacy to class theory as a vehicle for the analysis of twentieth-century developments. In an important but not absolutely critical sense, class died somewhere between the beginning of the twentieth century and the end of the Great Depression. It died with the absorption of class struggle into the democratic arena, with the emergence of the fascist and socialist states that so dominated civil society, with the institutionalization of corporatist deals that linked government, capital and labour into common projects, with the mitigation of the effects of the market through such institutions as citizenship and welfare, and with the domination of the planet by superpower politics. The development was not entirely critical because the effects of what we can call 'organized class', the successor to true economic class, could still be analysed sociologically. As a successor to class theory, class analysis is indeed therefore an appropriate and impressive intellectual development in which sociology can take just pride. However, we are now contemplating a second and more critical error. Sociology is continuing to offer class analysis as its main vehicle for the discovery of social inequality and struggle in the trans-millennial period. It is failing to recognize that oppression, exploitation, and conflict are being socially constructed around transcendent conceptions of individual human rights and global values that identify and empower struggles around such diverse focuses as postcolonial racism, sexual preferences, gender discrimination, environmental degradation, citizen participation, religious commitments and ethnic self-determination. These issues have little or nothing to do with class. In the contemporary period of history, the class paradigm is intellectually and morally bankrupt.

## Conclusion

We do not need to accept the heroic mantle of Bellerophon. The fire-breathing monster with the head of a lion, the body of a nanny-goat, and the tail of a serpent is now just a mythical fancy, a flight of the imagination. We do, however, need to convince ourselves that our worst nightmares are indeed over. We need to confirm that the events we once were able to analyse as class events are no longer with us and that our society is being driven by new and equally interesting developments. In so doing, we need not abandon our moral and ideological commitments. Indeed the causes of emancipation and equality will be better served by recognizing their actual sources rather than reducing them to an old comforting theoretical touchstone.

The remaining chapters of this book expand and develop this thesis. However, before we can mobilize what we believe to be a convincing body of evidence and argument, we need to indicate the shape of the theoretical debates within which we seek to position ourselves. The vigour and importance of these debates is indicated by the fact that we are obliged to devote two chapters to summarizing them.

## Notes

1 For summaries of these theories see Crompton (1993), Giddens (1973) on Marx and Weber or Waters (1990; 1991; 1994a: 322–43).

2 This parallels the identification of the membership of economic classes as those who perform the functions of capital and labour respectively by Burnham (1941) and Carchedi (1975).

3 The most widely used seven-class schema is constructed as follows (Goldthorpe 1987: 40–3):

| class I: | upper service class: large proprietors; higher professionals; higher administrators and managers |
|---|---|
| class II: | lower service class: lower professionals; technicians; lower administrators; small-business managers; supervisors of non-manual workers |
| class III: | routine non-manual workers |
| class IV: | petty bourgeoisie and farmers |
| class V: | lower technicians; foremen and shop supervisors |
| class VI: | skilled manual workers |
| class VII: | semi- and unskilled manual workers. |

Note that not all seven-class schemas are identical. In particular the one used by Erikson and Goldthorpe (1992) differs very considerably from this.

4 He also specifies a third stage in which classes self-identify and undertake sociopolitical action on their own behalf, becoming, as it were, *Klassen für sich.*

5 These findings were originally made for Britain but similar findings are gathered elsewhere: on France and Sweden see Erikson et al. (1982); on Britain and the USA see Kerckhoff et al. (1985); on Australia and New Zealand see Jones and Davis (1988).

6 Nisbet read the paper at the annual ASA meeting in Seattle, WA, in August 1958 and subsequently published it in *The Pacific Sociological Review* in 1959.

7 Originally written in 1964, it was republished in 1972, with an updating postscript, in a collection on ideology edited by Blackburn.

8 Bell (1988: 277) quotes Sombart's exclamation that: 'On the reefs of roast beef and apple pie socialistic Utopias of every sort are sent to their doom.' Sombart had been trying to explain why there was no class consciousness in America.

9 Also see critiques of class orthodoxy by Hindess (1987), Saunders (1989) and Holton and Turner (1989). All of these can be seen as indirect responses to powerful restatements of the class position made by Marshall (1988) and Wright et al (1985; 1989).

10 In fact, Lipset signalled this process of declining class politics as early as in his 1964 article on 'The Changing Class Structure and Contemporary European Politics' and, in a more direct way, in the revised edition of *Political Man* (1981: especially 459ff).

11 As will be clear from our previous publications, each of the authors has made a long intellectual journey towards the position espoused in this book. Like Lipset we have travelled separately from fideism through agnosticism to atheism, arriving only recently at a common destination.

12 The main critics addressed by Goldthorpe and Marshall (1992) are Hindess (1987), Holton and Turner (1989) and Sørensen (1991). At the time of writing, only Pahl (1991) and Holton and Turner (1994) have responded directly. Lee (1994) and Scott (1994) are broadly in sympathy with Goldthorpe and Marshall. Goldthorpe and Marshall (1992) have commented on the earlier comments and in so doing responded to another critical paper in *Sociology* that indicates that identities are no longer class generated (Emmison and Western 1990).

13 We outline many of the aspects of this historical framework in Crook et al. (1992) and Waters (1994b).

14 Our position on organized-class society is similar to that taken by early Frankfurt School theorists (see, for example, the contributions in Arato and Gebhardt 1978: Part 1).

# 2

# The Shifting Sands of Structure

In its original Marxist formulation, class theory promised to explain social inequalities, conflict and change. Its claim as an alternative to bourgeois sociology relied on a capacity to provide a universal explanatory key to economic, cultural and political relations, as well as to the sociohistorical dynamics. Moreover, it included an emancipatory promise to cure society's major ills.

At the heart of class theory, then, lies the notion of a basic structural fault in society that is generated in the production process and its relations of property ownership and markets. It specifies that the power of capital is the principal component of societal power. The endorsement of this theoretical option does not necessarily imply crude economic determinism. Nor does it presume any particular delineation of class or any particular model of the class structure. Rather it implies the acceptance of a general assumption that the relations people enter as producers, and the interests derived from their location in the system of production and the market, constitute the key determinants of structured social inequalities, of group interests and identities, of social orientations and conduct, and of struggle and conflict.

History has proved to be unkind to Marxist theory and eschatology. Actual social developments have defied both predictions of progressive class polarization and conflict and the emancipatory promise of socialist revolution. In this chapter we identify several old lags of arguments that are regularly trotted out by opponents of 'class', partly because we want to indicate our continuing commitment to them, and partly because many of the claims made in the rest of this book are rooted in them. They each specify a structuring principle for society that can be held to be independent of class.

Seven substantive developments pose particularly awkward problems for class theory:

- the increasing importance of the state and corporate elites, especially under communist and fascist regimes;
- the increasing salience of authority relations established in organizational contexts;
- the stratifying capacity of educational qualifications, professional knowledge and skills;
- the growing complexity of occupational divisions;
- the continuing saliency of race, ethnicity and nationality;
- the historical and contemporary significance of patriarchal gender structures; and
- the stratifying importance of the cultural dimension of lifestyle and taste.

This chapter reviews a century of attempts to wrestle with these problems by social theorists who seek either to reject or to refine the Marxian scheme. It focuses especially on the proposition of economic determination.

## Status and party

Criticisms of economism are as old as class theory itself. Perhaps the most significant one comes from Weber (1978). He acknowledges the central importance of class in modern Western capitalism where capital accounting predominates, and where property ownership and market endowments are the key determinants of life-chances. However, he stresses that this is neither the sole nor a historically universal principle of social structure. It can better be analysed in terms of power, where 'class', 'status' and 'party'[1] are the three principal forms of institutionalized power distribution. In turn they reflect three relatively independent structures: the economic-market grid, the cultural-conventional grid and the political-organizational grid. Weber's stratificational configurations are always the consequence of the intersection of the three grids, although typically one predominates. Thus the pre-modern European societies, as well as ancient China and India, were predominantly status stratified. Social inequality in these societies was represented through highly visible symbols and cultivated through distinctive lifestyles. The capacity to maintain high-status lifestyles, as Weber acknowledged, was in the long run dependent on wealth, but never to an extent that could justify a causal reduction. The principal causal determinants of the life chances of European noblemen, Chinese mandarins or Indian brahmins were not economic, not production-related, and not property based.[2] Rather they were anchored in cultural conventions and sanctified by traditions that were usually religious. Similarly, politics in such societies were predominantly status centred. Status conflicts, the defence and usurpation of social honour and of monopolistic privileges, were the central social conflicts.

Status stratification and politics were eclipsed in the rationalized and rapidly industrializing West by the emergence of class from the matrix of market relations. However, this was a historically unique occidental configuration, and its origins could not be attributed solely to economic transformations, much less to the 'forces of production' or property relations. In Weber's analysis, class division and conflict, though increasingly salient, did not replace or eliminate other cleavages. The formation of the modern state and the 'master trend' of bureaucratization in the West, in fact, enhanced the importance of a political stratification that was irreducible to class or status divisions. Prefiguring the arguments of the Frankfurt School thinkers and of contemporary elite theory, Weber affirms the potential, though not necessarily the predominance, of political-organizational stratification.

Thus, in Weber, class divisions are neither the sole nor even the central referents. Class is not treated as a privileged category. Class structure is not identified with the social structure in general. Class is not necessarily the central aspect of social inequality. Class relations, if analysed at any length, are always seen in a complex interplay with other aspects of societal structure. The social fabric always involves a warp of class relations *and* a weft of status relations *and* a rich embroidery of associative relations. While analytically distinct, these three aspects are never reduced to a single locus of determination and never treated in isolation.[3]

### Elites and the state

Sniping at the economic determinism of Marxist class theory is by no means a Weberian monopoly. In fact, the earliest and the most radical challenge to class analysis came from the classical elite theories of Mosca (1939), Pareto (1935) and Weber's student Michels (1958).[4] They offered an exact opposite of classical Marxism, stressing inequality and conflict between elite and masses, and the 'inevitability' of elite rule as a mirror image of the Marxist claim to an inevitably classless future. In elite theory, the core aspect of stratification is political power. The key division lies between a small, organized and powerful elite and an unorganized powerless mass. Politics is an elite game conducted in accordance with elite interests, and history is the graveyard of elite groups decaying and displacing each other.[5]

The idiosyncrasies of the numerous versions of elite theory are less important here than the general challenge that they pose to class theory and analysis. However, in a development that parallels the schism between class theory and analysis, the analysis of sociopolitical structures has survived beyond the eclipse of classical elite theory.[6] The first revival of elite theory was prompted by the formation of fascist and communist dictatorships that restricted the power of property, subjected markets to political control and generated a distinctive form of political stratification in which overall access to material and symbolic goods reflected a position in a party-organizational hierarchy. The second revival of the elitist paradigm is more recent. It coincides with the corporatization of politics and social structure in the industrialized West, the industrialization of Soviet-type societies, and the apparent success of the highly étatist and authoritarian 'Asian industrialization path'.

Neither the origins nor the collapse of the fascist dictatorships square well with the class paradigm. Fascist regimes emerged by political coups and their domination rested on the control of coercive apparatuses rather than the means of production. They generated a political form of stratification, with clearly articulated party elites and highly politicized criteria of rewards. These developments, and the interpretative difficulties they pose for class theorists, prompted a wave of Marxist, Weberian and elitist revisions that re-emphasized the importance of the political dimensions of stratification and conflict.[7] The latter followed the key tenets of classical elite theory by stressing the centrality and irreducibility of political power, as well as the capacity of party-political elites to wield this power by control of the state and the mass media.

The formation of the Soviet state in the 1920s, followed by similar developments in China after 1945 and the export of state socialism to Soviet-dominated Eastern Europe in 1944–8, posed even bigger problems for class theory and analysis. The communist takeovers in Russia and China defied the classical Marxist model of economic-class determination. To paraphrase Lenin, they proved that politics could determine economics. Moreover, although they were nominally class-destructive regimes, the communist dictatorships created distinctive and deeply inegalitarian stratification systems that in turn became the source of social conflicts that ultimately caused their collapse. This state-socialist stratification followed organizational-political lines. Economic rewards were distributed according to one's proximity to the party-state elite and one's capacity to influence state planners, and were entirely reminiscent of those observed under fascism. Power was heavily concentrated in the apex of the Communist Party Politburos and the organizationally circumscribed *nomenklatura*. Social divisions in terms of occupational prestige, skills, and sectoral, regional and urban–rural differences were dwarfed by these major organizational and party-political divisions. Access to material goods was, to a significant extent, politically dependent. Symbolic rewards also followed closely these political-organizational divisions.[8]

Unlike fascism, state socialism could not be dismissed by advocates of class theory as a historical diversion. The sheer size, longevity, and strength of state-socialist regimes propelled them to the centre-stage of theoretical debates and helped to rekindle the class controversy. The most plausible interpretations of state socialism either were couched in terms of elite theory (e.g. Aron 1968; 1988), or combined elite with class models (e.g. Voslensky 1984). The consensus suggests that the fundamental divisions in state-socialist societies are political-organizational rather than economic. The socialist ruling class of party *apparatchiki*, *nomenklatura* and planners is rooted in the command system rather than property relations. At the other end of the social spectrum there is a socialist 'working class' encompassing a very broad range of occupations, both manual and non-manual, but uniform in its subordination to political-administrative diktat. This configuration fits the elite–mass paradigm much more closely than it does class.

The elite–mass model was also embraced by many students of the post-Second World War American power structure. The apparent fusion of executive-governmental, corporate and military power during the Cold War into the so-called 'military-industrial complex' gave rise to the 'power elite' theories of the 1950s and 1960s, especially that of Mills (1956). Unlike orthodox class arguments, this elite account claims that power grows out of corporate hierarchies. It coagulates in the organizational apexes of state-military-industrial bodies rather than in broader property-based ruling classes. Although most American elite theorists, such as Hunter, Baltzell and Mills himself, remain very sensitive to the power of property and to the class connections of the corporate elites, they refuse to reduce organizational-political power to property or market relations. They are thus possibly more faithful to the spirit of Weber's analyses than are many contemporary neo-Weberians.

The latter were preoccupied in seeking reconciliations between class and elite schemes. The best attempts were made by Giddens (1973), and from a more orthodox Marxist angle, by Wesolowski (1979). For Giddens, the distinctive feature of capitalism is a 'separation of the spheres of political and economic hegemony' (1973: 118). While class-economic relations form the principal power grid, the degree of formal differentiation of authority and the forms of its mediation with class vary. Political elite structuration, like social class structuration, has its mediate and proximate aspects, and the variety of outcomes is therefore manifested in the variety of elite configurations – ruling class, governing class, power elite, leadership groups, and so on.

While Giddens emphasizes the diversity of political elite structuration, Wesolowski (1979) outlines the nature of class limitations on elite power. He sees elites as subordinated to the dominant class in three major dimensions: recruitment and social composition; decision-making autonomy; and the scope of issues subject to and excluded from political considerations. The last point was widely discussed in the context of Bachrach and Baratz's (1963) studies of 'non-decisional' power, the capacity to shape agendas, and Lukes' (1974) three dimensions of power. The power of class, they imply, the structurally determined capacity to shape outcomes, cannot easily be reduced to political decision-making; its principal sources rest outside the sphere of politics. Allegedly extra-political and 'deep' power resources, such as those implied by Lukes' third dimension, do not need to be of a class nature.

Contemporary theorists of the state (e.g. Evans et al. 1985; Skocpol 1985; Mann 1986b) and elite theorists (e.g. Field and Higley 1980; Etzioni-Halevy 1993) reject this metaphysics of power. They inisist on the transparency and autonomy of power relations and on the crucial importance of states and elites in shaping social inequalities and political outcomes, especially democracy and political stability. For Skocpol (1985), the state and state-controlling elites have to be brought back into social analysis as central structures and actors irreducible to class. For Etzioni-Halévy (1993), one of the harshest contemporary critics of class theory, and equally for Field and Higley (1980) the key players in political conflicts are elites. The degree and character of elite unity, and the extent of elite autonomy, including autonomy from mass pressures, are the key determinants of social and political configurations.

Political power relations lie at the centre of these étatocentric and elite-based accounts of stratification, conflict and change. They are proving more useful than class as theoretical tools for students of post-communist, Latin American and East Asian societies. Political power, state intervention and elite action are seen as the key determinants of social and economic change, especially in the Asian dragon societies (Amsden 1985). Class analysis offers, at best, only a backdrop for such sociopolitical analyses. Indeed in some accounts class becomes a mere dependent variable, the object of social and political manipulations by powerful and autonomous state elites (e.g. Trimberger 1978). While elite and class analyses are not intrinsically incompatible (see Giddens 1973; Wesolowski 1979), elite schemes that stress the autonomy and centrality of political factors contradict notions of class determination that stress the structuring role of production and market relations.

## Citizenship

The impact of the state is by no means limited to the arenas of the rulership. In a seminal paper on 'Citizenship and Social Class' presented in 1949, Marshall (1950) outlines a classical theory of citizenship that confirms the global and profound impact of legislative-political interventions on class inequality. His argument has subsequently been extended and adjusted to fit other liberal-democratic societies (see Barbalet 1988; Giddens 1985; Mann 1987; Turner 1990; 1993; Roche 1992). Class and citizenship, according to Marshall, have always been subject to contradictory tensions. He distinguishes three periods during which three components of citizenship, civil, political and social, were established in Britain.[9] The civil component of citizenship, 'liberty of the person, freedom of speech, thought and faith, the right to own property and to conclude valid contracts, and the right to justice' (1950: 71), was instituted in the eighteenth century in the form of independent courts of justice. The political component, 'the right to participate in the exercise of political power' (1950: 72), that is, to vote and stand for political office, developed throughout the nineteenth century. Parliaments and councils of local governments were the key institutional articulations of the political aspect of citizenship. Finally, the first half of the twentieth century saw the extension of citizenship into the social sphere of welfare and social security rights 'to live the life of a civilized being according to the standards prevailing in the society' (1950: 72). The institutions of the welfare state corresponded to this last stage of citizenship extension and corresponded with the erosion of raw class principles. The most important aspect of this third stage is the collective mode of definition and implementation. While civil and political rights were attributed to individuals, and in many ways were compatible with the operation of the capitalist class principle, welfare rights were defined within a collectivist idiom and extended under the impact of class organizations. Although their net effect was not the elimination of class, they did result in a substantial abatement of its impact:

> First, the compression, at both ends, of the scale of income distribution. Second, the great extension of the area of common culture and common experience. And third, the enrichment of the universal status of citizenship, combined with the recognition and stabilization of certain status differences chiefly through the linked system of education and occupation. (1950: 116)

For Turner (1986; 1990), the partial delegitimation of class inequality and the reduction of class division through the extension of citizenship are not as important as the legitimation of non-class principles of distribution, allocation and integration. At its heart lies the notion of entitlement linked with the universal status of citizen. Though the original Marshallian formulation is too narrow,[10] it is nevertheless correct in identifying citizenship as a major contender to class. Citizenship rights and entitlements are principally *status* rights and entitlements. More precisely, they constitute a political-legal domain within which status-like claims can effectively be made. Inequalities linked with citizenship rights cannot be analysed as class inequalities. However, the struggles for such entitlements that became the core element of contemporary politics could still be interpreted in class terms.

### Consumption

One offshoot of this argument has been elaborated by sociologists studying housing and consumption. Its inspiration comes from both the literature on the importance of state distributive interventions and a Weberian–Veblenian tradition that stresses the importance of consumption as a basis of social divisions. In Saunders' (1978; 1990) interpretation, the division between the 'privatised and collectivised modes of housing', in particular, generates a new and salient form of inequality and social division in Britain that renders problematic the key tenets of class theory. The 'established and enduring' process of restratification involves a shift of generative mechanism away from the relationship with the means of production and towards the relationship with the means of consumption, in particular housing. The key cleavage in contemporary British society (and perhaps also other societies), argues Saunders, is between owners and non-owners of dwellings. Interests, identities and political alliances centre on this aspect of social position. While this new division might be seen as a new class divide centred on the ownership of the means of consumption, Saunders prefers to regard it as a counter-class principle:

> We need to recognise that class is not the only major basis of social cleavage in con-
> temporary capitalist societies, for increasingly people find themselves involved in
> political struggles which emanate not from their class location but from their loca-
> tion in what Dunleavy . . . termed 'consumption sectors'. Seen in this context,
> home ownership does not alter people's class interests, but it is a major factor
> which helps to define their consumption sector interests. Consumption sectors,
> which are constituted through the division between owners and non-owners of
> crucial means of consumption such as housing, crosscut class boundaries, are
> grounded in non-class-based material interests and represent an increasingly sig-
> nificant form of social cleavage which in certain circumstances come to outweigh
> class membership in their economic and political effects. (1990: 206)

Saunders' work stimulated a wave of criticism (e.g. Marshall et al. 1988). The critics question the claim that the salience of home ownership is either new or enduring, pointing out the diversity and division within owning and non-owning categories, rejecting the diagnosis of the decollectivization and privatization of consumption, and criticizing the view as exaggerated. In spite of these criticisms, the notion of 'consumption sectors' is proving remarkably attractive both in empirical analyses of political attitudes and in further the-orizing the salience of consumption, lifestyle and taste.

## Organizational domination

A key feature of the development of industrial societies in the twentieth century has been an expansion of state activity. This development radically affects the system of social inequality. First, the state provides access to social resources and rewards that are autonomous relative to processes of production. Whatever social strata are generated by state employment and state benefits, they are not economic classes in the sense of being anchored in processes of production. Second, state action modifies social arrangements built around production processes so that economic areas previously defined as private and autonomous become subject to state control and regulation. States regulate labour and commodities markets; they intervene to provide capital infrastructure; and they sponsor corporatist relations between employers and employees (see Offe 1984).

These extensions of state activity into the economic sphere provide the basis for political restructuring of stratification arrangements. A bureaucratic-political elite controls the distribution of state resources and establishes consumption privileges on this basis – improved access to salaries, travel, working conditions, pension schemes, and so on. Below this elite, a less autonomous and less privileged public-service category of workers nevertheless enjoys a relatively high level of material security. The receipt of socioeconomic protection creates membership in a third and lower stratum of dependent citizens whose social location is entirely contingent on state activity. These are the recipients of welfare benefits, unemployment insurance, pensions, and so on. They include the structurally unemployed and underemployed, the physically and mentally disabled, female heads of households, and the aged. Membership in the dependent underclass is stable and reproducing. This is especially true where membership intersects with age, gender, race or ethnicity.

It is also possible to mount an argument that, even in the private sector, the critical stratifying feature is rather more to do with the distribution of domination than the distribution of ownership. The principal issue here is the 'separation of ownership from control' in which the functions of capital are increasingly performed by managers while stockholders merely own the corporation in a legal sense. Actual capitalists disappear from the production process and thus, it might be argued, class relations cannot be understood merely in terms of property ownership (Burnham 1941; Berle and Means 1967). Below the senior managerial level, increases in scale and specialization of organizations generate imperatives for co-ordination. A key characteristic of contemporary capitalism is its hierarchical and bureaucratic organization. In other words, organized capitalism offers a stable basis for the formation of intermediate strata defined by their access to domination.

## Knowledge and skill

The interpretative problems posed by state socialism and welfarism were eclipsed by the difficulties posed by organizational and occupational change in advanced capitalist societies. We leave aside old debates about the emergence of 'monopoly' and 'finance' capital, and leave until a later chapter debates on the separation of ownership and control, to focus on more recent debates on industrial society (Dahrendorf 1959), post-industrial society (Bell 1976), and professional society (Larson 1977; Perkin 1989).[11] Each of these challenges the economic-productive determinism inherent in all versions of class theory.

Many post-Second World War elaborations of the class paradigm seek to incorporate emergent stratificational features that are known in Marxist language as 'new classes': 'corporate elites', 'managerial classes', rapidly expanding 'professional and white-collar classes', and the fluctuating 'underclass' of state dependants and marginalized workers in insecure employment. Dahrendorf (1959: 36–66) summarizes these changes in six points: the decomposition of the capitalist class into owner-shareholders and managers; the similar fragmentation of the previously unitary working class into skilled, semi-skilled and unskilled segments, each with distinct interests; the expansion of the 'new middle class', itself divided into administrator-bureaucrats and service staff; increased social mobility that erodes class boundaries and dissolves class struggles into individualized competition; the extension of citizenship rights eliminating the most blatant forms of class privilege and deprivation; and the institutionalization of class conflict through collective bargaining and arbitration procedures. As the above section indicates, Dahrendorf stresses these developments cannot directly be attributed to the operation of the traditional class mechanism. They occur because the structuring and conflict-generating mechanism of industrial society is located in organizations that divide controllers from the controlled. These categories have opposed interests and are likely to form conflict groups.[12]

Bell's theory of the post-industrial society follows a similar line of argument to Dahrendorf but more radically. Bell (1976) suggests that a major revision of the class paradigm is necessary in order to make it suitable for the analysis of a society undergoing a post-industrial shift in the way its economy functions. This change from a goods-producing to a service economy is associated with the growing 'pre-eminence of the professional and technical class', an increasing 'centrality of theoretical knowledge', and the ascendancy of a technical-scientific knowledge class. The class mechanism, 'a system that has institutionalized the ground rules for acquiring, holding, and transferring differential power and its attendant privileges' (1976: 361), is changing:

> In Western society, the dominant system has been property, guaranteed and safeguarded by the legal order, and transmitted through a system of marriage and family. But over the past 25 to 50 years, the property system has been breaking up. In American society today, there are three modes of power and social mobility, and this baffles students of society who seek to tease out the contradictory sources of class positions. There is the historic mode of property as the basis of wealth and power, with inheritance as the major route of access. There is technical skill as the basis of power and position, with education as the necessary route of access to skill. And finally there is political office as a base of power, with organization of a machine as the route of access. (1976: 361)

The historical shift in the class base was from property to technical skills. Education and political mobilization replaced inheritance and patronage as the principal mechanisms and routes of access. The class system of post-industrial society is thus open and meritocratic. Although it does not dispose of the disparities of power and wealth, it nevertheless makes these disparities consistent with visions of classless inequality.

Bell's analysis demonstrates that educational credentials are an important component in stratification theory. Larson (1977) shows that the original basis for credentialism was the formal establishment of medicine, and later law and academia, as professions in response to the burgeoning specialization and monetarization of the market and to the growth of state bureaucracies engaged in its reproduction. Here, credentials found an important function in commodifying service provision by standardizing professional products as well as by arranging pricing structures in relation to them in a fee-for-service system. However, the rise of credentialism in the twentieth century is the outcome of efforts by employed occupational groups to imitate the success of free professionals in monopolizing closure in the market.

On a reading of social trends similar to Larson, Perkin (1989) theorizes the emergence of a 'professional society' where Dahrendorf and Bell theorize a (post-)industrial society. It is a 'logical continuation of industrial society', but it is based on a different stratifying principle and a different public ethos. Class society, which according to Perkin reached its zenith in England between 1880 and 1914, was property based, polarized and socially 'segregated by income, status, appearance, physical health, speech, education and opportunities in life, as well as by work and residential area' (1989: 27). A new professional society emerged in the 1920s under the impact of state-sponsored corporatism. This involved a partnership between government, employers and trade unions, and a 'trend towards equality' generated by welfare provisions and the redistributive activities of the state. The central process of professional society is state-sponsored mobility through education:

> A professional society is one structured around career hierarchies, rather than classes, one in which people find their places according to trained expertise and the service they provide rather than possession or lack of inherited wealth or acquired capital. (1989: 359)

In the political domain, it is dominated by professionalized party hierarchies; in the industrial sphere, by professional managers whose power rests on cultivation of human resources; and in the social sphere, by increasingly powerful welfare professions. Class divisions, images and identifications still persist, but in a 'weak, confused and changing' form. They are gradually displaced by professional divisions, identification and imagery. In the social fabric, the weft of class is less visible than the warp of professional interests.

There are striking similarities in these three views. Each diagnoses the collapse of class principles of stratification and conflict based on capital ownership and inheritance. They agree on the causes of this collapse: advanced industrialization, state intervention, especially in education and welfare, and social mobility. They also identify the symptoms of the new configurations in a roughly similar way, although they differ in the degree of radicalism by which they depart from classical class schemes. While Dahrendorf attempts to reconstruct it in a quasi-Weberian mould by emphasizing authority relations, Bell embraces an occupational, gradational and meritocratic class vision peppered by a rhetoric about domination by the allegedly ascendant knowledge class, and Perkin supplements the class scheme by adding a new professional principle.

## Occupational status

Conventional status is another contender in the conceptual contest to be at the centre of stratification arrangements. Here we shall understand 'status' in Weberian terms, that is as a coherent and shared lifestyle which consists of consumption patterns, forms of social intercourse, marital practices, associational memberships and shared value commitments. Status differentiation can therefore be based on formal education, hereditary prestige, and, most importantly for subsequent analysis, occupational prestige. An argument in favour of conventional status would contend that status groups can form across class divisions. Status groups can prevent the formation of classes in the market because they monopolize privilege and thus prevent the mobilization of property or skills in order to gain access to it.

The main vehicle for the mobilization of conventional status as the proper approach is the functional theory of stratification, which reduces economic differences of income and wealth to the prestige or importance that attaches to particular occupations. Parsons (1954) provides the theoretical underpinning for such a claim by specifying two premises: first, that mutual evaluation is a universal aspect of social practices and that, where evaluation occurs, a system of ranking must also occur; and second, that it is a condition of the stability of society that there should be a common value system in relation to which the constituent components are integrated. Therefore roles are ranked in terms of their significance as specified in the common value system (1954: 388–9). In capitalist societies, economic values are paramount; that is, the predominant basis on which the units and members of society cohere is their commitment to economic advancement. The structural subsystem which corresponds with these values is the occupational subsystem, so the principal dimension of inequality in capitalist societies is the occupational structure.

Parsons leaves unaddressed the issue of why some occupations are rewarded more highly than others. In seeking to explain the actual distribution of rewards Davis and Moore (1945) accept Parsons' view that the occupational structure has a functional relationship to the society as a whole: it is a universal necessity for societal survival. Differential rewards are necessary because some occupations are more important for societal survival than are others and people must be motivated to enter the more important ones: 'In general those positions convey the best reward and hence have the highest rank, which (a) have the greatest importance for society and (b) require the greatest training or talent' (1945: 243).

To summarize then, if one accepts that occupations are ranked by processes specified neither by production nor by a legal order, then they must be ranked or evaluated in terms of conscious negotiation between human beings. Indeed power groups and classes can be reduced to conventional 'socioeconomic status':

> The occupational structure in modern industrial society not only constitutes an important foundation for the main dimensions of social stratification but also serves as the connecting link between different institutions and spheres of inequality . . .The hierarchy of prestige strata and the hierarchy of economic classes have their roots in the occupational structure; so does the hierarchy of political power and authority, for political authority in modern society is largely exercised as a full-time occupation. (Blau and Duncan 1967: 6–7)

Importantly, in so far as: 'the occupation structure is more or less continuously graded in regard to status rather than being a set of discrete status classes' (1967: 124), status theory rejects the possibility of class formation. This helps to explain similarities in the occupational structures and stratification patterns in all industrialized societies, both capitalist and state-socialist, as well as broad similarities in social mobility patterns discovered throughout the 1970s and 1980s.

The functional theory of stratification inspired a wave of status-attainment studies that shifted attention away from societal conflicts and economic divisions, and towards the scaling of occupational prestige and the identification of the causes of individual occupational mobility. While the mainstream social mobility literature charts patterns of mobility, measures rates and distances, and debates the degree of social fluidity within and across generations, attainment studies focus on the question of determinants of individual success. Assessment of the relative causal impact of these determinants became possible owing to the application of a powerful regression analysis and the construction of path models of status attainment pioneered in Blau and Duncan's *The American Occupational Structure* (1967). The status-attainment models include such ascriptive factors as parental occupational position, and such achievement factors as education, all considered independently of each other in relation to the dependent variables that were typically operationalized in terms of occupational status.

Attainment studies confront class theory with a number of difficult questions and embarrassing findings concerning the alleged impact of class factors on life trajectories. They are able to measure the impact of parental class position, occupational status, income, property status, and education on the socioeconomic status of the offspring, as well as the impact of initial occupations on subsequent careers. In class societies these 'class factors' should have had a pronounced causal impact, generating detectable cycles of privilege and deprivation. However, this is not what the studies reveal in contemporary society. Rather, they show limited inheritance and confirm the expanding universalism thesis first formulated by Blau and Duncan:

The achieved status of a man, what he has accomplished in terms of some objective criteria, becomes more important than his ascribed status, who he is in the sense of what family he comes from . . . What it does imply is that superior status cannot any more be directly inherited but must be legitimized by actual achievements that are socially acknowledged. Education assumes increasing significance for social status in general and for the transmission of social standing from fathers to sons in particular. (1967: 430)

They also sound a warning that although the direct transmission of privilege and disadvantage is declining, indirect inheritance through education is increasingly effective. However, education lies outside the economic realm and under the sway of the state. Educational reforms, achieved mainly through political pressures, can affect the process of class formation by expanding universalism. Comparative studies in both state-socialist and social-democratic regimes confirm this capacity of the state to restructure and reduce social inequalities. A new generation of attainment studies confirms the expansion of universalism throughout the 1970s and 1980s, as well as a tendency towards the inheritance of educational advantage. Hout (1988), for example, observes that the effects of social origins on occupational destinations in the USA declined by over one-quarter over the 1962–73 decade, and by one-third over the 1972–85 period.

Attainment studies also identify variations in the extent to which social origins, including class origins, affect life trajectories (Heath 1981). The former state-socialist societies (e.g. Czechoslovakia, Poland) show the least ascription but some clear signs of inheritance of what Bourdieu subsequently calls 'cultural capital'. The settler colonies (e.g. Australia) and the 'middle-of-the-road' societies (e.g. Britain), which together form by far the largest membership in the advanced capitalist category, show high achievement and declining ascription. 'Traditional right-wing' societies (e.g. Spain) appear as more ascriptive than achievement oriented. This variation in pattern, as well as the relatively high openness in advanced industrial societies, is also hard to square with class determination.

### Race, ethnicity and nationality

The class paradigm has always found difficulty in accommodating the ascribed statuses of ethnicity, race and gender. Its principal coping strategy has been to assume that they are unimportant, irrelevant, irrational or non-existent and that economic class is the overwhelming structuring principle for modern society. In so far as it has done so, the class paradigm has itself contributed to ideologies of white male supremacism. Historically, gender has exhibited far more pronounced inequalities of power and material rewards. Gender inequalities may well offer more extreme examples of exploitation and brutal coercion than those between classes. It is also arguable that in the public sphere the extremes of discrimination that have occurred between races, and the passionate and bloody conflicts that continue to take place between ethnic groups, far outweigh division and struggle between classes.

Again, we stress that we find class analysis to be as culpable as class theory in this regard. In so far as it elects to emphasize the less salient effects of class as against the more salient effects of ascribed status, it denies the reality and importance of the latter.

In playing down the saliency of ethnicity and race, the class paradigm has always taken its lead from its intellectual ancestors. Marx viewed ethnic groups as 'national left-overs' and 'fanatic partisans of the counter-revolution' that threated to divide the working class and thwart its historical mission (Parkin 1979: 31). Equally Weber theorized ethnic group formation as a form of irrational action that ran counter to the technical rationalization of modern bureaucracies and markets. In a sense, the development of the state conspired in this view. Originally an expression of nationality, the nation-state operated to suppress national minorities and sought to assimilate the entire population into a homogenized national cultural community. Because sub-state nationalities were rendered invisible, sociologists often treated them as if they were unreal, as if they were only 'imagined communities' (Anderson 1983) relative to the structural realities of class.

Post-Second World War developments have made such interpretations more difficult to sustain. The persistence of racial and ethnic inequalities and conflicts, especially in the USA, stimulated an open challenge to the class schemes. The salience and autonomy of race and ethnic factors, according to Glazer and Moynihan, implied a reversal of class determinism: 'it is property that begins to seem derivative, and ethnicity that seems to be a fundamental source of stratification' (1975: 16). Racial and ethnic inequalities permeated identities and racial and ethnic conflicts clearly dominated politics. The civil rights movement, black consciousness movements, Québec Libre and other ethnic revivalist campaigns became the central features of the North American social and political scene. They also affected, although initially to a much lesser extent, the multi-ethnic and multi-racial societies of Western Europe.

The main class-theoretical strategies consisted either of denials (e.g. Poulantzas 1974; Westergaard and Resler 1975) or of rhetorical accommodations. In the latter case, class theory embraced the racial-ethnic factor as a sub-category of generic class domination. Race merged with class in the theory of 'internal colonialism' (Hechter 1975). Such interpretations depict the march of capitalism as involving a *divide et impera* tactic towards its working classes combined with a progressive expansion of class-exploitative relations. Racial and ethnic minorities are constructed as the intra-national victims of this tactic, the equivalents of external colonies. The contradictory aspects of the construct[13] are glossed over in such formulations. The accommodation of the reality is achieved by rhetorical devices that give little attention to theoretical consistency. Racial and ethnic inequalities are defined as a part of the general class landscape of expanding capitalism. They generate displaced antagonisms that must still be rooted in the capitalist mode of production.

Such views are now untenable. Three historical developments mean that the theoretical salience of race and ethnicity can no longer be denied. First, the previously colonized societies of the 'South' have managed to re-establish self-government, albeit in a form shaped by the 'Northern' colonizers. Part of the ideology that supported this move was an attempt to establish that racism was an unethical and irrational form of behaviour by claiming that inequalities of race far outweighed those of class. Second, one of the emerging features of the contemporary world is mass migration motivated by relative economic disadvantage. Flows from ex-colonies into colonizing societies and from Eastern and Southern Europe into Western Europe have radically altered the ethnic mix in societies previously claimed to be ethnically homogeneous, and these ethnic cleavages are now too apparent to be ignored. This can be confirmed by the fact that the class paradigm is least well established in a society with a large racial minority and relatively continuous immigration throughout its history, the USA. Third, during the past quarter of a century the state has gone through a series of crises that have weakened its powers, allowing the re-emergence of previously repressed national minorities. Nowhere is this more apparent than in the ex-socialist states of Eastern Europe and the former USSR where ethnic resurgence now threatens fragile political and economic arrangements.

## Patriarchy

If sociology turned a blind eye to ethnicity then it must have turned two to gender. Gender inequalities and exploitations were obscured by the 'naturalism' of sex-role theory and the triumphalism of a modernization theory that stressed the adaptive superiority of the nuclear family. In a weak sense the class paradigm can be regarded as less than culpable because one of its claims was that class processes transpired largely in the public sphere, and that because women were excluded from employment and politics they were irrelevent to class processes. This was a widespread view found for example in Parsons, 'The separation of the sex roles in our society is such as . . . to remove women from the kind of occupational status which is important for the determination of the status of the family' (1959: 80); in Giddens, 'Given that women still have to await their liberation from the family, it remains the case in the capitalist societies that female workers are largely peripheral to the class system' (1973: 288); and in Parkin, 'for the majority of women . . . the allocation of social and economic rewards is determined primarily by the position of their families – and, in particular, that of the male head' (1979: 14–15). In a famous article, Goldthorpe (1983) asserts that he will continue to measure the class of any woman by classifying the occupation of her conjugal partner because household income is largely determined by the male partner, because women's labour-force participation is intermittent, and because women's sociopolitical attitudes can be predicted more accurately by their partner's occupation than by their own, even if they are themselves employed.

Meanwhile such feminist critics as Britten and Heath (1983) and Baxter (1991) prefer an individualizing approach in which each person's class position is graded separately, although this does set up the conception of the cross-class family, incorporating the bizarre notion that members of different classes can cohabit. More radical feminists go beyond conventional class analysis into the sphere of domestic-familial relations and predominantly unpaid household work (e.g. Barker and Allen 1976; Delphy 1984). Many of these appropriate the class paradigm to suggest that women and men are classes determined by a domestic mode of production.

None of these positions is acceptable. Female participation in the employment sphere is now at a higher level, more stable and more influential than it has ever been. Patriarchy has been transformed into a 'public patriarchy' (Walby 1990) or 'viriarchy' (Waters 1989). The class paradigm is at a total loss in either predicting or explaining this development. Class analysis in particular seems to have great difficulty in analysing the intersection between gender and the labour market. Goldthorpe's current solution is what he calls the 'dominance' approach in which all members of a given household are classified according to the occupation of the member with the highest occupational standing. Clearly this is unsatisfactory because where two conjugal partners are employed it must be the intersection of their respective occupational standings that determines the location of a family within stratification arrangements and not the occupational attributes of any one of its individual members. This is because the gender dimension is impossible to incorporate into a class analysis that focuses on paid employment, occupational roles, and market relations.

Conventional class-analytic arguments that suggest that extra-domestic productive relations determine class, that the position of women is reducible to that of the household head, that class identities overshadow gender ones and are predominantly husband determined, all face increasing challenges. Such contemporary empirical analysts of class as Wright (1989), Marshall et al. (1988) and Baxter et al. (1991) admit to significant gender divisions that cross-cut class inequalities.[14] They try to explain them away by adopting such notions as 'mediated class relations' and 'cross-class families'. However these very attempts provoke more questions than they answer.

This analytic development raises the possibility of a more fundamental criticism. It suggests that the class paradigm has always been wrong in claiming pre-eminence as a structuring principle. The development of a class structure was only possible in so far as it was based on a domestic division of labour that allowed men exclusively to construct a public sphere. In these terms we must consider the possibility that gender is primordial as *the* structural principle and that class is merely contingent. Certainly one could make a more convincing case that gender has always structured society than one could that class has done so.

### Cultural capital

Bourdieu (1980; 1994) makes the most radical break with the economism of the original Marxist version of class theory:

> The failings of the Marxist theory of class, above all its inability to explain the set

of objectively observed differences, result from the fact that, by reducing the social world to the economic field alone, it is condemned to define social position with reference solely to the position within the relations of economic production. It thus ignores the positions occupied in the different fields and sub-fields, particularly in the relations of cultural production, as well as all those oppositions which structure the social field and which are not reducible to the opposition between the owners and non-owners of the means of economic production. (1994: 244)

Any Weberian sociologist would agree wholeheartedly with such a dictum. Social inequalities, it says, can be charted in a complex, multidimensional and open-ended scheme of 'social fields'. Cultural differences and symbolic actions gain due recognition. Relations of domination that are central in Bourdieu's scheme involve neither exploitation nor even open antagonism and conflict. Social power is the result of location in these relatively autonomous fields. Economic capital is an important dimension, but it is not privileged over cultural, social, symbolic and other capitals:

In reality, the social space is a multi-dimensional space, an open set of relatively autonomous fields, fields which are more or less strongly and directly subordinate, in their functioning and their transformations, to the field of economic production. Within each of the sub-spaces, those who occupy dominant positions and those who occupy dominated positions are constantly involved in struggles of different kinds (without necessarily constituting themselves thereby as antagonistic groups). (1994: 245)

Social agents can thus be located in the social space according to the type, composition and volume of their multiple capitals. This location in multi-dimensional social space allows Bourdieu to carve up classes as categories of agents who share a similar location in the social space. Because of this shared location, they are likely to have similar interests and dispositions, form social groups, and act in a solidary manner. In spite of Bourdieu's protestations, these 'classes' now closely resemble status groups.[15]

Bourdieu thus purges not only economic determinism but the privileged position of the general economic power grid from what is still nominally a class theory. For Bourdieu humans are symbolizers rather than producers; or, more accurately, material production is a sub-category of the more general and less definite category of the 'production of meaning'. The approach can maintain only a weak genetic connection to the original Marxist class project. The social-symbolic world of Bourdieu is torn apart by conflicts and struggles that rage against effective domination, but the domination and struggles are no longer primarily, let alone exclusively, generated in the sphere of property ownership, material production and markets.

### Conclusion

The inherent economic reductionism of class theory has proven to be untenable. Although high under early capitalism, the salience of relations of production has declined in relative terms and with it the power of capital. The evolution of theories of the class structure, with all their intellectual gyrations, their rhetorical claims and complex elaborations, is a failed attempt to come to terms with these developments.

Our review emphasizes three aspects of this process. The first aspect is legal-political, and is related to the growing power and interventionist aspirations of the state. Its peak was reached within the étatist formations of fascist and communist type, in each of which political ranking displaced class division. Under liberal forms of corporatism, the class principle and the generative power of capital also reduced, though to a lesser degree than under state socialism. Each marked a significant shift in the centrality of property and productive relations and posed an important challenge to class theory. Citizenship rights, introduced in response to untrammelled class relations, coexisted with class divisions. Such rights restricted the social impact of class by legal restriction, civil rights, broad enfranchisement, and the extension of welfare entitlements.

The second aspect of the process might be called 'market-meritocratic'. The increasing division of labour, organizational complexity and bureaucratization have enhanced the importance of education, knowledge and skills, none of which can be reduced to production relationships. The distribution and acquisition of education have become increasingly autonomous relative to class location. This is scarcely surprising in societies where education comes under the control of reformist states that are controlled by parties and elites committed to meritocratic principles. The consequent increase in skill stratification, the emergence of the structurally unemployed, the formation of educated categories variously identified as the intelligentsia, 'knowledge classes', experts, etc., all pose a continuous and serious challenge to class theory.

The third aspect of the process might be called cultural-symbolic. Again, the arguments are not new. Power based on 'status position' has long been acknowledged by Weberian sociologists. But the opposing notion that industrial capitalism has reduced the impact of status factors and subordinated them to the economic class dimension has more recently been called into question by the salience of ethnicity, race, gender, lifestyles and consumption patterns. Even within the Marxist camp, the epiphenomenal status of cultural factors has been questioned by such theorists as Bourdieu (1994).

Class theorists typically respond to these challenges by moving away from economic-productivist reductionism and abandoning notions of structural determination. However, a more radical theoretical overhaul is necessary. Such an overhaul should begin by disposing of the remnants of class theory and class analysis. It needs to acknowledge the structural complexity of contemporary society, the plurality and autonomy of power resources, and the diversity of contemporary power configurations.

## Notes

1 Political organizations exerting power directly through the state.

2 Although they may have been derived historically from functionally distinct economic roles.

3 Therefore the notion of 'Weberian class analysis' can be viewed as a contradiction in terms.

If such an analysis privileges class over other dimensions, it violates an essential principle of Weberian theory. If it does not, there is no reason to call it *class* analysis. Unfortunately, many contemporary neo-Weberians (e.g. Giddens 1973; Marshall et al. 1988; Goldthorpe and Marshall 1992) overlook this point.While declaring their Weberian preferences, they tend to ignore multidimensionality and focus almost exclusively on class. For them, Weberianism implies an acknowledgement of the complexities of class situations (as reflected in occupational structure), a division between property-based and income-based classes, and the articulation of social classes in the process of social mobility (e.g. Goldthorpe 1980; Marshall et al. 1988; Baxter et al. 1991). By contrast, Parkin's (1979) studies of class and status divisions and Turner's (1988) analyses of status politics take multidimensionality more seriously.

4 For summaries see Parry (1969) and, from a Marxist perspective, Bottomore (1964; 1994).

5 Some of these views were subsequently absorbed into Weberian versions of class theory, e.g. Giddens (1973).

6 See Field and Higley (1980) and Etzioni-Halévy (1993) for comments on the eclipse of and attempts to reconstruct elite theory.

7 Most notably the Frankfurt School thinkers and such mass society theorists as Horkheimer, Kirchheimer and Pollock (see Arato and Gebhardt 1978: Part 1).

8 For example, Voslensky (1984). The international structure of the 'communist bloc' reflects political-military rather than economic power.

9 Citizenship has been defined as 'a status bestowed on those who are full members of a community' (Marshall 1950: 70) with certain rights attached to this status.

10 Turner (1990; 1993) and Mann (1987) extend its universe of discourse by indicating a diversity of national paths in extending citizenship rights.

11 The prologue to the post-war debates began in the 1920s–1940s in the form of analyses of neo-capitalism by the Frankfurt School thinkers, debates on separation of ownership and control (Berle and Means 1967, first published 1932) and the 'managerial revolution' (Burnham 1941), as well as the studies of occupational prestige and 'class in the community' (e.g. Warner and Lundt 1941; Warner 1949). The common denominator in these debates was a vigorous movement away from economistic-deterministic theories of the class structure and polarized views of class conflict. But there was also a clear bifurcation between a neo-Marxist stream embracing the conflict-domination perspective and emphasizing political and organizational factors as important and autonomous structuring forces, and structural-functional theories embracing a consensus-integration perspective and stressing the sociocultural (value) basis of contemporary stratification.

12 In a more recent version, Dahrendorf (1988) adjusts this scheme to fit into a 'state dependants vs market dependants' conflict system. This for him is the key class conflict in contemporary society.

13 If the 'white proletariat' in tandem with its bourgeoisie exploited and dominated post-colonial migrant ethnic minority workers, little remained of the explanatory status of class relations.

14 The findings reported by Baxter et al. (1991) also suggest that class identity is shaped differently for men and women, that subjective class identification among women is weak and affected by both the nature of their employment (full-time or part-time) and the domestic-labour situation.

15 Bourdieu (1994) is openly critical of the concept of status group, but he interprets it in a historical fashion (as *Stände*). His criticism applies to historical studies of Weber, rather than neo-Weberian usages by such authors as Collins (1986) and Turner (1988).

# 3

# Fickle Formations

Classes are not merely abstract structural categories. In the classic Marxist version, they inevitably become tangible social entities marked by observable social divisions and ultimately, with the evolution from *Klasse an sich* to *Klasse für sich*, conscious and organized social actors. This development applies primarily to the two historic classes that will polarize into 'races wholly apart'. Early appearances confirmed the prediction. Describing British workers in Manchester in the 1840s, Engels observes that: 'The workers speak other dialects, have other thoughts and ideals, other customs and moral principles, a different religion and other politics than those of the bourgeoisie. Thus they are two radically dissimilar nations' (1892: 124). Similarly, in Thompson's classic study (1980) of the early development of the British class structure, classes are experienced realities, tangible social groupings that might be described as 'communities of fate' sharing collective experiences at the level of lifestyle, social solidarity and political activism. Here classes, then, are more than structural locations and economic categories.

This communitarian view of classes is criticized by Weber (1978: 302–10; 926–38). For him, classes are primarily economic life-chance categories. Classes can only become communities under the specific circumstances of transparency of domination, proximity, effective communication, and unifying political leadership and ideology. Weber, in fact, affirms that such conditions apply to the industrial working class. Normally, however, classes remain abstract market categories intersecting with status and associational-organizational structures. However, Weber specifies an intermediate formation, between abstracted class situations and class communities, that he calls 'social classes'. These are based on demographic stability, that is shared mobility prospects and social interaction, especially endogamy. Social classes are not communities or groups but distinctive social categories that transpire in social distance, in a degree of popular recognition and, above all, in sociodemographic continuity.

Issues of class groupness and community are matters of relativity. Class divisions are not, and never have been, the sole dimension of social differentiation and stratification. However, there would probably be a wide measure of sociological agreement on the view that class relations were more socially consequential in the past than they are today. These 'nations within nations' were not merely ideological projections but were segregated by working conditions, income, prestige, physical appearance, health, residence and styles of speech to a much higher degree than they are now. Boundaries were clearer and their consequences more tangible, especially where class overlapped with residual feudal estates, as in Britain and continental Europe. This is confirmed by the abundant testimony of literary and statistical documentation of which one example might suffice:

> Between 1880 and 1910 13-year-old working class boys in London and Glasgow were on the average 2.5 inches shorter than their middle-income group contemporaries, and 4 inches shorter than upper-class boys, and there was little evidence of much increase in average height or narrowing down of the gap between the two dates. The chances of living at all were twice as great in the highest as in the lowest class: infant mortality rates in the upper and middle classes as late as 1911 averaged 77 per 1,000, compared with 113 per 1,000 for skilled workers' children and 152 per 1,000 for the unskilled. (*Report of the Registrar-General*, England and Wales, 1913, in Perkin 1989: 35)

It is not only an amelioration of these dramatic inequalities that marks the decline of class. In advanced societies we are witnessing a decomposition and fragmentation of tangible class entities, a decline in class groupness. While the remnants of distinctive and homogeneous class formations, such as those identified by Engels and Thompson, survive in the isolated environments of mining towns and rural communities, they are increasingly rare.

Many contemporary class analysts, including Wright (1985), Goldthorpe and Marshall (1992) and Esping-Andersen (1993), acknowledge this shift. They relax the propositions of groupness and behavioural linkage (see Chapter 1) by stressing the relative autonomy of class formation, abandoning a communitarian view of classes, and rejecting the class polarization thesis. The class maps they construct are progressively more complex, and they converge on market segments and occupational gradations (see Waters 1991). Internal divisions within the 'major classes', as well as 'new classes', multiply in each consecutive scheme, thus making an empirical assessment of class divisions and an adjudication of the class debate extremely difficult. Therefore, our critical review of class formation must begin with a brief summary of the diverse maps of class.

### Class maps

Social classes, according to Weber (1978: 305), are clusters of class positions that become socially distinguishable in terms of social recognition, interaction and mobility boundaries. A social class is 'the totality of those class situations within which individual and generational mobility is easy and typical'. The term implies no standard pattern of class formation, no class polarization and no necessary class conflict. Weberian class maps therefore chart market segments, or, more precisely, the social consequences of market segmentation, in terms of social interaction and distance. While class places are fickle and numerous, social classes are more tangible, more stable and relatively few in number. In modern Western societies they move towards a fourfold formation: the manual working class, the petty bourgeoisie, white-collar and technical workers, and those privileged by property and education (1978: 305). This view is embraced by those who are most empirically oriented among contemporary class theorists and analysts. They focus attention on processes of 'class structuration' (Giddens 1973), 'social closure' (Parkin 1979), 'class formation' (Wright 1985) or 'demographic class formation' (Goldthorpe 1987; Marshall et al. 1988) that are manifested in patterns of social distance and intergenerational social mobility.

Giddens, for example, accepts that each capitalist society 'is intrinsically a class society' (1973: 20) in which 'class relations are of primary significance to the explanatory interpretation of large areas of social conduct' (1973: 132) and provide 'the key to the explication of the social structure in general' (1973: 127). He therefore insists that:

> Rather than speaking of the 'existence' or 'non-existence' of classes, we should speak of types and levels of what I shall call *class structuration*. The factors which influence the levels of class structuration are not to be traced to economic or technological complexity alone, or even primarily, and *cannot be directly inferred from the designation 'class society'*. (1973: 20, original italics)

The two main aspects of structuration are 'mediate' mobility patterns, and 'proximate' divisions of labour and authority within the enterprise and consumption patterns. The observable variations in social inequalities and social divisions are due to the differential processes of class structuration in each of these aspects. However, mediate structuration predominates, yielding, 'the basic three-class system in capitalist society: an "upper", "middle", and "lower" or "working" class' structurated respectively by property, credentials and labour power (1973: 167).

The Weberian connection in Giddens is masked by a Marxian rhetoric. While he begins by stressing the explanatory importance of property relations, class societies can vary on the extent and types of inequality, the levels of groupness, 'the nature and types of class consciousness (or class awareness) . . . the forms assumed by overt class conflict . . . and the typical character of class exploitation' (1973: 134). The analysis therefore rejects the most problematic assumptions of the Marxian class scheme, especially economic determination and inevitable class conflict. The cost is a progressive gap between a rhetoric wedded to a promiscuous and attenuated concept of class and an actual analysis that is indistinguishable from a general social analysis.

While Giddens seeks, at least nominally, to save key elements of Marxist class theory, Parkin makes an explicit and self-conscious break from it. The critical edge of his analysis is directed against a 'professorial Marxism' preoccupied with the realm of production to the exclusion of other generators of social collectivities, cleavage and conflict:

> The most damaging weakness in any model of class that relegates social collectivities to the status of mere incumbents of positions, or embodiments of systemic forces, is that it cannot account properly for those complexities that arise when racial, religious, ethnic, and sexual divisions run at a tangent to formal class divisions. Societies marked by conflicts between religious and racial communities do not exhibit the same type of class structure as societies lacking such conflict, notwithstanding similarities in their occupational systems and property relations. (1979: 4)

The explanatory power of the social relations of production, according to Parkin, must be critically revised in the light of both the diversity of capitalist stratification systems and puzzling similarities between the stratification systems of capitalism and state socialism. In a move that is similar to Giddens, Parkin employs the Weberian concept of social closure, 'by which social collectivities seek to maximize rewards by restricting access to resources and opportunities to a limited circle of eligibles' (1979: 44). Classes are *formed* by closure. Depending on the type of strategy of restriction or exclusion, collectivities may form as communal groups or segmental status groups as well as proper social classes. Usurpationary closure that is 'mounted by a group in response to its outsider status and the collective experience of exclusion' (1979: 74) gives rise to the collectivities of the disprivileged including workers' unions, women's movements, and racial and ethnic rights movements. Moreover, patterns of social closure can, and usually do, cut across property and market cleavages, giving rise to a complex pattern of exclusionary and usurpationary group formations that also involve the state. State powers, he claims, can

> be harnessed in support of many forms of exclusionary closure, not only those that promote and sustain class exploitation. The closure model conceptualizes the state as an agency that buttresses and consolidates the rules and institutions of exclusion governing all relations of domination and subjection. Indeed, a class, race, sex, or ethnic group only accomplishes domination to the extent that its exclusionary prerogatives are backed up by the persuasive instrument of the state. (1979: 138)

While Parkin analyses classes as socially closed market segments, Goldthorpe (1980) sees them as occupational clusters. His seven-class schema (described in Chapter 1) was originally inspired by an earlier scale of the social desirability of jobs (Goldthorpe and Hope 1974). It was later modified in the light of Lockwood's (1958) study of clerks to focus on objectively common levels of access to rewards and to autonomy and control in the workplace. Here a class is any aggregation of occupations whose incumbents are: 'typically comparable, on the one hand, in terms of their sources and levels of income and other conditions of employment, in their degree of economic security and in their chances of individual enhancement; and, on the other hand, on their location within the systems of authority and control governing the processes of production in which they are engaged' (Goldthorpe 1987: 39). Marxists criticize it as 'overtly Weberian' but the author defends it as basically compatible with Marx's original formulation (1987: 40).

It is unclear whether Goldthorpe intends his schema to be entirely heuristic but certainly this is a major focus of the contribution. His analysis is driven by an ideologically based interest in establishing just how much equality of economic opportunity is available in contemporary capitalist societies, how 'open' they are, and he is convinced that this must be measured by class analysis rather than by analysing movement up and down a continuous social hierarchy. However, the fact that he switches between eleven-, seven-, five- and three-class schemas according to the problem at hand would suggest that these classes are more like convenient aggregations of occupations than bounded or coherent collectivities. Indeed he goes on, in an argument reminiscent of Weber's analysis of 'social classes', to specify processes of 'demographic class formation'. By this he clearly means a capacity to monopolize labour markets, to effect intergenerational and career closure and thus to monopolize privileges:

> For any such structure of positions, the empirical question can then be raised of how far classes have in fact formed within it, in the sense of specific social collectivities; that is, collectivities that are identifiable through the degree of continuity with which, in consequence of patterns of class mobility and immobility, their members are associated with particular sets of positions over time; and in turn, the further issue may be pursued of the degree of distinctiveness of members of identifiable classes in terms of their lifechances, their lifestyles and patterns of association, and their sociopolitical orientations and modes of action. (1983: 467)

This process of the demographic class formation focuses especially on patterns of intergenerational social solidity. The formation of classes is indicated by tendencies to the inheritance of positions, endogamy and friendship. While, as the Featherman–Jones–Hauser hypothesis (Featherman et al. 1975) indicates, the overall pattern of mobility is similar in industrialized Western societies, relative mobility rates vary, and result in specific patterns of class formation. These formations are identified by Goldthorpe and his associates in a series of comparative mobility studies (e.g. Erikson and Goldthorpe 1992; Goldthorpe 1980; 1987; Halsey et al. 1980; Heath 1981; Marshall et al. 1988).

There are two ways of assessing whether class formation has occurred. Either one can examine the absolute composition of 'classes' in a schema to establish whether their members have heterogeneous origins, or one can seek to control for variations in the size of the class categories by examining relative chances of staying within any one of them, in either career or intergenerational terms. Goldthorpe does both of these things and we can now examine his findings with a view to establishing whether labour-market classes have indeed been formed. Here we shall focus our attention on two of the 'classes' in Goldthorpe's five-class schema: the 'service class' of professionals, administrators, managers, technicians and supervisors, and the non-skilled working class, what in other analyses might be thought of as the true proletariat.

Findings about absolute mobility rates give very real cause for doubt that market classes exist. Because the 'service-class' category is expanding very rapidly its members have highly heterogeneous social origins, and indeed far more of the influx is long range from the very bottom of the class structure than class analysis would predict. At the bottom, absolute mobility rates give some cause to support market-class theorists, at least to those living in Britain. Because industrial labour is declining very rapidly in that society, the non-skilled working class has homogeneous origins but members can rise out of the category during their career as opportunities open up in the classes above. Nevertheless Goldthorpe feels able to conclude that the service class is indeed 'in formation' and that this is a key process in the development of twentieth-century class structures.

Goldthorpe reaches this conclusion, at least in part, on the basis of relative mobility rates examined on an internationally comparative basis against inheritance chances. He and other members and associates of the CASMIN project have successfully established a common pattern of mobility across industrial societies. They find the greatest degree of occupational inheritance among farmers, followed by the petty bourgeoisie, followed by the service class; classes are more solid the higher one moves up the social hierarchy; inheritance is lowest among routine white-collar and skilled working classes; and short-range mobility is more common than long-range mobility (Kurz and Müller 1987).

There are six further comments that can undermine a claim that this pattern represents a confirmation of the existence of labour-market-based classes:

- The greatest level of solidity comes from the inheritance of property in the farming and petty-bourgeois categories. However, property is itself of declining significance generally and we can expect a further decline in these instances. Farming is becoming increasingly corporatized, and the petty-bourgeois category is becoming infused by expertise. Moreover these currently represent small proportions of national populations.
- A key claim is made about the solidity of the service class. However, this is only a relative solidity. Goldthorpe makes much of the finding that the chances of inheritance of position in the service class are vastly greater than the chances of mobility to this class by sons of non-skilled workers. But this is too much of an insistence on long-range mobility. We can find that, for example, the chances of a category III (routine white-collar) origin providing a category I destination are about the same as those of a category I origin.
- Goldthorpe's data are well out of date. Both the British and the international data were collected in the early 1970s and typically the analysis is restricted to men above the age of 30. By far the greatest proportion of the contemporary male labour force is now made up of men not included in the population studied. Changes in the organization of work and production since the early 1970s have been very considerable, including the quite profound set of changes known as post-Fordism or flexible specialization. These have removed some of the distinctions that might be made between semi-skilled, skilled and technical service workers.
- In so far as Goldthorpe analyses the situation of women he analyses it separately from that of men. A key development in the pattern of occupational allocation has been the way in which, since the 1970s, women have managed to penetrate the apparently closed labour markets of the service class.
- In so far as there are segmented labour markets the segmentation now appears to be constructed on bases other than class. The existence of a

secondary labour market, membership of which is specified by gender, race, ethnicity, age, migration experience or role in family support, is now widely accepted but can find no confirmation in Goldthorpe's findings because it privileges class analysis.

- Goldthorpe's insistence on examining only exchange mobility as a measure of openness introduces an unacceptable bias into the findings. Saunders puts this nicely: 'there seems no good theoretical reason why improved chances of success for working class children should be recognised in a measure of fluidity only if there is a corresponding deterioration in the chances of success of service class children' (1995: 26).[1]

Wright's class schemes also demonstrate similar flexibility and convergence in addressing the familiar problem of reconciling the formation with the theorized structure. He makes several attempts to rescue class from the declining influence of property. The first (Wright 1978) makes an explicit effort to use Poulantzas' notion of contradiction to define classes. Curiously, however, it is not property or even exploitation that does so for Wright but what Weberians would call domination: control over money capital, control over physical capital and control over workers. However this formulation provides Wright with several problems: by specifying Weberian domination as the structuring principle he denies his own ideological and theoretical commitments; and he also finds no possibility of societal transformation in so far as the proportion of the population in the historic classes is low and declining.

This creates more problems than it resolves. Wright's emphasis on 'indeterminacy' and 'contingency' in class formation and struggle must raise serious doubts about the explanatory potential of 'class structure'. If the relationships between the class structure on the one hand, and class formation, consciousness and struggle on the other, are complex and contingent (1985: 14; 1989: 27) then analytic distinctions between class and non-class phenomena become impossible. It raises the question of how much indeterminacy and autonomy such a class scheme can tolerate without undermining its own logic. A further difficulty arises from the specification of 'contradictory locations within the class structure' that, on a Marxist logic, ought to be irrelevant. Apparently these 'new classes' 'embody a principle of class relations that is quite distinct from capitalist relations and that potentially poses an alternative to capitalist relations' (1989: 27). This radically alters the core element in Marxist class theory and raises the question of theoretical consistency. The main challenging class is not only formed outside the capital ownership relations but is *not* an exploited class. Exploitative relations are not held to be central in explaining conflict and change and so the scheme veers towards another theory that Marxists would find problematic, that of 'middle-class radicalism' (e.g. Parkin 1968; Gouldner 1979).

Wright was not too far wrong in this first formulation: in so far as twentieth-century stratification can be called a class formation it is indeed based on domination and not on property, and a societal dynamic based on struggle between property classes is well on the historical wane. However, as is also discussed in Chapter 1, he moves on to establish a twelve-class model based on relations of exploitation (Wright 1985). The scheme recognizes the property problem by intersecting three principal types of 'asset': real property, control of organizations, and credentials. Although the property division is emphasized in graphical depictions of the scheme, the great majority of the population is in the nine propertyless classes. More importantly, variation in such matters as income is greater outside the property division than across it. Wright's second scheme can account for 20 per cent of the variance in male earnings in the USA (Hout et al. 1993: 263), an unconvincing figure even if gender had not been held constant. But Halaby and Weakliem (1993) show that earnings can be predicted much more effectively if domination is treated as a continuous rather than a discrete or class variable. Halaby claims that he has shown that there is little external evidence to suggest that the class boundaries proposed by Wright 'matter anywhere but in his own mind' (1993: 35).

Wright's modifications of his class scheme (1985; 1989) bring it dangerously close to its neo-Weberian competitors. The multiplication of classes from six to twelve increases its similarity to Goldthorpe's occupationally based model of seven main classes plus four sub-classes. It is also much closer than any other neo-Marxist class scheme to occupational prestige scales which may explain its relative acceptance by empirically oriented sociologists. However, Wright's scheme offers rather more intuitive appeal than the abstract and simplistic schemes of more orthodox Marxists (e.g. Poulantzas 1974; Westergaard and Resler 1975).

## Fragmentation

The classical Marxian formulation suggests a historical tendency towards polarization along the capital–labour fault line. It also makes a series of quite specific predictions concerning certain universal trends in the development of capitalist class structure, including the articulation of class from structural category to political community, polarization, concentration of ownership, and proletarianization. Most of these forecasts have proved to be substantively incorrect, and the 'explaining away' of counter-factuals is a major preoccupation of contemporary Marxists. They must cope with blurring class divisions, the fragmentation of the major industrial classes, the managerial ascendancy, the expansion of the middle class, and the shrinking of the proletariat.

These modifications and *ad hoc* repairs eventually led to the emergence of a new consensus that underlies post-Second World War studies of class. The class formation is now held to be much more complex than Marx specified. But, in the eyes of class fideists, this complexity is not allowed to undermine a conception of the overall integrity of the class paradigm. One can allow that the capitalist class did fragment into owners and top managers, financial and industrial segments, old and new, but continue to maintain that it achieves social integration through networks, positional interlocks, dense social links and lifestyle commonalities (see classical studies by Baltzell 1962; Domhoff

1967; and the more recent analysis of Scott 1991). Similarly, one can admit to the expansion of the middle class but this can be attributed to diverse processes affecting its different elements in different ways. Thus, the ascendancy of the 'post-industrial' classes (professional, managerial, expert and 'knowledge' classes) is matched by the reduction and subordination of routine white-collar workers experiencing deskilling and proletarianization (see e.g. Braverman 1974) and the decline of the 'old' middle class or petty bourgeoisie (see Mills 1956; Raynor 1969; Edgell 1980; Wright and Martin 1987). The working class can also be seen as fragmenting into high and low skilled, industrial and service, operative and trade, or traditional, deferential and privatized (Lockwood 1958), but these multiple divisions can simultaneously be seen as overshadowed by common relative disadvantages in working conditions and mobility prospects. Indeed they can be overcome by the unifying appeals of such class organizations as trade unions and leftist parties. This broad consensus on class diversification is reflected in the proliferation of increasingly complex class maps and a theoretical convergence between the neo-Marxist, neo-Weberian and neo-functional camps (Waters 1991; Edgell 1993).

Social developments in the 1980s and 1990s are testing the limits of this consensus. First, it is being undermined by the globalization of the market, the dismantling of corporatist deals, and post-Fordist strategies of labour control and flexible specialization. These challenge the proposition of behavioural linkage according to which economic rewards and life chances are firmly attached to class positions. Second, non-economic processes of social and cultural differentiation are raising questions about the viability of any further multiplication of classes without a wholesale revision of the core assumptions of class theory. Third, the unifying impact of class organizations is declining with de-unionization and the rapid decline of class-oriented parties. These changes impact on four regions of the class map: the upper, intermediate, working, and emerging 'new' classes.

### The upper class

The theoretical debates about the bourgeoisie can be established by the diverse terminology employed to describe it. It is variously called: the 'capitalist' class, implying capital ownership and exploitation (Poulantzas 1974); the 'dominant class', indicating broad social domination, including ideological domination (Althusser 1977); the 'ruling class', to signal a dominant political position (e.g. Connell 1977); and the 'upper class(es)', a term typically associated with the graded-occupational schemes or even with aristocratic feudal residues (e.g. Scott 1991). Moreover, in empirical studies the plural form, 'classes', is used more frequently than the singular. The old divisions between financial and industrial capitalists or between ownership and managerial classes have been accepted by both post-Second World War class theorists and their critics. For both Dahrendorf (1959) and Poulantzas (1978), for example, the 'power of control' is as important as the legal ownership of capital.

The emergence of a powerful public sector of state-controlled corpora-tions creates further difficulties. Controllers of state corporations, especially under social-democratic regimes, can hardly be described as members of a capitalist class. They are dependent upon political leadership and susceptible to partisan pressure. Moreover, the étatist trends that give rise to state-cor-porate elites have been unequal and diverse in their development. Liberal forms of capitalism (e.g. in the USA) generate a different upper class than do European (e.g. French) or Asian (e.g. Japanese) étatist configurations. The strictly corporatist European states such as Austria (see Katzenstein 1984; 1985) are different from post-feudal Britain, which is different again from the former settler colonies (Scott 1986; Useem 1984).

The debate about the salience of the owner–manager division is showing clear signs of exhaustion. Wright (1985: 18) places 'expert managers' firmly in a distinct class but indicates political affinities between them and owners. Scott identifies a single dominant 'capitalist class' but simultaneously divides it into four 'distinct class segments', reminiscent of Weber: entrepreneurs, rentiers, executives, and finance capitalists, the last two of which may be propertyless (1991: 72). The theoretical status of these 'distinct segments' remains unspecified. Lastly, Goldthorpe (1987: 40) places both managers and owners in a single 'service class' but identifies differences between their market situations, thus raising the question of the consistency of its composition.

### The intermediate classes

While the growth of the middle class presents an obvious problem to Marxist historical materialism it can also be a little difficult to accommodate within Weberian analyses. The cartographical elaborations of both the Goldthorpe and the Wright schemes are largely attempts to come to terms with the pro-liferation and diversification of 'middle-class' occupations. There are several simultaneous shifts going on that increase the tendency to fragmentation.

First, there has been a rapid growth of middle administrative and man-agerial occupations that are difficult to separate from 'service-class' executives and administrators. The post-Second World War rise in the number of pro-fessional and technical workers has been little short of spectacular. In most advanced societies they constitute more than 20 per cent of employees. One of the central problems for recent class theory has been how to explain the emergence and proliferation of these 'new middle class(es)' (Abercrombie and Urry 1983). They have been variously interpreted by class theorists as a 'knowledge class' (Bell 1976), a 'service class' (Goldthorpe 1982), a 'new petty bourgeoisie' (Poulantzas 1974), a 'new working class' (Mallet 1975), a 'contradictory class' (Wright 1978), 'expert classes' (Wright 1985), a 'new middle class' (Giddens 1973), a 'professional-managerial class' (Ehrenreich and Ehrenreich 1979), or simply a 'new class' (Gouldner 1979). Perhaps Barbalet's attempt (1986) to rescue a bipolar Marxist class theory by sug-gesting that professional and technical workers constitute a Weberian status group is the most convincing class-theoretical account of professional employees, but it convinces only because it steps outside class analysis in order to rescue its conclusions.

A second development is an unanticipated reversal in the fate of the petty bourgeoisie. It was traditionally seen as an archaic and precarious class, a remnant of the past that clogs the wheels of progress: 'The lower strata of the middle class – the small tradespeople, shopkeepers, and retired tradesmen generally, the handicraftsmen and peasants – all sink gradually into the proletariat' (Marx 1977: 227). However, recent research shows that those once thought drowned are again rising to the surface. The petty bourgeoisie is thriving on the current wave of market-oriented, neo-liberal public policy. The proportion of workers who are self-employed is increasing rapidly in all OECD countries (OECD 1992). The number of small firms, including family firms, is also increasing, as is the proportion of people employed in them. Moreover, many of these small companies are doing anything but rot: rather, they operate at the cutting edge of technological progress. The self-employed are also differentiating very rapidly, moving away from the image of the traditional-patriarchal family firm. Within the contemporary petty bourgeoisie one can find traditional artisans as well as new breeds of contractual and often unskilled manual workers, affluent consultants, and specialized hi-tech niche producers (see e.g. Piore and Sabel 1984; Steinmetz and Wright 1989).

The fact is that class theory and class analysis are inadequate in specifying a class location either for professional and technical workers or for the post-industrial petty bourgeoisie. This is because, in class terms, their locations are highly diverse. They exhibit a wide range of relationships to the state, for example, from state employment through state-authorized monopoly and state licensing to formal independence. Their organizational location is also diverse, encompassing participation in both large-scale state or private-sector bureaucratic systems and small-scale partnerships, and incorporating various relationships to the system of authority including hierarchical, specialist staff, collegial, and consultancy relationships. Finally, particular individual workers have differential locations in authority and reward systems.

### The working class

Perhaps the most contentious issue in debates about class fragmentation is that of the identity, size and unity of the 'working class'. While diagnoses of divisions among workers are as ancient as the class paradigm itself, many recent developments have radical implications. First, there has been a progressive market segmentation of manual workers resulting in internal differentiation not only according to skill and sector (private/state and primary/secondary/tertiary), but also along regional-territorial lines, between primary and secondary segments, and on race, ethnicity and gender. True disadvantage, according to Wilson (1987), no longer embraces the entire category of manual workers, but is restricted to the incumbents of diverse sub-categories of racially stereotyped, ethnically segregated and 'gendered' positions. Second, there has been a steep decline in the number of traditional manual jobs. The image of a typical manual, male, factory or mining operative is increasingly at variance with reality, because the manufacturing sector is shrinking and because women are increasingly entering manual employment. The manual depletion is matched by an expansion of routine non-manual labour. These career clerical positions, that are often low-status, low-paid and typically held by women, can be located in the lower class region but are clearly not 'proletarianized' in any traditional sense (for contrasting views see Crompton and Jones 1984; Stewart et al. 1980). Third, there are significant regional and national differences within manual-worker patterns of employment (see e.g. Esping-Andersen 1993). Highly skilled and relatively homogeneous industrial workers in Germany, for example, can be contrasted with the diversity of skill levels and wages among heterogeneous and largely service-employed workers in the USA.

In so far as it is no longer the proletariat that stands at the receiving end of class exploitation or at the lowest ranks of the class hierarchy, it has been displaced by various 'underclass' categories of welfare dependants, marginalized service workers, postcolonial migrants, *Gastarbeiter*, and workers disadvantaged by age, ethnicity or gender. This new outsider category is different from both Marx's lumpenproletariat and 'the unemployed' because it includes the racially stigmatized, the unemployable and 'permanent state dependants' (Rex and Tomlinson 1979). This means that the 'underclass' is not generated by production relations. However, leaving them outside class schemes would be difficult since they constitute an increasing proportion of the populations of affluent societies. Equally, their incorporation poses theoretical problems. In some class schemes they can appear as 'decommodified' social categories (e.g. 'students and pensioners' in Offe 1985). In others, such as Wright (1985), they are partly incorporated as exploited and subordinate classes.

### Old and new classes

While more orthodox class fideists simply multiply the old class and sub-class categories, several 'new-class' theorists postulate altogether different and new mechanisms of class formation. The meaning of the term 'new class' varies widely between the three main Western streams of new-class theorizing: the anarchist stream that outlines the dangers of a new state-controlling 'intellectual class' (Kristol 1979); the technocratic-bureaucratic stream, popularized during the mid twentieth century (e.g. Burnham 1941), that identifies the new class with managerial positions; and the post-industrial stream of the 1970s and 1980s (e.g. Bell 1976) that specifies the new class as scientists, technocrats and intellectuals.

The Yugoslav dissident Djilas (1957) proposes what is perhaps the best known theory of the new class, a theory that later was elaborated by two Hungarian dissidents, Konrad and Szelenyi (1979). Indeed, although it was originally a concept for the analysis of state-socialist formations, it also influenced new-class theories in the West. Djilas embraces an orthodox Marxist paradigm in which the new class derives its power from command over the means of production and, although recruited from the ranks of the proletariat, continuously exploits workers. Konrad and Szelenyi offer a Weberianized version, in which the central socioeconomic planning that determines the societal *telos*, combined with command over the bureaucratized party-state apparatuses, transforms the intelligentsia from a mere status category into an increasingly dominant class. By contrast, in West European theories, especially those following Gouldner (1979), the new class represents the major challenge to the bourgeois order. New forms of protest activism, especially the emergence of 'new social movements', are in broad terms typically interpreted within the Gouldnerian framework of radical intellectuals so that the new class is typically identified with highly educated people employed in public-sector jobs (e.g. Eckersley 1989; Rootes 1990).

The theoretical status of the new class, in all its versions, is highly problematic. New-class theories reverse the logic of class analysis. While class analysis explores the political articulation of the economic class structure, new-class theories see classes as sociocultural and sociopolitical categories. They locate the origins of class in education, political organization, industrial-sectoral location, symbolic skills and cognitive capacities. The problem is not the argument that sociocultural factors can generate sociopolitical groupings, but that such processes can be uncritically interpreted in class terms rather than in terms of, say, elites or status. This undermines the identity and integrity of class theory, blurs the distinctions between class and non-class formations, and increases the conceptual stretch. In these theories class can be anything that is socially distinct and important.

If they were not interpreted within a class paradigm, the points made by Djilas, Konrad and Szelenyi, and Gouldner and their followers would not be controversial. The political power both of the modern state and of large corporations has to be treated as an important, though relatively autonomous, social generator, and large-scale political organizations, such as party states, may be the basis for the formation of important social categories. Similarly, we can admit that the educational and mass-media revolutions have given rise to emergent collectivities. However, to label such categories and collectivities as 'classes' creates confusion. Western versions of new-class theory that stress the importance of symbolic and cognitive skills are as unconvincing as their East European counterparts. As Bell (1979b: 22) and Pakulski (1993a; 1993b) elsewhere point out, they confuse classes with status categories and confound sectional mentalities and cultural trends with structural divisions.

## Boundaries

Identifying classes and drafting class maps involves the specification of boundaries. This has always been a contentious issue. For Marxists, the class structure and objective class interests are essential realities even if the class formation is inchoate, so that boundaries are less important than exploitation and struggle. However, because non-Marxists tend to see classes as *social*

entities, reward differentials, mobility barriers, social isolation, mutual identification, endogamy and political conflict are all key indicators of the degree
to which class divisions are real and sharp. While there is considerable dispute
about which of these boundary markers is the most important there is nevertheless some agreement on the indispensability of social mobility and
endogamy.

The problem is that neither of these potential barriers separate classes very
well. Social mobility studies do reveal discontinuities, but the boundaries are
highly permeable and they do not necessarily coincide with theoretically
drawn class divisions. The most pronounced mobility barriers are found at
the two extremes of the social hierarchy, among what Sorokin (1964: 478)
calls the 'hereditary rich' and 'hereditary poor'. However, the identification of
these relatively small categories with the class structure as a whole would be
highly problematic. Moreover, comparative studies of social mobility have
identified a similar pattern of immobility in the marketless and formally
classless state-socialist societies of Eastern Europe (e.g. Zagorski 1976).
Mobility between classes, especially intergenerational movements between
'middle classes' in advanced capitalist societies, is high. This is partly due to
structural shifts, first diagnosed in the 'Lipset-Zetterberg hypothesis' as a
universal trend associated with industrialization (Lipset and Zetterberg 1956;
Lipset and Bendix 1959). The trend they identify is the multiplication of
skilled and white-collar occupations at the expense of blue-collar and agricultural jobs. This trend has eroded class boundaries and increased the
openness of industrializing societies. Contemporary mobility studies generally confirm these regularities: while absolute mobility rates vary between
societies, rates of exchange mobility remain constant and high across all
advanced societies (Featherman et al. 1975). Generally, mobility barriers are
weak, and are being further eroded by structural mobility. They remain most
effective around the elite, small owners and the 'underclass' (see Featherman
et al. 1975; Heath 1981; Erikson and Goldthorpe 1992; Jones and Davis
1988; Kirkhoff et al. 1985).[2]

Studies of occupational and inter-sector mobility (e.g. Featherman and
Hauser 1978; Zagorski 1984) show that mobility barriers coincide more
closely with occupational and sector categories than with class categories. The
professions, in particular, manifest a high degree of closure, while the intermediate categories of middle management and sales and clerical labour are
relatively open. Similarly, skilled manual categories are considerably more
open than unskilled ones. Even supporters of the class paradigm acknowledge
this 'class heterogeneity' and the 'low level of demographic identity'
(Goldthorpe 1987: 332, 336, 337). Nor do status-attainment studies (see
Chapter 2) offer much support to a clustering effect that might provide evidence of class. Although optimistic predictions of continuous increases in
universalism and meritocracy may have been exaggerated (for a recent example see Saunders 1995) there is precious little evidence of extensive inheritance
of social positions among men and women.[3]

Studies of marriage patterns raise similar doubts about the strength of the social class formation.[4] There is a considerable degree of social homogamy in advanced societies but this is seldom a class homogamy. First, the level of class homogamy is generally low and it varies across the social hierarchy. Like occupational inheritance, it tends to be greatest at the extremes and among farmers. Second, homogamy patterns coincide with the status divisions of education and culture rather than with class divisions (see Tyree and Treas 1974; Rockwell 1976; Jones and Davis 1986). There is also considerable evidence of racial, religious and ethnic homogamy, as well as some occupational homogamy. Class endogamy, by contrast, is very difficult to demonstrate.

This should not be surprising considering contemporary processes of partner selection which are much less affected by traditional class-reproductive institutions than in the past. An increasing proportion of young people select spouses within relatively universalistic educational contexts. As marriage serializes and moves later into the biography, it is increasingly brokered through schools and universities, singles bars, computer-dating services, newspaper advertisements, lonely-hearts clubs, and marital agencies rather than through the class-reproductive agents of kinship, community and the workplace. Partner selection now follows affiliations of educational proximity, residential and territorial propinquity, culture (especially ethnicity and religion) and, increasingly, tastes, needs, values and beliefs (Eckland 1970). To the extent that these dimensions are progressively disengaging from class (see Chapter 5), class endogamy is likely to decrease.

### The democratic class struggle

Marx and Engels state in *The German Ideology* (1964: 49) that 'The separate individuals form a class only in so far as they have to carry on a common battle against another class; otherwise they are on hostile terms with each other as competitors.' Thus a key principle of class theory is that classes attain their greatest level of articulation under conditions of conflict and struggle. For some Marxists, this passage means that classes can be articulated *only* under conditions of acute socioeconomic antagonism, and that class and political conflict are related. The analysis of politics, especially the politics of conflict and change, is the domain in which the class paradigm can find its confirmation and prove its utility (e.g. Miliband 1977).

History has proved unkind to this expectation, inviting a scepticism that came in three waves. The first coincided with the failure of proletarian movements to polarize capitalist societies and to trigger world revolution in the early part of the twentieth century. This led to revisionist reformulations and the birth of reformist social-democratic ideologies, parties and regimes. Class politics was thus released from revolutionary associations and placed firmly within the context of national party politics. The second wave followed the experience of Stalinist communism and Nazism between the 1920s and the 1960s, and helped to disaggregate alliances of the left so that social democrats could stand opposed to revolutionary socialism. These two waves combined to create, in Lipset's (1960) celebrated formula, a 'democratic form of class struggle'. The third wave was triggered by class and partisan dealignment and the emergence of new politics throughout the 1960s, 1970s and 1980s and is posing the most serious challenge to the class interpretation of politics.[5]

According to Lipset's (1960) original scheme, the major party-political cleavage between left and right, the main political parties and movements, and the associated ideological constructs, are all the political correlates of the major industrial classes, including the inchoate intermediate classes:

> In every modern democracy conflict among different groups is expressed through political parties which basically represent a 'democratic translation of the class struggle.' Even though many parties renounce the principle of class conflict and loyalty, an analysis of their appeals and their support suggests that they do represent the interests of different classes. On a world scale, the principal generalization which can be made is that parties are primarily based on either the lower classes or the middle and upper classes. This generalization even holds true for the American parties, which have traditionally been considered an exception to the class-cleavage pattern of Europe. (1960: 220)

This political articulation of classes occurs, according to Lipset, at many levels. Political cleavages are actively organized around issues of economic inequality and redistribution including wages, working conditions, and political and welfare rights. The political appeals of the major parties are increasingly glossed in class discourses and elaborated into class programmes focusing on such ideologies as socialism, liberalism, conservatism. Lipset interprets the universalization of appeals and of constituencies not as class-disaggregating but as part of the universalization of class relations. On this view, mass constituencies can be conceived of as class constituencies so long as they are formed by such class-framed appeals and reproduced through inter-generationally stable partisan loyalties.[6]

Lipset modifies his view in what has become known as the Lipset-Rokkan model (Lipset and Rokkan 1967). The core of this proposal is that party-political divisions are anchored in the stable social cleavages of class, ethnicity and religious affiliation. It links emergent party systems both with these original divisions and with subsequent trans-generational social reproduction of partisan allegiances. Stable political regimes reflect the freezing of such cleavages owing to their effective articulation and to the stable intergenerational transmission of partisan loyalties and identifications.

This scheme matches the Western, post-Second World War configuration of a bipolar, stable and highly organized politics. Its formulation coincides with the formation, strengthening and bureaucratization of the state administrative apparatuses, that organized politics into an orderly, bureaucratized electoral contest involving large, socioeconomically based parties. The rise of an increasingly interventionist welfare state, seeking to reduce inequality and mitigate conflict, institutionalized the aspiration that a political class compromise might form a lasting resolution of the class struggle. Few social scientists objected to the imbalance implicit in the fact that the argument mainly concerned the parties and policies of the left. The fact that the orderly class contest was punctuated by violent ideological-political conflicts equally failed to diminish its appeal.[7]

Notwithstanding Lipset's assurances, the model of the democratic class struggle proved to be procrustean when applied to the USA. Corporatist deals were prevented by popular suspicion of the state, entrenched pluralism, the effectiveness of New Deal policies and, above all, a disorganized national class politics. In American society, as Nisbet (1959) indicates, classes only ever functioned in the context of local status hierarchies. Class politics was localized and class sociology was largely confined to the realm of community studies. Popular visions of the American national power structure were couched in elite rather than class terms (e.g. Mills 1956). It is not surprising therefore that the earliest diagnoses of 'death of class' and the 'end of ideology' were formulated in the USA.[8]

### Status competition

The main foundations for a revised analysis of social conflict can be found in Parkin's (1979) and Giddens' (1973; 1981) critiques of Marxism and Turner's (1986; 1990) analyses of citizenship and 'status politics'. Turner combines the theoretical insights of Weber and T.H. Marshall with contemporary work on citizenship and lifestyles to question the political importance and centrality of class relations in advanced societies, and to focus instead on *status*. He understands status as a political-legal process that legitimizes state-directed and state-sanctioned claims for entitlements. Status thus cuts across class relations.

G. Marshall, Newby, Rose and Vogler (1988: 198) follow a similar line of argument, distinguishing between class and status principles of conflict. Class conflict is generated at the level of production and struggles over the control of property and the allocation of rewards for skills. It has no 'moral dimension' because it has the natural qualities of a 'matter of fact' that reflects the 'dull compulsion of economic relations' (1988: 200). By contrast, status conflict is conventional-legal. It is generated at the level of sociopolitical and sociocultural arrangements in relation to social conventions and legal rights to claim deference and privilege, and transpires in social and cultural divisions about moral rights, traditions and legitimate entitlements.

Armed with this distinction, Marshall, Newby, Rose and Vogler indicate a persisting political relevance of class in contemporary British society. Specifically, they claim that:

- Sectionalism, privatism and instrumentalism are not new because classes have always been internally divided and fragmented by status divisions (1988: 201).
- Class identity and solidarity persist among the working class: 'Social class is to the fore among conceptions of collective identity. It is still the case that important differences in shared beliefs and values are structured more obviously by class than by other sources of social cleavage' (1988: 267).

- changes in voting patterns are the result of 'superficial' and conjectural processes but they are not symptoms of decline of class: 'there has been no secular decline in the tendencies for collective identities and collective action to develop on a class basis' (1988: 268).

There are several problems with these claims. By the logic of Marshall et al.'s own typological distinction, trade unions operate almost exclusively according to the class principle. They appeal to class constituencies, utilize class rhetoric and apply class strategies. By contrast, professional associations operate on the status principle, by mobilizing occupational constituencies and cultivating a sense of honour through elaborate ethical codes and social rituals. Professional appeals are couched in the moral terms of rights and entitlements. If this is the case, then the decline in trade unionism combined with the rise of professionalization cannot but undermine Marshall et al.'s insistence on the 'persistent relevance of class'. Class divisions, in fact, are fragmenting into a multiplicity of status claims rooted in the moral economy and sanctioned by the state.[9]

### Beyond class struggle

Some new accounts of political struggle are explicitly and self-consciously opposed to class interpretations. We conclude this chapter with a brief review of developments that suggest alternative political cleavages.

*Generations*

There is a broad consensus among observers of such political movements as fascism, American civil rights, Polish Solidarity and green movements that youthfulness is the distinctive feature of their social constituencies (see, for example, Merkl 1980; Adamski 1982; Van Liere and Dunlap 1980; McAdam 1988; Baker et al. 1981; Pakulski 1986; 1993a). One explanation for this regularity is that of 'youth radicalism'. More sophisticated versions utilize a concept of generation that is more firmly grounded in classical social theory (e.g. Mannheim 1952). Generation theory suggests that age cohorts sharing certain formative experiences can carry their orientations and value preferences forward into their biographies. Divisions between generations reflect sociohistorical watersheds. Some of these watersheds are cross-societal thus producing globalized generational categories. We can identify, for example, a 'post-Second World War generation' that experienced the 'long boom'.[10] Other generational watersheds are society specific.

Perhaps the best known generational theory is Inglehart's 'post-materialist' interpretation (1977; 1991) of cultural and political shifts in advanced societies. Political orientations and behaviour, he argues, correspond to general value orientations that in turn reflect generationally specific formative experiences. In advanced societies, a generational shift is resulting in a new form of political cleavage that pitches older 'materialists' against younger 'post-materialists'. This cleavage is reflected in conflicts about civil rights, ecology, peace and women's rights, as well as the dissolution of the old left–right polarity. Such explanations alter the emphasis from socioeconomic to sociocultural factors, from structural configurations to sociohistorical experience.

## Status

The best known version of status politics is formulated by Turner (1988):

> [T]he classical conflict between the working class and the bourgeoisie . . . has disappeared with the relative decline of the urban, industrial working class, the restructuring of ownership of capital in the twentieth century and by an expansion of the formal entitlements of citizenship within a liberal-democratic framework. The simple divisions between classes have been replaced by a much more complicated and complex social structure involving . . . the endless struggle of status communities and status blocs for access to the welfare cake under the auspices of the state. (1988: 54)

The contradiction between the principles of economic class and political-legal legitimacy is the central feature of modern industrial societies, both capitalist and state-socialist. The formation of 'status columns', 'blocs' and 'groups' is a central sociopolitical process in advanced societies. It is articulated in struggles between feminist, civil rights, gay rights, indigenous rights and new-nationalistic movements on the one hand, and new Christian right, pro-life, flat-tax, and economic-rationalist movements on the other. A postmodernizing shift in culture and social structure adds further complications to the systems of inequalities and conflicts:

> The conventional hierarchies within the cultural system appear to be more fragmented and diversified than in any previous period. The cultural realm becomes somewhat dissociated from the economic and the political system, and the competitive struggle within the cultural field produces an explosion of cultural signs and a cacophony of lifestyles. (1988: 77–8)

## Action systems

According to Melucci (1988), political activism now takes place in a new field of conflict that is cultural and symbolic and focuses on claims to identities and autonomy. The new symbolic conflicts are about 'frameworks of sense', social norms and symbols:

> codes, formal regulators of knowledge, and the languages which organise our learning processes and our social relations . . . take place principally on symbolic ground, by means of the challenging and upsetting of the dominant codes upon which social relations are founded in high density informational systems. The mere existence of a symbolic challenge is in itself a method of unmasking the dominant codes, a different way of perceiving and naming the world. (1988: 248)

The actors in such conflicts lack permanence and organizational identity. They form loose and ephemeral 'networks submerged in everyday life'. The networks are both media and messages, since their very form carries 'alternative frameworks of sense', alternative experiences and the messages of symbolic defiance. Because of their symbolic focus, success or failure in such conflicts cannot be assessed in terms of impacts on decision-making. Rather, the stakes are cultural innovations in the norms guiding 'language, sexual customs, affective relationships, dress and eating habits' as well as the capacity to generate new elites (1988: 249). In a post-industrial society politics is therefore losing its substance. Diffuse systems of action are disconnecting themselves from social groups and such organizations as parties and interest groups. There are no actors, but only social accomplishments. The key task for the sociologist is to identify these accomplishments, that is the processes through which the unity of action is accomplished.

This constitutes a radical break not only with class but also with a traditional sociology that views action as socially embedded and structurally rooted. Melucci's classless and actorless sociology cannot even be seen as a sociology of politics. It is a radical sociology of action *in statu nascendi*.

*Civil society*

The concept of civil society emerges from a critical re-evaluation of Marxist analysis. Such re-evaluations are often called 'post-Marxist' because they claim to transcend class theory and Marxist political eschatology. Post-Marxist theory stresses the autonomy of culture and politics and the complexity of group formation. Its vigorous anti-reductionism is most transparent in accounts of politics, especially of the new social actors:

> Contemporary actors abandon what they see as the 'productivist' cultural model of the Old Left, as well as its modes of organisation. Instead of forming unions or political parties . . . they focus on grass-roots politics and create horizontal, directly democratic associations that are loosely federated on a national level. Moreover, they target the social domain of 'civil society' rather than the economy or state, raising issues concerned with the democratisation of structures of everyday life and focusing on forms of communication and collective identity. (Cohen 1985: 664–7)

The concept of civil society lies at the centre of post-Marxist theorizing. It encompasses social relations that develop in the processes of self-identification and self-organization of such spontaneously formed social subjects as informal groups, protest movements, and local associations. These form around five points of reference: space (national, regional, neighbourhood community groups); gender (feminist and women's rights groups); religion and ethnicity; occupations (unions and professional associations); and generations (Urry 1981: 70–3; Keane 1988: 13–29). The most radical post-Marxist critique of class comes from Cohen and Arato (1992; Cohen 1982), whose analysis of civil society relies on the notion of spontaneous social initiatives that are independent of the state and are aimed at self-determination.

Curiously the key elements of civil society, legality, tolerance and pluralism, share their nineteenth-century origins with class. They were articulated within social movements for legal and political rights. The formation of civil society, in fact, coincided with the development of bourgeois society and its principles were subsequently institutionalized in parliamentary procedures, democratic constitutions, citizenship rights, and legal norms of due process. They were further enhanced by the development of free associations and media-related public opinion. In Cohen and Arato's view, then, an authentic politics can only transpire in civil society. The key challenge in contemporary society is the defence and protection of civil society against the encroachments of state-authoritarian and commercial institutions. Therefore, the most important strategic battles for the survival of a vigorous civil society have occurred under the most étatized fascist and communist regimes. The defeat of facism and the 'velvet revolutions' in Eastern Europe were the most important episodes in these battles.

Civil society accounts deal a serious blow to class theory, not necessarily by superior explanatory power or empirical evidence, but by stealing its ideological thunder, by denying to class theory the high moral ground as the main representative of progressive and emancipatory theorizing.

## Conclusion

The arguments presented here go one step further than standard critiques of the Marxist class theory that only question the relevance of the *old* class divisions for understanding contemporary conflicts and change. They foreshadow our argument about a radical dissolution of class in all its crucial manifestations, including economic determination, social and cultural clustering, and political identification and action. A process of social *restructuring*, especially associated with étatization and mass production and consumption, is the first phase of the dissolution. Processes of social *fragmentation* and cultural *differentiation* mark the second phase, in which class declines as a tangible social entity. Social distance, association and interaction, and the normative and symbolic structures underlying them, lose their internal cohesion and economic-productive foundations. Class communities, neighbourhoods and cultures are eroded and fragmented. Finally, the dissolution can be diagnosed in respect of identification and action. The processes of political and ideological *decomposition* mark the waning of class politics and class ideologies. To paraphrase Sombart, the key social question at the end of the twentieth century is no longer the class question.

## Notes

1 Saunders' (1995) response to Goldthorpe involves the claim that it is unacceptable to measure 'openness' independently of 'ability' which should be held constant. We are unable to endorse his position fully because of the unavailability of a class-independent measure of ability. Saunders' use of IQ as a measure of ability leaves him particularly vulnerable in this respect.

2 The 'topological models' developed by Hauser (1978) and Hout (1983) confirm that immobility is greatest among owners of capital and land.

3 In their review of the mobility literature, Kurz and Müller (1987: 436) conclude that despite concerted efforts to identify patterns of class mobility the question of 'demographic class formation' remains largely unsettled.

4 Schumpeter (1951: 141) defines class as a collectivity in which 'intermarriage prevails among its members, socially rather than legally'.

5 We are treating Lipset's original class-interpretative scheme that was formulated in the

1950s (1960; 1981) separately from his recent arguments on the declining relevance of class (Clark and Lipset 1991; Clark et al. 1993). The latter are reviewed in Chapter 1.

6 Lipset even accounts for extremist movements and regimes in class terms (1960: 131). He takes other cleavages (religious, regional, ethnic, etc.) to be either fused with class issues and appeals, or less organizationally articulated and politically pronounced (see also Lipset 1991).

7 The European fascist parties stressed common *national* interests, virulently opposed liberal democracy (as well as communism) and promoted an anti-liberal, non-class form of national corporatism.

8 We agree with Hindess' (1987; 1992) view that neither the categorical interpretation of class as a foundation for political attitudes and behaviour, nor the 'class-actor' interpretation, withstand theoretical and empirical scrutiny. One reaction to this failure has been a redefinition of class analysis by scaling down its scope and explanatory aspirations. Marshall et al.'s (1988) study provides a good illustration of a sophisticated version of such modified class analysis that endorses some central features of the Weberian perspective. Another reaction is to abandon a class analysis of politics, conflict and social change altogether, a strategy adopted by Lipset himself (Clark and Lipset 1991; Clark et al. 1993).

9 For a discussion of Marshall et al.'s (1988) claims about class and identity see Chapter 6.

10 The concept of generation is deployed in the analysis of 'new politics' in the West in the recent work of Baker et al. (1991), Dalton (1988), Inglehart (1990), and Abramson and Inglehart (1992). The role of generational replacement in changing the face of contemporary politics is also stressed by Franklin et al. (1992: 410).

# 4

# Subsiding Economic Foundations

The issue of economic allocation lies at the centre of the debates that we review in the preceding two chapters. Both class theory and class analysis presuppose that access to position and reward is predicated on one's own, or perhaps more precisely one's parents', location in systems of production, distribution and exchange. In a class society this is indisputably correct: that is, one's entire identity – preferences, life chances, access to power, freedom from constraint, lifestyle, and political behaviour – is determined by one's economic relationships. At least, this is true unless one happens to be female or black or both, in which case it is determined by that fact. If economic relations are the *fons et origo* of class, then this too is where we must begin to demonstrate that sociology must now embrace the view that class has done its dash.

## Private property

It is a curious feature of class theory that it stresses the allocation of property as the fundamental basis of stratification. This is true of each of its main streams. Marxist class theory stresses productive property in particular. There are only two possible relationships that a person can have to productive property: one can own it or not own it, as Engels explains in that famous footnote to the *Communist Manifesto* (Marx 1982: 16n). However, Marx qualifies this statement immediately by the specification of a differentiated petty bourgeoisie that is propertied but nevertheless excluded from the grand bourgeoisie because its members do not exploit the labour power of others. Property then is already insufficient to differentiate classes from one another. By contrast and given its reputation, we would not expect Weberian class theory to be as insistent on property differences as the source of class differences but it nevertheless is so. '"Property" and "lack of property" are', Weber says, 'the basic categories of all class situations' (1982: 61). In an argument reminiscent of Marx's fragment on classes in *Capital* (1982: 20–1) that asserts the existence of *two* ruling classes, the aristocracy and the capitalists, Weber specifies two hierarchies (*Besitzklassen* and *Erwerbsklassen*) based on different types of property, physical property and fiscal property. However, for Weber property is significant not because it allows one class to exploit another in systems of production, but because it allows that class to enjoy privileged access to markets.

These arguments are curious not simply because they have now become *passé*, but because in an important sense they were *passé* at the time they were written. Capitalist society succeeded a feudal system constructed around a hierarchy of land ownership linked to fixed legal and religious statuses. Under feudalism, human beings were fundamentally defined by land tenure. The emergence of capitalism actually represented a loosening of the centralized organization of property ownership, so that property in fact had a reduced capacity to fix social membership. This is confirmed by the increased mobility and salience of class in directly post-feudal societies that has been noticed by more recent authors (e.g. Beck 1992: 96; Giddens 1973: 207; Mann 1973: 40–1; Mayer 1981; Moore 1973). Classes based on property were more effective in the early capitalist societies of the nineteenth century than at any time since. Indeed, in many instances relationships of exploitation and resistance between owners and non-owners were explicit, intense and personal, especially towards the end of that century. Capitalist enterprises were frequently small to medium, post-artisanal, individual or family firms in which there was a large measure of contact between owner and worker. Relations between firms were highly competitive both in the sense of a large number of competing producers, and in the sense of an absence of state regulation. Class differentiation was real and present and the need for capitalists to exploit their workers to the maximum presented itself tangibly in the threat of eclipse or absorption by competing firms. However, these classes were at their most effective when armoured by the status system of aristocracy, as in Britain or Germany, than when not, as in the USA.

If a society organized around the struggle between property classes is the class society *par excellence,* then its decline began relatively early. No sooner had capitalist society been established than it began to evolve into a new form in which property declined as the critical factor in economic group formation relative to the development of hierarchically ordered systems of domination, i.e. bureaucracies. In Marxist theory this shift is interpreted as the emergence of monopoly capitalism (e.g. Baran and Sweezy 1966). The production unit under monopoly capitalism is the 'giant corporation' that we would now identify as the multinational enterprise. Baran and Sweezy (1966: 15–16) argue for three main characteristics, although these do not go uncontested in other theoretical analyses. The first is that control is in the hands of management, by which they mean directors and chief executive officers, who are said to hold real power in the corporation and whose interests are inextricable from it. Secondly, management is a self-perpetuating group that establishes corporate career structures to recruit and promote new members independently of stockholders. Thirdly, corporations achieve financial independence by the internal generation of funds and thereby can become independent of finance capital. Marxists account for the emergence of monopoly capitalism in terms of its capacity to prevent the tendency for the rate of profit to fall by depressing wages: the problem of immiseration of labour is resolved by the maintenance or enhancement of individual wage levels but with a declining number of workers per firm.

The emergence of monopoly capitalism had serious consequences for the formation of classes around property ownership. Marx himself recognized that the emergence of corporate capital would change the structure of the ruling class (Clegg et al. 1986: 105; Sweezy 1942: 257). The principal consequence is what is known as the separation of ownership from control in which the exploitative functions of capital are performed by controlling managers while stockholders merely own the corporation in a legal sense. This position is represented in Burnham's (1941) well-known formulation of the 'managerial revolution' but is argued most effectively by Berle and Means (1967) who show that the senior managers of corporations own minorities of their assets. The point is confirmed by Galbraith (1967) who shows that managers have distinctive motivations and ideologies. However this does not necessarily imply that all stockholders will be small ones, that family stockholding will disappear, and that all stockholders will be private individuals. As Clegg et al. (1986: 105–22) show, such developments were only partial. Rather the general trend is from family ownership to ownership within 'institutionalized intercorporate relations', in which there is a coalition of interests between finance-capital holding companies and production firms integrated by interlocking directorships and mutual stockholding.

Increases in scale and specialization in an organization generate imperatives for co-ordination and, by extension, control. A key characteristic of monopoly capitalism is its hierarchical and bureaucratic organization: 'concentrated/centralized capitalist enterprises became permanent "bureaucracies." Capitalist accumulation increasingly depended on organizational coherence, long-term planning, political stability, cooperation between large corporations and the state' (O'Connor 1984: 80). This has two minimum effects in relation to the class structure. Firstly, it mediates the relationship between capital and labour, increasing the level of surveillance and blurring the dichotomous division between them. Secondly, and in order to achieve this, firms must delegate control of the technical division of labour down the organizational hierarchy so that: 'The way the process of production is organized is a productive resource distinct from the expenditure of labour power . . . organization – the conditions of coordinated cooperation among producers in a complex division of labour – is a productive resource in its own right' (Wright 1985: 79).

Simultaneously, monopoly capitalism is a major means for the control and division of the working class. Control is vested in the drive towards increasing technological rationalization in an effort to reduce the amount of surplus allocated to labour and to compete in the market for commodities. The effect, as suggested by Braverman (1974), is to reduce the capacity for resistance in the industrial sphere by the manual working class and the development of a status-differentiated clerical labour force. Highly technologized production offers both the possibility of direct control of labour power without the necessity for human surveillance and the routinization of tasks which increases the substitutability of labour.

## Public property

The growth of the state during the twentieth century also has implications for the distribution of property and the restructuring of class. Most Western societies have such high levels of state intervention, state regulation and state production that the official theory of Western capitalism given in state-social-ist societies was that they were constituted as 'state monopoly capitalism' ('stamocap'), an alliance between state interests and ruling-class interests. However, nowhere did the state play as important a role in class formation as in state-socialist societies themselves where individual private ownership of the means of production was abolished.

However, the state played an increasing part in structuring the distribution of property and economic rewards in the West as well. The example that is likely to offer the most challenging test to this argument is the USA, which has had one of the lowest levels of state intervention in economic life in the Western world. It has had few nationalized industries and an underdeveloped welfare sector. Nevertheless, by the 1980s there were 16.9 million government employees, or 15.4 per cent of the labour force. In addition, transfer payments (pensions, welfare benefits etc.) amounted to 13.8 per cent of total personal income (US Bureau of the Census 1986). If we combine recipients of transfer payments with state employees, a reasonable estimate of the proportion of the population whose material condition was entirely or largely dependent on the actions of the state might fall between 25 and 30 per cent.[1] The material condition of at least one-third of the members of this, the most privatized of societies, already had very little to do with the distribution of private property. In other societies, this development was much more advanced. In the state-socialist societies, for example, the proportion of the population whose class location was determined by private property was very low indeed; while in corporatist Western Europe, state intervention was also very considerable.

However, the state also influenced the remaining 70 per cent of the population in the private sector. Offe (1984: 125) identifies three ways in which the state impacts upon economic structures in advanced or mixed capitalism: firstly, processes of state regulation establish rules of competition within markets in order to ensure the survival of the commodity producers on which the state relies for its existence; secondly, processes of state intervention provide a capital infrastructure, principally for activities that reproduce labour as a commodity; and thirdly, processes of state-sponsored corporatism seek to minimize class conflict by the joint organization of capital and labour.

So, by the middle of the twentieth century, property had been reorganized. Its distribution was no longer simple, and class theorists could no longer provide evidence of a clear separation between plutocratic capitalists and an utterly immiserated and disempowered working class. Productive property was shared through corporate and institutional holdings and state ownership. Indeed in many societies the traditional staple industries in which the class struggle might be expected to take hold – coal mining, steel, shipbuilding, transportation and even car assembly – were the primary targets for public ownership. Elsewhere the leaders of such industries were locked into corporatist deals with worker representatives that gave the latter considerable control over the societal application of productive property.

## Organizational property

The amount of property owned by such industries could become very large indeed. In part this was due to the discovery of the economies of scale involved in mass production. In the early years of the century many American industrial organizations went through a famous transformation. The Ford Motor Company of the USA invented the moving assembly line and thus established an ideological paradigm for economic organizations that recently has come to be called Fordism. Fordism advocates the mass production of standardized items for mass markets made affluent by high incomes. It aims to reduce the cost per item by intensive mechanization and by economies of scale in the utilization of capital equipment. Fordism became the idealized system of production not only in the capitalist West but in the socialist East.[2] In so far as Fordism was exported by multinational enterprises, and in so far as it was mimicked, it became a major feature of the global economy in the period just after the Second World War. However Fordism owed its success not only to its capacity to produce and market goods on a wide scale but to its social and political consequences. It was an extraordinarily effective means both of controlling the labour process and of satisfying workers' aspirations at a material level. In the terms of Goldthorpe, Lockwood, Bechhofer and Platt's well-known formulation (1969), it turned proletarians into instrumental workers.

But Fordism was not a complete paradigm. In particular it left untouched the vast issue of who makes decisions and by what processes. In many instances this issue was resolved in terms of a parallel paradigm of work called Taylorism that specified a radical differentiation between the functions of management and labour. However, Taylorism did not achieve the level of acceptance that Fordism did, partly because it was challenged by a humanistic though equally manipulative paradigm called 'human relations'. Industrial organizations could therefore vary according both to the pattern of state action in regulating, co-ordinating, subsidizing and socializing the economy, and to cultural prescriptions of appropriate economic behaviour (see Lash and Urry 1987). So, for example: in the USA, large companies were run by ex-engineers making highly rationalized technical decisions in relation to technology and markets; in Germany, firms were organized and influenced jointly by state managers and finance houses; in France, large firms were centralized, state-managed bureaucracies; in Britain, there was a concentration on the maintenance of the managerial status group, at the possible expense of relative industrial effectiveness; and in Scandinavia, there was a deliberate effort to dedifferentiate managers and workers.

For Bell (1976: 276), whose analysis of corporations has much to offer, the giant corporations that were created by these managers were a 'new social invention' that was able to institutionalize, to an ultimate degree, a commitment to maximizing productivity by an increasingly efficient use of resources. A central feature of this commitment is a stress on an ideology of Taylorism or human relations in order maximally to control and thus to exploit the worker. However, Bell is convinced that, in the second half of the twentieth century, corporations have begun to be reconceptualized as social organizations of people and as the site for much of each person's lifetime experience rather than simply as a means for the production of goods and services. They are no longer exclusively committed to profitability and now pay much more attention to quality of working life and employee loyalty.

With not a little hindsight, for Bell this development was 'historically inevitable'. As the traditional institutions of community, church and family have declined the corporation has became the focus for social aspirations to status, security and justice. Corporations become complicit in a much more humanistic approach to employees precisely because these employees themselves, rather than stockholders, have become its main source of capital. Although theoretically corporate capitalism involves risk-taking investment by entrepreneurs, in fact most capital is raised by the internal generation and reinvestment of funds. This in turn depends on the labour, the skills, and the knowledge and ideas of its employees, in other words, on human capital. Ownership is therefore becoming a legal fiction because shareholders do not control the operation of corporations. Rather their status is more akin to that of a lender: 'the corporation may be a *private enterprise* institution but it is not really a *private property* institution' (Bell 1976: 294, original italics). Corporations are actually possessed by their employees.

Bell proceeds to draw an analogy between the emerging business corporation and the university in which the management and the board of directors are theorized to be equivalent to university trustees. They hold the corporation in trust, certainly for stockholders, but also for workers, consumers, and the public at large. Although this argument, which suggests that the contemporary corporation is becoming 'subordinated', subjected to external influence and internal democratization, is on the fanciful side, the view that it is ceasing to be the determining institution of society is not far from accurate.

It might be argued against Bell that some 'employees', that is executive managers, are clearly more powerful than others. However this is only a class-forming effect on the assumption of a continuation of monopolization and Fordism. There is widespread agreement that in about 1970 Fordism met a crisis of saturated markets. The organizational response has been downscaling, deconstruction and disamalgamation into smaller, more mobile firms that can rapidly and flexibly respond to niche-market opportunities. 'Flexible specialization', as it is called, relies on the extinction of the lumbering Fordist dinosaurs. One means of achieving this is their dissolution into networks of relatively small but skilled-up production companies that engage in product innovation on a competitive basis. The best known example of this development is the North Italian clothing industry (see Piore and Sabel 1984: 213–16). Another strategy is radically to overhaul a company so that progressively fewer employees are held in permanent relationships while others are hired on short-term or piecework contracts in response to shifting demand. The object of either of these post-Fordist configurations is to concentrate on economies of scope, that is, to produce the widest possible range of products.

Post-Fordism implies a further reduction in the saliency of property in structurating social inequality. Capital property can no longer secure domination of the society for those who control it precisely because their own accumulation possibilities are vulnerable to competition from firms whose owner-employees have better ideas that can penetrate markets more effectively. Perhaps more importantly, post-Fordism is reducing the scale of organizational property, or at least its relative capacity to determine patterns of economic allocation. In 1970 the *Fortune* 500 (largest companies) accounted for 20 per cent of American GDP but by the early 1990s they accounted for only 10 per cent (Naisbitt 1993: 13). The possibilities for the reproduction of a managerial capitalist class are correspondingly reduced.

### Redistribution

Our critique of property as the basis of class formation could end comfortably with this discussion of the political-organizational character of property arrangements that applied in the mid twentieth century. However, several further statements need to be made about property relations. First, we need to emphasize Parkin's point (1972: 21) about the redistribution of real property down the occupational hierarchy. Rather too much political mileage can be, and indeed has been, made about the extension of shareholding to wider sections of the population through share floats and the privatization of state-owned companies. Saunders (1990: 37) goes so far as to describe it as 'a dramatic redistribution of wealth from the state to private individuals'. Writing about Britain, a society in which privatization was developed both as a deliberate strategy to divide the democratic-socialist and liberal electoral bloc and as an expression of ideology, he indicates that the shareholding proportion of the population increased from 5 per cent in 1979 to 19 per cent in 1987. Of course, he does admit to an obvious problem that many of these shareholdings are tiny and uninfluential and that proportionately fewer shareholders are found at the bottom of the occupational hierarchy than at the top.

In fact the widening direct ownership of capital and financial property is merely a hint of the developments in property ownership that are under way. Indirect ownership is far more important. In Britain, Saunders says, more than half of all workers are covered by private pension schemes that invest funds in real property, equity and interest-bearing deposits. And a striking phenomenon of capital holdings in most Western societies has been the rapid spread of mutual funds and insurance-based investments to widening sections of the population. In the ten years up to 1992, the proportion of American shares owned by individual investors fell from 66 to 50 per cent while the proportion held by pension funds, insurance companies and mutual funds increased from 28 to 44 per cent. Over similar periods the distribution in Britain shifted from 28 per cent individual and 52 per cent mutual to 19 per cent individual and 55 per cent mutual, in Japan from 25/11 to 17/11, and in Germany from 28/4 to 19/7 (Bishop 1994: 4).[3] In the USA the number of mutual funds increased from 1,241 holding assets of $400 billion in 1984 to 4,500 holding just under $2 trillion in 1993 (*The Economist* 22 January 1994). While none of these data necessarily indicate a spreading of capital assets, the fact that such funds are created with a view to attracting small investors means that their growth is consistent with the argument advanced here.

However the key issue in the redistribution of property ownership is housing. Perhaps the prime example of a society experiencing an expansion of home ownership is Britain, although the patterns under inspection there are also evident elsewhere. The shift over the course of the twentieth century is quite stark. In 1914 about 90 per cent of the British population lived in private rental accommodation. During the course of the century state housing provision increased very considerably but generally the predominant trend lay in the direction of owner-occupation, so that by 1990 less than a third of the population lived in rented accommodation (Saunders 1990: 314). Housing, according to Saunders, represents not merely a consumption good but a domestic capital asset. It can accumulate in value, it can replace rental spending, it can be inherited, it can be realized to supplement or replace income in hard times, and it can serve as loan collateral. Saunders stresses the first of these, showing that home owners have received rates of return on their investments that might be the envy of any industrial 'capitalist'. Unlike other forms of private property, home ownership is widely distributed across the social spectrum, by occupation, by ethnicity, and even by gender.

These changes may individually appear to be minuscule and trivial. The claim that more people own their dwelling or have small investments in a unit trust might be argued to be only weak evidence of the dissolution of property classes, because their individual influence is so slight. However this is exactly the point of impact that must be stressed: the influence of property ownership is indeed in decline precisely because it is being distributed more widely. The redistribution of property is not making more people powerful but is making property a decreasing source of power.

Taken in the aggregate, the change is very profound indeed. There can be little doubt that in most 'capitalist' societies, by whatever measure one uses, the distribution of wealth has become progressively more equal during the course of the twentieth century. The evidence is so overwhelming that even such an unreconstructed Marxist as Miliband (1989: 54–5) must make the grudging admission that 'the share of wealth owned by the richest 10 per cent of the population of these countries appears to have declined in the last fifty years', while insisting that 'The system itself constantly reproduces great – at the extremes staggering, monstrous – inequalities of wealth, income, and power.'

The capacity of property to structure exploitation has been seriously diminished by its redistribution. There are numerous methodological problems in analysing the distribution of household wealth. The normal process is to examine its distribution by quantiles but there is no rule about what size of quantile one should use or whether one should look at the lowest or highest quantile. The question of what kinds of property constitute wealth is also unclear because of the issues of whether one should include means of consumption as well as means of production and whether one should include such non-disposable items as vested private pension or state pension rights. However, by whatever measure one uses it is clear that the distribution of wealth has indeed trended in a more egalitarian direction during the twentieth century. Figure 4.1 shows the proportion of disposable wealth owned by the richest quantiles in three Western countries. The trend is consistent and universal across countries and at different quantile levels. This runs against all arguments about the polarization of property ownership or that wealth redistribution is the consequence of the ideological orientations of particular parties or political cultures. More importantly it tells us that if contemporary societies are structured into classes then the basis for that structuring cannot be property. Property can no longer offer a foundation for cleavage and struggle.

Although the long-term trend in the distribution of property is clear there is some evidence that a reversal of the trend may now have become apparent, certainly in the Anglo-Saxon advanced societies during the 1980s and 1990s. The explanation normally given is the ascendancy of economically rationalist political regimes that have deliberately sought to redistribute wealth, particularly by the manipulation of capital-gains tax law and the relaxation of inheritance taxes. The first thing that needs to be said is that, if the explanation is correct, it cannot be an economic-class explanation but is organizational-political in character. More importantly the facts, and the possible explanations, need to be examined in slightly more detail.

The secular trend in the USA is described by Wolff: 'wealth concentration fell substantially during the mid-1970s and then increased sharply during the late 1970s and early 1980s. During the mid-1980s, wealth inequality remained more or less stable' (1992: 553). The net effect does not appear to have been severe. Ericksen (1988: 243) estimates that the wealth holdings of the top 0.5 per cent increased from 25 per cent in 1963 to 27 per cent in 1983. If mass-media reports of a new study by Wolff are correct (*The Australian* 19 April 1995) there has, however, been a sharp reversal of the trend in that society. In 1989 the richest 1 per cent of households owned 39 per cent of wealth. However, the same report states that the British top 1 per cent owned only 18 per cent of assets, which indicates that wealth inequality in that society is stable and relatively low.

The discrepancy between the trends casts considerable doubt on explanations made in terms of the ideological colour and practices of a particular political regime. Rather, short-term fluctuations are probably influenced much more by the changing cash value of assets than by the redistribution of

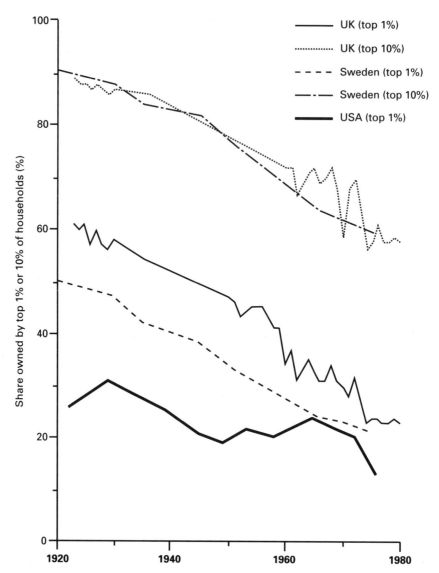

Figure 4.1   *Distribution of household wealth, Sweden, UK and USA,*
*1920–80 (data from Wolff 1987: 32, 60, 74–6, 81; 1991: 109)*

Data employ traditional measures, i.e. they exclude private and public pension
assets. UK data are for England and Wales only to 1972, and are for individuals
rather than households.

their ownership. The two main factors that affect this value are the price of
equities and the price of housing. An increase in the former tends to favour
the top of the distribution, but an increase in the latter favours its middle
ranges. In the 1980s and 1990s, 'black Monday' notwithstanding, there was a
general increase in equity prices and a downturn in housing prices. Two other

factors influence these particular fluctuations. First the USA has a lower rate of home ownership than the UK and other societies, so that there equity prices have more of an impact on the wealth distribution. Second, household income distributions will be affected by patterns of family formation, so that an increase in single-adult families, for example, will exert an anti-egalitarian pressure on the distributions no matter what the genuine distributional trend appears to be. This pattern of family formation is a widespread development in the second half of the twentieth century.

### Cultural property

The above issues are only relevant within a modernist or capitalist view of property. This chapter argues that if class is dependent on the distribution of material property then an equalized redistribution of that property is consistent with the decomposition of class. However, it is possible to go much further in suggesting that real or financial property is progressively ceasing to be an axial structural principle even in the arena of production. Here our claims are consistent with the influential but much contested proposal made by Bell (1976) that societies are entering a post-industrial phase. A post-industrial society is characterized not by the production of physical commodities but by the production of services. Therefore its chief production patterns depend not on investment of physical plant and machinery, real property, but on human commitment and intellectual technology. The means of service production cannot be 'possessed' in the same way that the means of goods production can. In contemporary society, human beings and their ideas and commitments cannot be owned, accumulated and traded in the way that shares are. While the commodification of human capital and intellectual property can be achieved by the use of patents and copyright, they are far more contestable and susceptible to redundancy in the marketplace for ideas.

This argument can be taken even further, however. The emerging pattern of goods production appears to be following a similar course to that of services; that is, it is becoming increasingly contingent on applications of ideas and human commitment and is thus becoming more informatic in character. The argument is captured neatly and possibly more accurately in Lash and Urry's (1994) theory of 'reflexive accumulation'. While Bell projects a shift in production from goods to services and an increasing interdependence between goods-producing and service-producing industries, Lash and Urry suggest that commodity production has actually become more like service production. Information structures, they argue, have become not only central to but coextensive with production systems. Theoretical expertise is a condition of successful material production. Flows of information and expertise give an information system the character of a material economy: 'In information structures cultural capital can be accumulated (in training and education) and spent as information flows are applied in problem solving' (1994: 108).[4] Lash and Urry try to show that the success of the German and

Japanese economies relative to Anglo-American ones is precisely that their production systems are information-rich, involving extensive training systems, high levels of education, continuous reflexive monitoring of organizational and engineering systems, and the engagement of employees in problem-solving and quality control.

Lash and Urry add a further dimension to the post-industrialization thesis that is drawn from what might be called the postmodernization thesis (see e.g. Crook et al. 1992; Harvey 1989). In contemporary societies, flows of aesthetic symbols have also multiplied and accelerated. The increases in scope, penetration and impact of the culture industries have created new arenas beyond traditional goods and service production for the creation and accumulation of cultural capital. They show that the production of cultural objects (books, television programmes, films, recordings) has become highly dispersed and localized, as well as reflexively engaged by its producers. By contrast the distribution systems of the culture industry, which relies on such capital-intensive technologies as fibre-optics and satellite broadcasting, have become increasingly concentrated and globalized. Here capital accumulation employs the judicial processes of intellectual property and the market-closure processes of branding, advertising and long-term contractualization.

Lash and Urry's critique of the culture industry, specifying the constraints of the distributional system and the excluded third of junk-job workers, also contains a more or less explicit approval for the diversity, competitiveness and fluidity of aesthetic production. Certainly, in a deregulated era, Dennis Potter could get his plays broadcast and Jean Baudrillard his books published. The public sphere, *pace* Habermas, is much more active and critical than it has ever been. This is consistent with a view that, while the culturalized society is riven by inequality and disadvantage, it is more open than a property-class system would ever allow. Independent producers are indeed autonomous, and however few distributors there may be they remain dependent on them for product. Unlike industrial production systems, distributors can own cultural products but they cannot own the capacity to produce. This restricts accumulation possibilities for each individual and thus distributes them more generally.

The accumulation constraints that apply to the culture industries are centred on the process of distribution rather than the level of production. In many national European television markets a few broadcasters can control and immiserate any number of small producers. However, distributional systems are themselves diversifying and amalgamating and thus becoming increasingly competitive. The American distributional system is now an enlarged mixture of big networks, satellite channels, local stations, community cable-vision co-operatives, and so on, all of which are programme-hungry and many of which seek to serve niche markets. The progressive aggregation of European and Asian mass-media systems should lead to similar developments.

## Markets

Let us now turn to the issue of the openness of society.[5] The picture of organized capitalism painted by the class paradigm specifies a concentration of power in the hands of the chief executives of monopolistic enterprises and of large-scale state agencies that regulated and segmented labour markets (see e.g. Blackburn and Mann 1979; Gordon et al. 1982). The principal problems in this argument are threefold. First, it assumes that these executives operate as a single collective actor in the market. In fact, cartelization was a relatively early phenomenon of organized capitalism, most often practised in relation to external commodity markets and only ineffectively in relation to the labour market. The relationship between firms has become increasingly competitive as markets have merged and as they have diversified their products. Second, power in large-scale organizations cannot be wielded exclusively by small groups. To the extent that what Wright (1985) has called organizational assets (authority) must be distributed down hierarchies there has been a dilution of competitive advantage in the labour market and it becomes increasingly difficult to 'own' jobs and to ensure their familial inheritance. Third, it ignores the fact that organizations can become so large that competitive internal labour markets can develop within them. In general, large-scale organizations relying on individual initiative, expertise and skill tend to contribute to a more open labour market rather than its opposite.

In another, perhaps less central occupational field the openness of labour markets also expanded under state protection. 'Professional' practitioners in law and medicine had previously been divided between central quasi-aristocratic monopolies, on one hand, and locals with community recognition of practitioner status, on the other (Larson 1977: 12). There had been no phase of 'open competition' because no market for professional services had ever existed. Rather, professionals sought to commodify their services by creating a standardized 'product' that relied on uniform professional training for its legitimation. Having standardized the product they then needed to create a market for it; that is, they needed to persuade consumers that they needed or wanted medical or legal services. However, the key factor in seeking to achieve market closure was not commodification but state recognition and public legitimation of credentials. In so far as the professions accomplished this they established a general market for credentials that was, in principle, limitless. Quite early, Weber was writing with disdain of the 'universal clamour' for educational certification (1978: 999–1000) and by the late twentieth century Collins pronounced the credential system in the USA to be 'inflationary' (1979: 191).

Consider now the overall change that had occurred within the transition from 'liberal' to 'organized' capitalism. Previously there were two fundamental economic roles, employer and unskilled labourer. The latter would often be trapped in a hermetic company town, ranch, mining community, plantation, or single-industry city (see Chapter 5). In most cases diffuse ties, lack of awareness of opportunity, or material constraint prevented occupational mobility. Where geographical mobility could occur it was virtually pointless because rewards were undifferentiated. Under organized capitalism, with all its very real barriers and protections, competitive market forces activated the labour system and gave some market power to employees. Workers could try to perform at a higher level in order to achieve promotion; they could seek to improve their skills and credentials in order to get a better job; they could aspire to the ownership of wealth; they could seek to educate their children; if opportunities were blocked they could move sideways and try to climb another occupational ladder; they could aspire to the most senior positions. The more that organized capitalism developed and elaborated, the more these opportunities became available. It needs to be stressed that this argument does not endorse the altogether apologetic functional theory of stratification (Davis and Moore 1945). The labour markets of organized capitalism were riven by segmentation, mobility barriers and the reproduction of disprivilege, especially for manual workers, although even here there were industrial and skill differentials. However, compared with the previous historical period, its occupational variety and the differential rewards attached to occupations offered something much closer to an open labour market.

More significantly, the organization of capitalism represented an important step in the commodification of women's labour. The appearance of an elaborated occupational system meant that social reproduction began to look like far too important and difficult an activity to be left in the hands of private individuals, especially women. The development of the welfare state was a deliberate attempt to socialize this function (Brenner and Ramas 1984). It provided an entry point for middle-class women into the labour market in such emerging though feminized occupational roles as nurse, teacher, and social worker. Simultaneously, compulsory education partially released 'working-class' women from the supervision of children, allowing entry into the labour market on part-time and non-permanent bases, although again in feminized occupations as clerk, sales assistant, cook, cleaner, etc. Clearly, although women had indeed entered the labour market it was by no means on an equal footing with men. Nevertheless it was also clear that organized capitalism had thus breached a powerful status constraint.

Changes to the labour market were matched by increases in the power of consumers. The conventional view of the class paradigm is that, under organized capitalism, monopolization allowed sellers increasingly to control prices. But even oligopolistic sellers can compete, and that competition led to an expansion of markets and to an increased substitutability of products within them. A critical feature of organized-class society then is mass consumption. Prior to the First World War, consumption patterns were, for the most part, oriented to subsistence needs. This was changed by three social technologies: Fordist assembly-line production, mass marketing, and easy consumer credit (Bell 1979a: 66). Now consumption became oriented to substitutable, replaceable luxuries. In so far as consumers could select whether to buy a new car this year, have the kitchen remodelled, or take an overseas vacation, monopolization in any single product area could no longer succeed in controlling prices except where demand was highly inelastic (e.g. tobacco, oil). Mass marketing became a highly competitive process and consumers were unwilling to accept black Model Ts for very long. While this did not make the consumer a sovereign it had a very considerable effect in increasing consumer influence. Indeed, in many societies, mass-consumption culture has proved highly resistant to elitist impositions of taste and choice from any source, including the state.

We are claiming then that the markets of organized-class society were much more open than those that preceded them. However, by about 1970 mass-consumption markets had become saturated because of rapid rises in productivity (Crook et al. 1992: 173; Harvey 1989: 141). At the same time states suffered a series of crises in which they proved unable to meet clientilist demands from underproductive sectors without severe fiscal consequences: states were experiencing market failure. States and markets both started to change as markets began to disassemble state arrangements that they had previously only influenced. States began to shrink, shedding functions to both local and global levels of government and to the private sector. Equally, markets both expanded by global merger and underwent a process of 'hyper-differentiation' (Crook et al. 1992: 32–3). Under the latter process, the range of products and types of labour service diversified to an extreme degree. While the process is by no means complete, its hypothetical end point would be one in which every single product was unique and competitive with every other product; and in which each worker provided individualized services that could compete in the labour market with those offered by every other worker. Even by the 1980s, capitalist societies had moved so far down this road that some observers began to speak of a 'disorganized capitalism' (Lash and Urry 1987; Offe 1987).

The critical competitive feature of the new consumption market that emerged as a response to this crisis is not simply its massive scale. This is a long-standing characteristic. Rather, consumption has now become a reflexive practice. It is becoming the standard by which individuals judge others and themselves. Consumer goods become signs of association and lifestyle. They are consumed for the images they convey, rather than because of utility or aesthetics, much less out of necessity. Few consumers would seriously believe, for example, that they can make a difference to the environment, much less to a clean domestic environment, by using 'green' household cleaning materials, but they can, by consuming them, indicate a commitment to environmentalist values. The tendency to multiply brand names, to inscribe them on the outside of clothing and cars in large letters, is an indicator of the signifying pattern of consumption (see Baudrillard 1988: 19). Consumers are caught in what for the producer is a happy paradox: what they wear must be both unique and recognizable as an instance of a particular style.

Similarly post-Fordist, flexible organizations have profound implications for the labour market. An increasing proportion of the labour forces of most Western societies is self-employed (Hakim 1988a; Steinmetz and Wright 1989). Equally there is considerable evidence that many companies are downscaling their operations (e.g. Murray 1988); rates of part-time and temporary employment are rising (Hakim 1988a; Pollert 1988); and homeworking is also increasing (Hakim 1988b). All of this bespeaks an increasingly deregulated labour market. Here unions are unable to control the supply of labour services because employers can outflank them by increasing rewards to skilled employees and by contractualizing unskilled work. While the current recession in employment would suggest that employers can influence wages more than employees can, an increasing number of employers as well as possibilities for self-employment might bring the situation into balance.

The deregulation of labour markets has not, however, been an even development. Worker categories recently entering the labour market, women and migrant ethnic minorities in particular, find themselves in the highly competitive segments of contractualized, outsource manufacturing and low-grade, consumer-service occupations. Meanwhile multiskilling has enabled some 'professionalized' workers to establish the closure pattern known as 'lifetime employment'. Again, by contrast, the employment market in the post-industrial service sector has moved in the direction of more open competition as small-scale service providers increasingly compete for short-term contracts in an increasingly downscaled, decentralized and informatic production arena.

The opening up of these markets has had ambivalent consequences for the ascriptively disprivileged because the emergence of a post-industrial service proletariat or underclass means low reward levels. However, their increasingly competitive nature has reduced possibilities for ascriptive closure. If social worth is based on profligate consumption, or commitment to lifestyles or values, then gender, race and ethnicity must play a reduced role in shared estimations of social worth. Equally, if contributions of skills and knowledge become more critical to product innovation than a secure and compliant labour force, the possibilities for demonstrating such qualities must improve. For Beck (1992: 104–5) these universalizing effects of the market are felt in a personalization of identity in which one reflexively self-identifies ('I am myself') in preference to locating oneself as a member of a social category or class. In an 'individualized society of employees', status constraints on the labour market would disappear.

It bears repeating that the labour market is full of barriers, exclusions and privileges. Ascriptive and status constraints continue to be more effective than any occupational grouping in structuring the market. To these we can add the constraints of patriarchal relations and the burdens of raising children. More importantly, any apparent residue of class in the labour market might more successfully be analysed by using a variation on the theme of the so-called 'underclass'. To repeat, this is not a class in the production-centred sense but rather is identified by the incapacity of its members to engage in status as opposed to subsistence consumption. Its membership is not prescribed by a common relationship to the production process because it includes aged pensioners, state-supported single parents, the 'working poor', ethnic and racial minorities, people challenged by reduced physical abilities, women excluded from masculinized occupations, working youth, recent migrants and 'guest' workers, the unemployed, and the homeless. The bases for the exclusion of such people from high-reward labour markets is to do not with class but with both ascriptive and conventional statuses.

One final point needs to be made against the class analysts' insistence that, if only for those who are in an employment relationship, identity and action are class determined. It assumes that work is coterminous with the life experiences that construct an identity. This is clearly no longer the case. Between 1850 and 1950 the average working week in the USA declined from about 70 to about 40 hours, from seven ten-hour days to five eight-hour days (Galbraith 1958: 334). The social impact of this decline becomes apparent when we translate it into an experiential profile. In the mid nineteenth century an average worker spent more than 60 per cent of active life in the work environment under a workhouse or factory regime. Considering the working conditions, the remaining 40 per cent can scarcely have been more than an appendage to work. A similar point can be made about biography. A working life began at the age of twelve or fourteen and, given a relatively low average age of death, retirement could not be expected to be long and fulfilling. Indeed, only a few decades earlier women and children had experienced similar employment experiences to those of men.

A long lifetime filled with work endowed a person with the proletarian identity of a 'worker', one whose habits, activities and perceptions necessarily were dominated by the employment situation. A century later, work occupied only a third of anyone's active time. Employment often does not begin until one's early or mid twenties and lasts, except for judges and politicians, only until the age of 65. Given that life is now longer and healthier, the period of retirement might last for ten or twenty years. The remaining time is colonized by the non-work roles of citizen, consumer, student and family member. It is difficult to share the assumption made by class analysts that these roles should have less impact on identity and action than the employee role that is often filled instrumentally.

### Collective class action

In classical class theory as specified by the four propositions set out in Chapter 1, union organization and industrial conflict are class phenomena. They allow us to view classes as collective actors struggling against each other in the economic field. Indeed, even in market-class theory, where there is no requirement that workers need to be solidaristic in a *für sich* sense, one would still expect that the most effective way for a class to accomplish market closure would be by collective action. So the pattern of industrial action represents a very important test of the effectivity of class structures.

In about 1970 there was an enormous upsurge in industrial conflict that included a near revolution in France in 1968, the Italian 'hot autumn' of 1969 and the British coal mining strikes of the early 1970s, as well as less significant strike waves in North America and even Scandinavia. To many class theorists this must have appeared as continuing evidence of the salience of class in determining collective action, a corrective to the embourgoisement/business-unionism thesis that was then beginning to take hold and that argued that proletarians would only engage in collective action when it was in their individual material interests to do so. Crouch and Pissorno (1978) for example pronounce it to be a resurgence of class conflict, even if they did manage to conflate the political action of students, women and anti-war protesters to class. Even such a dispassionate observer as Hibbs (1978) is convinced that the prevailing thesis about the withering away of industrial conflict is inconsistent with this evidence. However, whatever confirmation it offered must have provided only temporary support for class analysis because since that time a withering of industrial conflict has indeed occurred and along with it the very 'working-class' organizations that gave rise to it.

In fact Hibbs' analysis (1978) of strike trends in capitalist societies up to the 1970s tends to confirm the general historical proposal that in the twentieth century classes were reorganized into political and organizational collectivities, as opposed to socioeconomic collectivities. These collectivities were fundamentally oriented to distributive rather than to ideological issues. Hibbs argues that in some societies, especially in Scandinavia and Northern Europe, the working class was able to organize itself to such an extent as to dominate government. When a social-democratic party is in power it is able to shift the locus of control of the distribution of rewards from the private to the state sector. When it does so, the level of strike activity declines. This Hibbs confirms both cross-societally (societies with social-democratic governments have fewer strikes than those without) and cross-historically (there are fewer strikes during periods when such governments are in power than when they are not). Hibbs explains the upsurge of 1970 in terms of a decreased commitment, even by social-democratic governments, to étatist redistribution. He quite incorrectly predicts that the upsurge in industrial conflict will continue.

The evidence in the opposite direction is overwhelming. Strike activity is declining whether the government is socially democratic or not and whether it seeks to effect redistribution or not. This is because industrial conflict takes place between collective class actors and the structural basis for such action has disappeared. Unionization or union density, the proportion of the labour force that belongs to trade unions, is declining in most Western societies. The general trend of unionization since the Second World War is as follows (Goldfield 1987; Visser 1992; Western 1995): the unionization level was roughly constant until the late 1960s when the upsurge of class action attracted more members, but thereafter a general decline in unionization rates occurred and this decline accelerated in the 1980s. There are national exceptions to the pattern (Belgium, Denmark, Finland, Norway and Sweden) but these are outside the G7. Indeed in the late 1980s Belgium, Denmark and, unprecedentedly, even Sweden experienced falls in union membership.

Experts in the field adduce several possible causes for this decline: the declining size of the manual working class and the growth of new white-collar occupations; the entry of difficult-to-unionize women into the labour force; the economic recession and its accompanying unemployment; the demise of social-democratic governments (an argument that runs directly counter to Hibbs' evidence); increased global competition for jobs; and the advance of enterprise bargaining and other forms of labour-market deregulation. Western (1995) quantifies many of these and finds that they are indeed effective in explaining the onset of unionization decline. However, such findings need not be disputed in order to suggest that they are expressions of the general proposal advanced here. No longer can unions effectively moderate the predominant forms of inequality found in contemporary society because they are not class inequalities. As they are currently constituted there is no hope for a long-term revival in union fortunes because the class struggles that underlie them now have minimal significance.

### The international division of labour

One of the reasons why unions are proving increasingly ineffective is that they have traditionally focused on redressing inequality within nation-state societies and that these are becoming much less self-contained and self-sufficient than they used to be. Stratification and inequality have long been internationalized but they are now becoming globalized. In an international system of stratification, intra-societal classes can be sustained by external exploitation, but in a globalized system, inequality and its exploitations transpire on a planetary scale. Class-collective actors can no longer cohere in an increasingly chaotic and borderless world.

Marx's original argument about international stratification, elaborated in Lenin's analysis (1939) of imperialism, claims that international capitalist monopolies divide the world between themselves both economically and, through the agency of the colonial state, territorially. Imperialism differentiates the working class into an upper stratum of affluent workers and the lower stratum of the proletariat proper which is increased by immigration from the colonies (1939: 105). Lenin's thesis, in turn, has been extended by such neo-Marxist authors as Frank (1971) and Amin (1980), but the most influential contemporary version is Wallerstein's analysis (1974; 1980) of world systems.

The world system is a unit that has a capacity to develop independently of the social processes and relationships that are internal to its component societies or states. A critical feature of Wallerstein's argument, which differentiates it from the dependency theory of Frank and Amin, is that the focal point of pressure in the world economy is the state structure. The state helps to stabilize capitalism by absorbing its costs and managing the social problems that it creates. This shifts the fundamental process of stratification away from classes and onto states. The capitalist world system stratifies into core, semi-peripheral and peripheral states. There is a division of labour between these: 'tasks requiring higher levels of skill and greater capitalization are reserved for higher-ranking areas' (1974: 350). Class is explained by this international division of labour in so far as the ability of core states to remain at the centre depends on their capacity to maintain capital accumulation in the face of working-class claims for redistribution.

⌐ Wallerstein's argument is an appropriate corrective for sociological analyses of inequality that focus only on the internal mechanisms of the nation-state society, and this has come through into the specification of a new international division of labour. Fröbel, Heinrichs and Kreye (1980) develop this concept to explain declines in German manufacturing employment. Investment and technology were flowing offshore to newly industrializing countries and manual-work jobs were going with them. In the new international division of labour the former First World is increasingly post-industrial, hosting educational, cultural, managerial and administrative service production whose workers exploit and are serviced by a migrant-enriched 'post-industrial proletariat' or 'underclass' while commodity production is relocated in the newly industrializing and less developed countries.

Although it is a little of an overstatement to suggest that Germany, Japan or the USA no longer has a manufacturing economy, this argument points to the fact that flows of finance, commodities, technology and labour are now much more mobile than previous theories allow. It means, however, that the differences between say Germans and Colombians are far greater, more significant and conceivably more exploitative than differences between German service workers and German manual workers or farm labourers. Equally, the 'underclass' in Germany is structured far more by nationality, citizenship, ethnicity and gender (i.e. most frequently by *Gastarbeiter* relationships), that is by status-based exclusion and appropriation, than it is by simple market monopolization, much less by control of production.

### Conclusion

Let us now reconfirm the historical processes that we flagged in Chapter 1. In what is called economic-class society there was a radically unequal distribution of property between capitalists and workers that enabled the former to exploit the latter. Property was largely owned privately and familially, rather than by the state, and was inherited dynastically. In organized-class society property was still distributed unequally but the sharp break between ownership and non-ownership disappeared in favour of a gradient that, over time, progressively became less steep. An important element in this redistribution was the intervention of states in patterns of property ownership. Under the aegis of socialist, communist and fascist ideologies, states often appropriated the means of production on behalf of the working class. In other societies property ownership was reorganized by the formation of shareholder corporations that tended to separate ownership from control and to facilitate the dispersal of the former. In the emerging status-conventional society this redistribution continues, especially in the context of privatization. More importantly, the character of property is changing so that it is much less easy to accumulate and monopolize. Intellectual property is becoming more important than material property, and the economy of intellectual and aesthetic signs is increasingly fluid and competitive.

Labour and consumption markets have followed a similar path. The original property classes were mutually exclusive in terms of recruitment and able to confer radically different consumption privileges. In organized-class society the key role in market participation was the occupation. What many sociologists now call classes were in fact groups of similar occupations effecting an unreliable closure against external recruitment and battling to climb the ladder of consumption privileges. The critical contexts for occupational advancement were the hierarchies of authority and responsibility established in state agencies and business corporations. It was here that mobility barriers were erected and that participants strived for sufficient income to reproduce their standing by providing adequate educations for their offspring. In the contemporary phase, markets have become casinos. Each individual is now their own market player, needing to make educational and occupational career decisions in contexts that defy parental advance planning. We are moving into a situation in which what you get depends on how you perform, although there is very little evidence that this means that the markets necessarily will judge performance on a just calculus.

### Notes

1 Frankel puts this point nicely in his critique of Althusser's and Poulantzas' view of the state: 'they do not seem to comprehend the millions of state sector workers as more than mere administrators and reproducers of capitalist relations – that is, they do not fully acknowledge the transformation of the material conditions of existence of millions of people who do not themselves produce surplus value, but whose economic relations would dramatically affect the private capitalist units of production should their numbers increase dramatically, or be reduced by half' (1982: 260–1n, italics deleted).

2 Fordism was indeed paradigmatic and idealized rather than generalized. It never accounted for more than 10 per cent of manufacturing labour, even in the USA (Crook et al. 1992: 172).

3 The remainder are held by corporations or banks or are outside the country.

4 Of course, cultural capital is never 'spent' but rather applied. As it is applied it is not exhausted but actually accumulates with the benefit of experience. This makes it rather different from material capital.

5 This section is drawn from Waters (1995b).

# 5

# Crumbling Communities of Fate

Chapter 4 shows that the economic basis of class has changed very radically since the inception of capitalist society. This chapter begins the process of examining the consequences of these changes. It considers the shifting relationship between class divisions and their social consequences. It asks how class is affected by the scale of the community in which it is constructed, what its relationship is with the gender system, and what consequences these developments have for the latent reproduction of inequality and conflict. The chapter addresses, then, the issue of the articulation of class in space and time.

We agree with many class theorists who suggest that class is at its most real when it is experienced in day-by-day confrontations and struggles with members of other classes. So class is most apparent and most salient when it occurs in complete and bounded communities based on a few industries. Here patterns of exploitation and domination can easily be apprehended and class interests can readily become recognized and shared. The chapter shows that such communities have progressively disappeared from modern societies. With their eventual decay classes were aggregated into political organizations at the level of the nation-state. More recently these class organizations have themselves attenuated with the shrinking of the state.

The reality of class also presupposes its reproduction across time. Certain class processes must result in a continuing, although possibly expanded, structure of positions and in allocations of individuals to them. The critical arena of social reproduction is domesticity and its associated patterns of patriarchy and kinship. We are guided by the proposition that the reproduction of classes will be most certain where the family is solely responsible for the reproduction of labour power or where there are other specialized class-reproducing institutions such as exclusive schools. Where responsibility for the reproduction of labour power is shared between families and universal education systems, class reproduction will be correspondingly attenuated. Under current circumstances, the family is more or less entirely losing its functions of social and cultural reproduction, thus undermining the continuity of both class and patriarchy.

## Communities of fate

If class is the product of capitalist industrialization then its arrangement in space and its reproduction over time must be understood in relation to urbanization and the emergence of the industrial city. The nineteenth century saw a rise in the level of urbanization to unprecedented levels (Elliott and McCrone 1982: 61; Gold 1982: 57, 67). In 1700 the largest city in Europe was London with a population of over half a million. In the next 100 years it grew to 900,000. It was pursued over the next 50 years by industrial cities in the midlands and north of Britain: Birmingham, Liverpool, Manchester, Leeds, and Glasgow. The Industrial Revolution occurred rather later in the USA but there cities grew even faster as their populations were swelled by immigrants from Europe. By 1851 there were nine cities in Britain with populations over 100,000; in the USA there were also nine by 1860 but 56 by 1910.

There were three factors that brought about the rapid growth of these industrial cities: the mechanization of agriculture that released labour in rural areas; the reduction of craft work to mechanized processes that could be performed by unskilled labour; and the large-scale social organization of work in specialized factories. Economies of scale demanded that these should be close to sources of supply of raw materials and to mass markets. Factories therefore tended to be concentrated geographically.

The cities that emerged were unplanned, disease-ridden, pestilent, and dangerous for many of their inhabitants. Housing stock was frequently shoddy and often overcrowded. Public sanitation, public transportation, and law-and-order systems were rudimentary and inadequate to meet the demands placed upon them. Victorian cities established for the first time a classic separation between the commercial district or the central business district on the one hand, and the manufacturing area on the other. This also enforced a pattern of residential segregation. Working-class housing developed in inner-city areas close to manufacturing employment while the middle class was able to live on the other side of town, or even well out of it.

However, it would be incorrect to suggest that the city drove out 'premodern' structures of community. The picture painted by Chicago School urban sociologists of a civic existence constructed around an anomic and atomistic struggle for survival has long since been dispelled by studies of urban working-class communities that stress cohesion and mutual support. In Britain, for example, Young and Willmott (1962) showed that the inner London, working-class area of Bethnal Green was bound together by kinship, a stable population, and economic and class homogeneity. Young and Willmott's Eastenders were neither impersonal nor lonely because they worked, shopped, and recreated with the same people. Aid and support were available through the neighbourhood and kinship networks when they needed them. Meanwhile in the USA, Gans (1962) discovered a similar communal enclave in Boston, but one based on ethnic rather than class homogeneity. Gans' ethnic Italians protected themselves against the encroaches of corporatist America by establishing their own institutions that overlapped one another in membership. Gans calls his subjects urban villagers, and the term 'urban village', with its communalistic connotations, survives as a way of describing such residential patterns.

Smaller towns were also class divided, and indeed, some may remain so to the present day. Lynd and Lynd's (1959) classic study of the small industrial town of Muncie, Indiana (population 35,000) in 1925 and its restudy in 1935 offers one example. The restudy in particular assesses the workings of the local stratification system. The community was dominated by a classic ruling class, a small local elite, all of whose members were united in the bosom of a single family (the 'X' family) that based its dominance on the ownership of the local manufacturing business. A much quoted statement made by one of the Lynds' informants sums up the pattern of class domination:

> If I'm out of work I go to the X plant; if I need money I go to the X bank, and if they don't like me I don't get it; my children go to the X college; when I get sick I go to the X hospital; I buy a building lot or a house in an X subdivision; my wife goes downtown to buy clothes at the X department store; if my dog strays away he is put in the X pound; I buy X milk; I drink X beer, vote for X political parties, and get help from X charities; my boy goes to the X YMCA and my girl to their YWCA; I listen to the word of God in X-subsidized churches; if I'm a Mason I go to the X Masonic Temple; I read the news in the X morning newspaper; and, if I am rich enough, I travel via the X airport. (Stein 1964: 57–8)

The Lynds' study is highly significant because it shows, for the first time, that traditional communities were structured in terms not simply of familiarity and harmony, but also of domination and subordination, and divided interests and conflict (Bell and Newby 1971: 82–91; Stein 1964: 47–69).

In this sort of company town class was apparent and real, expressed not only in domination and control but in lifestyle and domestic arrangements. In such communities there is an intimate link between class and patriarchy, as Williams (1981) shows in her study of a surviving company town in Australia that she calls 'Open Cut'. This is also a working-class town but it is located in a more isolated context, built to house miners and their families working the coal seams licensed to the Utah Development Company at Goonyella and Peak Downs in central Queensland. Williams shows workplace class relations to be highly antagonistic. This is partly because the isolated nature of the work context means that workplace relations are reproduced in the community. But it is also predicated on a punitive management style and an increasing level of technological control of labour on the one hand, and a highly instrumentally oriented, homogeneous and concentrated labour force on the other. The reality of class differences was clearly recognized by the company and the state government in the way in which the town was planned:

> Wages workers and their wives were to be housed in new low-set houses with three bedrooms; foremen were to be housed in new four-bedroomed high-set houses, selectively located amongst the low-set houses, while higher management were to be housed in the large, almost palatial dwellings situated on the slight incline in the centre of town which were to be serviced by professional gardeners . . . Management Row. Despite the fact that a proportion of the houses were built and paid for by the Australian taxpayer through the Housing Commission, this ranking was duly followed in the Government houses as well . . . These houses are rented from Utah at a nominal rent. (1981: 112–13)

Indeed, Williams argues that many workers experience Open Cut not as a residential community but as an occupational community. Men typically separate themselves from women to socialize and to talk about work. This is reinforced by the fact that for most of them it is not regarded as a permanent place of residence. It is a merely a site where family capital can rapidly be accumulated by engaging in intensive, laborious and isolated but high-paying work for a limited period.

This links to Williams' second main theme, that of patriarchy. In Open Cut men regard themselves as instrumental providers for their families. Mine work is surrounded by a discourse of toughness and hard labour. Yet men are also confronted by the contradictory experience of their own subordination in class terms. So domestic life is a retreat from this experience. The men who experience the highest level of job dissatisfaction in terms of tension, stress and pressure are also those most likely to make extreme patriarchal statements about domestic life. Williams interprets the subordination of working-class women, then, as compensatory action on the part of working-class men for their own subordination in the workplace. Patriarchal domestic relations are thus seen as a safety-valve for the injuries of capitalist class relations.

Many Marxist-feminist scholars have generalized this argument, that patriarchy is the basis for the social reproduction of class, to entire societies. Perhaps the most extreme and explicit example is offered by Barrett, for whom: 'The family-household system of contemporary capitalism constitutes not only the central site of the oppression of women but an important organizing principle of the relations of production for the social formation as a whole' (1980: 211). This position is worked out in her analysis of the relationship between household organization and capitalism (1980: 204–26). She begins with an assumption that the family is the site for the definition of gender identity. This is primarily an ideological process in which families both respond to and contribute to representations of the family especially in religion and the mass media. The ideology is constraining – no matter what individual family members choose to do, the representations are fundamentally gendered. However, the household is also a site of material production with a gender-specific division of labour. The assignment of child-rearing duties to women places them in a relationship of material dependence on and inequality with men.

She can now make the link between household structure and the ideology of the family on the one hand, and capitalism on the other. The family-household system has the following consequences: it prevents the revolutionary unity of working-class men and working-class women; the dependency of women and children on a male wage means that working-class men are less likely to engage in acts of protest or revolt; it provides an apparently intimate haven for men who daily face the debilitations of wage labour; it reproduces masculine labour power; it provides continuity in the face of social upheavals; and it provides a site for the maximal consumption of commodities. So the link is essentially a functional one. The family-household system contributes to the maintenance of capitalism and, concomitantly, of bourgeois hegemony. It does so in terms of contributions to reproduction, political stability, economic demand, and ideologically induced conformity.

The functional articulation between masculine domination and bourgeois domination is expressed even more explicitly in the work of Eisenstein (1979; 1981). Subscribing to a somewhat discredited private–public dichotomy, she specifies society as the arena of commodity production and the family as the arena of (domestic service) production, reproduction and consumption. The sexual division of labour in the family has two specific functions for society: it provides a pool of unpaid and low-paid labour and it 'stabilizes' the society (1979: 30). The practices by which this stabilization is achieved include the fulfilling of domestic roles, the biological reproduction of new workers, and consumerism (1979: 29). Within 'capitalist patriarchy' the domestic sphere follows the particular form of a nucleated family structure and the confinement of women to the domestic role of housewife. Thus the structural arrangements of patriarchy are contingent on the structural arrangements between men constituted in the class system.

These reductions of patriarchy to class, in which patriarchy is consigned to the realm of epiphenomena and ideologies, verge on the bizarre if we try to apply them outside the period of early capitalism. Even if we were prepared to accept the logical problems of functionalist explanation, we would still be left with the difficulty of explaining how patriarchy managed to survive for perhaps a million years before class arrived on the scene. This difficulty is expressed in a debate, one side of which is taken by Marxist feminists, about why it was that during early capitalism there was a shift from commodity production, as a shared task, to gender differentiation between domestic production and commodity production. Two alternative positions are available. In line with Marxist feminism, Hartmann (1982) argues that male workers actively sought, through their unions, to exclude women from the employed labour force in order to protect their own jobs. This can be viewed as a variant on the 'reserve army' thesis mobilized by Barrett and Eisenstein in so far as masculine exclusivity forms part of a struggle between bourgeoisie and proletariat about returns to labour. However, for the argument to receive support, employers would have had to have been complicit in the arrangement because women were not merely organized out of employment, but were legislated out of it. As Pahl (1988) argues, such a view leaves us with an uneasy choice between a bourgeoisie-proletariat conspiracy and an equally unlikely masculine altruism in protecting wives and daughters against the class depredations of capitalism.

A second explanation, from Brenner and Ramas (1984), is much more convincing. Their argument is materialist and biological. Under pre-industrial conditions, production and reproduction could easily be fitted together because production itself occurred in domestic contexts. The organization of production into factories directly threatened possibilities for reproduction. If all the members of a household had to spend most of their lives governed by the rhythms of machines, then biological and social reproduction would be impossible. Brenner and Ramas insist that there was no alternative to the establishment of the differentiated household and its attached division of labour. A high level of female participation in employment would have required the market provision of low-cost prepared food, child-care, laundry services, etc. and these simply were not available. Moreover the severe biological constraints of gestation and lactation meant that it was not possible for men to be the child-carers.

This argument is important not merely because it is a corrective to more ideologically driven alternatives but because it can admit change. In the nineteenth century, working-class labour was directly and simply reproduced precisely because that reproduction took place in encapsulated domiciles dominated by working-class men and enfolded within working-class communities and their cultures. When reproduction was detached from the household two developments followed. First, women could be released from the absolute imposts of biological and social reproduction. It would no longer be impossible for women simultaneously to work in the public sphere and to bear children within a conjugal relationship. Second, the reproduction of class would no longer be simple and direct. As working-class children began to be socialized in non-working-class milieux, the possibility arose for an extended pattern of reproduction that began to break down class communities. The boundaries of community expanded beyond locality to the nation, and biological and social reproduction began to be organized at the nation-state level.

## Imagined communities

This was nothing short of a revolution, even if it was non-violent and gradual. Its main causes are set out in the classical literature: commodification; an increasing division of labour; corporate industrial organization; urbanization; and bureaucratization. Its key symptoms are the decomposition of rural communities and the decline and dissolution of the urban villages that formed around the early industrial and trade centres. The metropolitan social landscape, described with artistic sensitivity by Simmel (1964), was too fluid and diverse to accommodate lasting and homogeneous social enclaves of a *gemeinschaftlich* type. The result was an erosion of communities of fate or, to be more precise, their dissolution within the more abstracted and universalistic imagined or quasi-communities of nation and nationalized classes.

Although class and nation have often been depicted as 'alternatives' in the sense that they compete for identities and loyalties, they are, as Mann (1993; also Anderson 1983) indicates, intimately connected: they share historical origins in the process of industrialization and military conflict; both are highly universalistic and open; they are imagined rather than real communities because they are much too big to allow for even the most diluted of face-to-face interactions; and both rely on foundational myths and highly abstracted notions of commonality that have to be constructed and maintained through a systematic organizational effort. They are a deliberate and intentional rather than a spontaneous emergence. They are rooted not in the shared, localized, everyday experiences of their members, but in organizational activities extending across space and time and in abstracted ideological formulations that are systematically produced and disseminated by specialized agencies. The central organizational generators of these imagined communities are nation-*states* and class *parties*, the latter including such organizational forms as trade unions and national social movements.

Class communities of fate are small, homogeneous, well bounded and clearly circumscribed. Even if their members do not know each other personally, they have clear and visible criteria of membership. Commonality of experience, territorial proximity and dense relations make them tangible and powerful so that they generate clear and specific identities and envelop their members' lives. Shared interests transpire in a direct and obvious way through shared lifecourse and lifestyle. Norms, symbols and identities reflect these life situations. Collective action comes, typically, in response to threats or violations of these shared interests and communal lifestyles. There is little need for formal organization, if the threat is clear, and if political mobilization does not require elaborate ideological constructs. Mobility is low and mechanisms of social reproduction are obvious and direct because community and family are closely co-ordinated and they create exclusive lifeworlds.

By comparison, the imagined communities of national classes, e.g. the English working class, the French bourgeoisie, the American middle class, are altogether different phenomena. They stretch over vast national territories and encompass people with very diverse experiences and life situations who must be persuaded systematically and repeatedly that they have common interests, often against their everyday experience of internecine difference, division and animosity. Openness and mobility contribute to this diversity, blurring social boundaries and posing constant challenges to unification efforts. Organizational and symbolic unification is only possible because of the appearance of organization and mass communication within what Carr (1964) calls the 'third period' of nation-state formation, 1870–1945.

Modern nation-states make the formation of imagined communities of class both possible and necessary. The possibilities are expanded by the organizational extension of the state, and its penetration of the economy and previously autonomous areas of social life, including education and family support. The appearance of a daily press, popular literature and radio greatly facilitates this bureaucratic extension and penetration. Equally, national class formation becomes necessary because nation-states rely heavily on bureaucratic standardization and regulation. They unify territories, legal systems, currencies, fiscal systems, and administrations, and even standardize and promote 'national' languages and cultures. Wars and internal social upheavals encourage this gradual shift from the 'night-watchman state' to the 'nanny state' by making standardization and unification an essential condition of military success. As the nation becomes a standardized field of state intervention, national classes, represented by national class organizations, become the standardized referents for intra-national political intervention and regulation.

This is a two-way process of forming and firming a national 'political community' mainly through the extension of suffrage, and of constituting

standardized, organized and nationally oriented sub-units of social and political management: 'Thus formal electoral participation seemed to increase in
some rough symmetry with the state's greater penetration and the range of its
activities, adding to its authority and stability' (Grew 1984: 97). National
classes are defined as the 'natural constituencies' of national political units,
primarily through 'people's parties', that is 'parties of national integration' or
*Volksparteien,* but also through trade unions and large-scale interest groups.
These national units reshape sectional interests so that they can fit an étatized
and institutionalized system of conflict resolution. Such a system presupposes national-scale interest aggregation and redefinition, as well as
legitimation through systematic persuasion. The classical functions of popular parties thus involve not only policy formulation and execution, but also
public education and the mobilization and structuring of electoral support.
These aggregated interests are then articulated at a very high level of gener-
ality into consistent policy lines that are legitimated by reference to such
global ideological constructs as socialism and liberalism. These thus come to
be identified with 'class interests'.

We must stress that this is an ideal-typical representation of a highly uneven
and tension-ridden process. Organizational articulation progresses fastest in
the strategic area of industrial production. The two main industrial classes,
the working class and the industrial bourgeoisie, lead the field in providing
the lineaments of the social and political structure. The non-industrial classes
develop much more gradually, and they have much less impact on national,
state-sponsored arrangements. The fact that the peasant class and the petty
bourgeoisie, those most distinctive and homogeneous formations, articulate
with the state relatively slowly, testifies to a clear hiatus between class communities and nationalized classes.

There can also be fierce competition for the right to represent a given
'class'. The right to organize and represent the working class was claimed at
the turn of the twentieth century by competing revolutionary, syndicalist and
social-democratic organizations, each defining class interests differently. The
formation of the welfare state, and the subsequent corporatization of state
policies, settled these disputes. Legitimate representation was restricted to a
few incorporated organizations, usually social-democratic or democratic
communist parties, that gained privileged access to state-controlled resources.
Others either dwelt on the political fringe or had to subordinate their claims
to mainstream 'licensed' bodies.

Any view of *national* class formation as a spontaneous process emerging
from an 'economic base' of property or production relations and localized
communal relations cannot withstand critical scrutiny. In fact, such 'spontaneous' processes, as Bauman (1982) indicates, split and fractured classes
along the multiple lines of region, trade, occupation, and industrial sector.
Nor can national class formation be viewed as the product of the foresight or
strategic wisdom of local-community class leaders, because these leaders were
as divided as their followers, perhaps more so. They fought a rearguard battle
against the process of nationalization that actually served to undermine their

(often quasi-charismatic) power. The new national class leadership that emerged in the organizational political domain had only tenuous links to local class communities.

## The corporatization of class

This process of class articulation in the form of national quasi-communities reached its zenith with the extension of the welfare state and the corporatist trends of the mid twentieth century. Under liberal corporatism, the national classes had gained unparalleled legitimacy, consistency and influence owing to their political organization and their near-monopolistic position as referents for state policy. The tension between class and national interests, between class struggle and democratic proceduralism, had, by mid century, been overcome. The liberal political contest in the Western 'polyarchies' could now widely be perceived as having been transformed into a 'democratic class struggle' (Lipset 1960; Korpi 1983).

The welfare state was both the reproducer and the product of national classes. Welfare interventions were national in their scope and standardizing in their effects. They defined class-national stakes and interests in a highly universalistic manner. Perhaps most importantly, the extension of welfare provision, especially in the areas of working conditions and education, undermined both the commonality of fate of the original class communities and the key patriarchal and community-centred mechanisms of class reproduction. Many of the welfare provisions, in turn, were the products of conflict and competition between the class organizations that emerged under the process of nationalization. The political and ideological leaderships of these organizations defined welfare provisions as class goals and interests. This attribution was an essential element in national class formation. Support for 'class interests', thus defined, and for the organizations that represented them, became the boundary markers of national classes. Improvements in working conditions and the extension of welfare provisions, rather than, say, collective ownership of the means of production, became the core of working-class interests and politics. Similarly, the liberal and conservative parties defined the domains of bourgeois interests and politics as involving support for low taxation, entrepreneurial activities and profit accumulation.

Liberal corporatism easily accommodated these shifts. The state became an arbiter in a peaceful and orderly class contest, and the central arena for the democratic class struggle. The rules of the contest were clearly set out and were safeguarded by an elaborate system of legal and political institutions. The status of the contestants was clearly circumscribed and typically restricted to state-legitimated organizational representatives of the major industrial classes. By giving them privileged access to policy-making, the state formally redefined the class structure. It re-created quasi-communities of interest around the general policy lines pursued by the licensed class organizations. It reinforced the political articulation of these quasi-communities by supporting their representative organizations: granting them formal recognition; legitimizing their political roles; and carefully restricting the entry of potential competitors. Lastly, the corporatist state actively participated in the reproduction of these politically defined quasi-communities through administrative interventions into socialization and through ideological appeals. Classes were sanctioned not merely politically and socially but also ideologically. The ideological meta-narratives of socialism, liberalism and conservatism were institutionalized as the referents of quasi-communal classes. Indeed, they were elaborated by the class-representing bodies and by party leaders and intellectuals, and they were disseminated by the state- and party-controlled media.

Thus the (largely West European) corporatist Great Armistice represented not so much the elimination of class and class struggle, as the national reorganization of classes and the absorption of class conflict into an orderly contest under the aegis of the state. Subject to such reorganization and political restrictions, class quasi-communities could blossom and the democratic class struggle could continue in a relatively uninhibited way. Crackdowns were seldom necessary, owing to broad incorporation that left excluded only a few minority interests, and even fewer capable of effective mobilization. Violations of corporatist deals were effectively repressed by coercive apparatuses and political vilification which invariably caused electoral backlash against alleged transgressors.

This helps to explain a paradox identified by Hindess (1987). Classes understood as aggregates of people in structurally defined class locations could not be political actors. Class politics is always organizational politics because only organized bodies are capable of intentional conduct. Yet, the link between organizations and class positions, and hence the class nature of action, is eminently contestable. In a similar vein, Etzioni-Halévy (1993) criticizes class accounts of politics, arguing that the real subjects of politics, the real makers of history, are organizational elites. Both arguments are in line with the view presented here. Although corporatist politics is indeed a class politics, the classes are neither communities nor structurally defined aggregates. They are imagined communities organized 'from above' by their alleged representatives. Twentieth-century class politics is thus an organizational politics, a politics dominated by state elites, mass parties, trade unions and corporate executives.

This also helps to account for American exceptionalism. American society did not embrace corporatism and, significantly, did not develop a class politics of the type found in inter-war Europe. Despite a concentration of executive power, the growth of state interventionism, and the concentration of business power, there was much less corporatist organization and state penetration in American society than in its European counterparts. Neither the industrial lobby nor labour achieved the organizational coherence and prominence that they did in Europe. Equally, the most vigorous denials of classness have come from the USA. Indeed, American society must closely approximate what Ossowski (1963) calls 'classless inequality'. Class divisions are scarcely visible at the national level. They are identified mainly by community studies and they are declining as single-industry communities and urban villages are eclipsed (Nisbet 1959).

The reason for this apparent classlessness in American society lies mainly in the absence of organizational articulation and the corporatist reinforcement of class. As in early industrial Europe, class divisions in America were originally articulated at the communal level. However, here they coexisted with prominent racial and ethnic divisions, unlike in Europe where classes evolved in relation to pre-industrial estates. The decomposition of American class communities, however, did not coincide with national-organizational articulation. There was no strong class organization, no class party in the USA. Neither of the major American parties resembles a European 'people's party'. There was no organizational creator of class quasi-communities and hence no visible class in the social and political sense. The organizational articulation of race and ethnicity was much more pronounced, especially with the formation of black organizations during the civil rights movements of the 1950s and 1960s. Race rather than class predominated as the basis for the main sub-national 'imagined communities' in America.

In summary then, a welfare state is a highly interventionist state, and corporatization means that interventions became highly centralized and organized. When combined with processes of societal modernization, corporatist trends undermined localism and class-communal relations. Simultaneously, these processes of étatization generated new social entities, the imagined communities of national classes, that could dominate social space for half a century. These entities coexisted with the remnants of old communities that survived mainly in the isolated enclaves of company towns and small-scale city and rural localities. Class became synonymous with national class, a quasi-community often identified with occupational clusters.

**Patriarchy and class reproduction**

Although the community studies discussed in the first section of this chapter were undertaken in the mid twentieth century they in fact represent residual patterns from a previous formation, and are introduced here only to provide a perspective on what class communities must have been like. In fact, as the preceding section argues, the corporatized nature of most of the organized societies of the twentieth century focused on the nation-state as the significant community of interest and meaning.

The residential system was progressively declassed through processes of suburbanization. As production became centralized in cities and as professional and technical occupations expanded, most Western societies experienced migration by middle- and upper-middle-class people to 'rural' areas. In most instances these migrations were partial. People resided in the 'country' but worked in the city, or they had a town house or city *pied-à-terre* and a hobby farm in the country for weekends and holidays. Pahl's *Urbs in Rure* (1965) shows how commuting workers living in rural areas outside London reproduced city social structure in those areas. Similarly, Wild (1974) shows that those moving from Sydney to the small town of Bowral lived in a state of mutual isolation with the well-established townspeople. This type of move to rural areas represents a form of capture by the city. It further breaks down community boundaries and institutions and draws established communities into the atomism of city relationships. The rural community becomes a satellite settlement of the city.

But suburbanization did not apply only to white-collar and professional workers. One of the principal guarantees that corporatized states typically made to their manual-worker claimants was the provision of a decent standard of housing. This often meant the demolition of both slums and urban villages and the relocation of their populations to newly constructed housing estates, apartment blocks, 'garden cities' and 'new towns'. These planned residential environments could indeed offer that minimum provision, but typically they also signally failed to offer any opportunity for the emergence of meaningful community relationships. Indeed, by many accounts, such interventionism often destroyed any possibility for class solidarity and rather reconstructed the lives of manual workers and their families into rounds of petty crime, substance abuse, social apathy, and domestic disorder and violence. Certainly it turned manual workers into mobile individuals who would not necessarily live close either to their family of origin or to work.

The consequences of these developments can be witnessed in small towns as well as in cities. Stacey's study (1960) of Banbury, a small market and manufacturing town in central Britain, shows that the local pattern of class cleavage altered considerably during the twentieth century. Although Banbury had become established as a market town during the Industrial Revolution it was not actually industrialized until 1933 when an aluminium plant was established. The impact of this new industry on a traditional community structure drew Stacey's attention in particular. The workers in the new plant were immigrants from the depressed staple-industrial areas of the north. They made up a quarter of the working population of the town which had an overall population of 19,000 when it was studied. The original, traditional community had been integrated not by common attachments to the locality or by a shared value system of any kind. Rather it had been riven by status cleavages that had cross-cut one another, so that allegiances shifted depending on situation. There was a major 'horizontal' class cleavage between middle-class merchants and shopkeepers, on the one hand, and workers on the other. But there were also vertical religious and political divisions, between Anglicans who voted Conservative and religious Nonconformists who voted Liberal, that applied to both the main classes. So groups that were allied in religious terms could be opposed in class terms. The introduction of the aluminium factory added an additional cleavage to this existing structure, a division between the traditionals who were oriented to the local community, and the newcomers who were oriented to the wider society. The crucial indicator on which the groups could be separated was, as our discussion of national class formation would suggest, political allegiance, the newcomers tending to vote for the Labour Party. Stacey says: 'the town is bisected in two ways: it is cut down the middle by a line which divides traditional from non-traditional; it is cut across the middle by the line which divides the middle from the working class' (Bell and Newby 1971: 183). This, then, was a much more twentieth-century pattern of stratification than that found by the Lynds in Muncie: the cleavages were numerous and cross-cutting; there was no ruling class because the community was not isolated; some of the status groups drew on the wider society for ideological stimuli and looked to the nation-state for alteration of their conditions of life; and there was a middle class.

Habermas interprets the corporatist expansion that promoted the eclipse of community as an aspect of a process of 'internal colonization' in which 'subsystems of the economy and the state intervene with monetary and bureaucratic means in the symbolic reproduction of the lifeworld' (1987: 356). This process is highly explicit in the area of social reproduction. In an organized-class society the level of technological and organizational complexity of industrial production increases sharply. Families are therefore increasingly defined as inadequate in the social reproduction of labour power. They are unable to provide the abilities, skills and commitments adequate to an advanced industrial economy. Under pressure from employers these social-reproductive functions are progressively acquired by state-organized educational systems.

For such class theorists as Bowles and Gintis (1976) educational policy is therefore a product of quite explicit intentions on the part of employers, and is not the product of either citizenship or altruism or individual aspiration or increased working-class political power. Its objectives, they argue, are: 'the production of labor power and the reproduction of those institutions and social relationships which facilitate the translation of labor power into profits' (1976: 129). On Bowles and Gintis' argument, the ruling class constructs educational institutions to meet these objectives in four ways. First, schools develop skills appropriate to the adequate performance of job tasks. They do this by developing appropriate general aptitudes including literacy and numeracy as well as skills specific to occupations. But they also do it by encouraging a pattern of personal demeanour and self-presentation that is appropriate to the workplace, teaching people how to live in hierarchically organized, disciplined systems. Second, schools legitimize economic inequality because they are competitive systems that grade abilities. This grading reflects a social inheritance of inequality in which family backgrounds are translated into educational qualifications which are then regarded as evidence of 'real' ability. Third, schools credentialize abilities in a hierarchical way that matches hierarchical participation in the labour market. The lower levels of the school hierarchy, junior and secondary schools, emphasize obedience and rule-following, a necessity for all workers; community, technical and teachers' colleges give somewhat more emphasis to independent work, training a capacity for self-supervision; while universities emphasize problem-solving that can be employed at the top of the production hierarchy. Progress from level to level in the educational hierarchy is contingent on mastery of the previous level. Fourth, schooling fragments working-class communities and cultures. It is competitive and individualistic rather than collectivistic, so it sets individual against individual. Moreover, it educates different sectors of the working class differently – blacks differently from whites, girls differently from boys, minorities differently from majorities.

It is the last of these points, the bizarre claim that schooling reproduces class by fragmenting it, that must detain us. It tells us that the change wrought by the expansion of education was principally a disruption of the processes of simple class reproduction that had previously succeeded in the domestic sphere. Rather reproduction entered a more complex or expanded cycle in which the process actually altered the structure in the future. The class paradigm needed a more subtle theory of reproduction that could accommodate this shift. Bourdieu (1977) provided such a new theory by introducing the notion of 'cultural capital', arguing that it is possible to appropriate and to accumulate symbolic goods in the same way that it is possible to do for material goods. Thus, the greater the extent to which one has access to what is conventionally described as 'high culture', the greater the possibility of obtaining further access to high culture. The capacity to engage in high-cultural practices is received in educational experience. Access to education is in turn differentially distributed according to class origin. Bourdieu says that persons in cultured families have a privileged access to this educational key. Therefore education serves to reproduce differentiated cultural patterns. The fact that a dominant economic class is able to demonstrate its superiority in terms of its access to high culture legitimates its position of superordination. Persons who are members of subordinate classes are not merely constrained to be so, they are also culturally, and therefore morally, inferior. The facts of a system of social inequality are thus legitimated.

Ultimately, the inheritance of economic capital is a far more solid guarantee of social reproduction than is inheritance of cultural capital. However, where such unequal inheritance is called into question, for example where there is separation of ownership and control in corporations, on Bourdieu's argument, a dominant class can progressively capture the means of cultural reproduction as a way of securing its own social reproduction. So, for example, where university qualifications in medicine are regarded as indispensable in medical practice, the sons of medical practitioners will tend to enter university courses in that area.

Bourdieu's idea that education, far from ameliorating structured inequality, actually serves to reproduce it, is now a central component in the class analysis of educational processes. The general view taken by educational reproduction theorists is that 'dull compulsion' and state power are alone insufficient to ensure commitment adequate to the provision of labour power to capitalist enterprises. This position stands opposed to liberal theories of education which claim that it is a vehicle for individual opportunity and attainment (see Parsons 1959). The claim made here lies much closer to the latter position. In order to validate this claim we need to look further at the evidence that is accumulated by its opponents. This evidence can be divided into two groups: data on the relationship between parental class and child's

education; and data on the relationship between education and subsequent
class membership.

There can be no doubt that parents are extremely adept at seeking and providing educational advantage for their children, and there is considerable
evidence that their capacity to do so is affected by their material circumstances. In an American study, for example, Jencks (1972: 138–9) finds that
the correlation between parental occupational status plus income on the one
hand, and educational attainment on the other, is 0.55. This means that about
half the children born into the 'upper middle class' will end up with more
schooling than 80 per cent of all children, and half of the 'lower-class' children will receive less than the schooling received by 80 per cent of all children.
The former will average about four more years of schooling than the latter.
Jencks estimates that about one-third of educational differences are
accounted for by IQ test scores, but about half of this is mediated through
class effects. Other international studies confirm that this is a widespread
pattern.

There is slightly less convincing evidence on the effect of education on
occupational status and incomes (taking these as proxies for class). Jencks
reports that, in the USA, occupational status is clearly related to educational
attainment, and that this effect is independent of family background (1972:
191). However, he also reports that while each year of secondary schooling
accounts for a 6 per cent increase in income, each year of undergraduate
education for 12 per cent, and each year of graduate education for 7 per
cent. If the effects of family background are discounted, these figures come
back to 4, 7, and 4 per cent respectively (1972: 222–3). Educational inequality, he concludes surprisingly, explains little of the variation in income
inequality between occupations, and he prefers to explain this by such
randomly distributed factors as desire, luck and chance.

Using a basic three-class model, Halsey, Heath and Ridge (1980: 184) find
more convincing results for Britain. Of 'service-class' members (Goldthorpe's
classes I and II) 72 per cent attended private or selective schools, 58 per cent
received a secondary leaving certificate and 20 per cent attended university. In
the intermediate class (III, IV and V) the respective percentages are 40, 24 and
5; and for the working class (VI, VII and VIII), 24, 12 and 2. Service-class
children make up more than half the university educated. Broom, Jones,
McDonnell and Williams' Australian data (1980: 37) approximately confirm
this effect. The correlation coefficient between 'social background' (a basket
of family characteristic variables) and 'basic education' (level of attainment
before commencing work) is 0.601; that between background and additional
post-school education is 0.165.

Stewart, Prandy and Blackburn (1980) address this argument by disas-
sembling their British data by means of simple contingency graphs. In general
they show an increase in status score with father's occupation. However, for
those attending private or selective schools, the increase was steeper than for
those who did not. Also, in general, for those with qualifications, there was a
steeper increase for higher qualifications than for lower ones (1980: 234).

They also plot income against various qualifications by age. The curves they develop show that income differentials, while minimal or even reversed at the early stage of a career, become very pronounced late in career. At the age of 21, for example, a degree provides a lower level of income than does an absence of qualification, but by the age of 50 the situation is reversed and a degree provides a two-and-a-half-fold advantage (1980: 256).

On the basis of this overwhelming evidence, there can be no doubt that education differentially reproduces labour power, in the sense that it provides skills and attitudes that are employed in different areas of systems of production, but there must remain very real doubt that it reproduces class. In any set of data produced on the issue the class-education connection seldom accounts for more than half the relationship. This means that the rest must be accounted for by other factors, the principal candidate being the capacity of the education system to motivate and hone individual abilities. Indeed, education never completely replaces the domestic milieux that can be deeply rooted in class. The critical first three to five years of 'primary socialization' typically remain firmly in the domestic context, and it is here, if anywhere, that class is likely to be reproduced. Education attacks the class-reproductive effects of domesticity and we should not be surprised if it only half succeeds.[1] Indeed it is altogether surprising that it succeeds as much as it does.

The interventions of the state in social reproduction and the takeover of social reproduction by specialized educational institutions also vitiate the strength of the link between class and patriarchy that can readily be admitted for the liberal-state period of the nineteenth century. In so far as most female labour in that period was committed to social reproduction, the appropriation of that function by the state has resulted in some reorganization of the gender division of labour. Brenner and Ramas (1984) outline the principal forces that were at work:

- Increasing bourgeois control of the reproduction of labour power was exercised by the state through its agencies, the schools and welfare bureaux, which reduced child-care responsibilities for women.
- Technological developments in the area of biological reproduction (contraception, abortion, etc.) relieved women from repeated childbirth but placed increasing control of biological reproduction in the hands of state agencies, hospitals and medical practices.
- The labour power of women was thus released and made available for exploitation both in commodity production and in the state agencies of reproduction, which replaced their own domestic activity.
- The subordination of women was maintained by making them responsible for biological and social reproduction while relieving them of control of these processes which, in turn, meant that women's careers were disrupted by child-bearing and often confined to component-wage jobs.

During the twentieth century, then, women increasingly entered the labour market, but in a pattern that cannot adequately be conceptualized in class terms. Rather, it must be couched in terms of the intersection between domesticity and the state. Women entered the public sphere largely under the control of men, that is in subordinate, menial or 'caring' occupations, occupations that can be characterized as quasi-domestic. Men reproduced domination in three typical ways: they retained control of domestic means of material subsistence so that they could in turn control the domestic labour of women; they controlled cultural representations of women in the arts, the mass media, and education to ensure that women were idealized for their sexual and aesthetic qualities rather than their instrumental abilities; and they practised informal discrimination.

The structure of society therefore remained at least as much gendered as it was classed. Several conceptualizations are available to describe this new masculine gender system: Holter's (1984) 'reorganized patriarchy' stresses the masculine construction of the market and male domestic hegemony; Walby's 'public patriarchy' (1990) stresses subordination in the public sphere; Mann's 'neopatriarchy' (1986a) stresses cultures of masculinity and femininity; and Waters' 'extended viriarchy' (1989) focuses on labour-market segmentation and domestic power differentials. More importantly, however they are conceptualized, patterns of masculine domination could no longer be theorized to function in the reproduction of class. The persistence of patriarchy, its migration to the public sphere, must be regarded as evidence of its autonomy.

### Disétatization and globalization

To observers of the post-Second World War decades in Europe, this corporatist-welfare configuration must have looked looked like a happy 'end of history', the social equivalent of a *perpetuum mobile*.[2] Three decades of unprecedented social and political stability also served to cement the quasi-communities of class. If there were social upheavals, these were seen as minor imperfections that could be eliminated by a renegotiation of corporatist deals and further fine-tuning of state intervention.[3]

However, in the 1970s and 1980s corporatist welfarism began to crumble, mainly under the impact of what can be diagnosed as self-generated disfunctions. As a consequence the major class organizations, especially trade unions and the class parties, began to unravel. The latter are both losing support and abandoning their class idiom, thus ceasing to function as organizational reproducers. In many ways, this is the result of their spectacular success. Deep social intervention requires tight controls over the national economy and society which can, in turn, result in an overexpansion of the state that, in turn again, can decrease its sensitivity to expanding claims. The 'citizenship strategy' of organized lobbying for sectional entitlement has almost become a popular sport. While early welfare provisions were directed towards 'class' constituencies, later ones are proliferating into hyperdifferentiated status categories claiming the status of quasi-communities. The publicizing effects of interventionism have led, on the one hand, to a proliferation of claims based on the illusion that social life can be fully rationalized, and, on the other, to an accumulation of blame which is the other face of a belief in state omnipotence. Welfare disfunctions can be pinned on the state and its corporatist agencies, thus undermining the legitimacy of welfarist deals. Corporatist exclusion, which is a precondition for successful settlements, has now prompted political activism among marginalized and excluded categories. Perhaps most importantly, social differentiation, especially market segmentation and communal fragmentation, is eroding national class façades.[4]

The response to the 'crisis of welfare corporatism' is a massive wave of disétatization, decorporatization and 'rolling back of the state'. In authoritarian states, it takes the form of a horizontal or functional decentralization and a territorial redistribution of authority. In more liberal regimes disétatization occurs under pressure from below in the form of a revival of civil society and the mobilization of mass social movements. Where the interventions are deep and the public sector extensive, massive marketization, deregulation and privatization programmes tend to be initiated.

In the third quarter of the twentieth century, therefore, the corporate welfare state has hit a multiple and widely recognized crisis. In summary, its components are as follows:

- Popular demands have escalated beyond the capacity of the state to meet them. The right to make a claim against the state has been separated from the capacity to make an economic contribution to it. Moreover the state has educated and politically enfranchised its population. The volume and effectiveness of collective claims against the state are clogging the political process.
- The locations of real state power have become hidden. Politicians focus on mediating claims and cultivating support while the real power is exercised behind the scenes by bureaucrats and technicians.
- The administration of welfare is consuming an increasing proportion of the welfare budget. Moreover the welfare system is cultivating its own clients by creating a culture of state dependency.
- The interventions of the state in economic matters are tending to destabilize the markets that they were intended to preserve. Economies are populated by weak and failing industries and underemployed workers.
- The state can no longer offer security: trade and financial markets are internationalized; drug syndicates and terrorists no longer respect borders; the 'natural' issues of AIDS and ecology are not susceptible to state action; and the individual state is no protection against the risks of chemical and nuclear weapons.
- Lastly, through international alliances, the state has created more danger than security. It divided the world into hostile camps whose commitments to the acquisition of military technology appeared to have but one purpose. (Crook et al. 1992: 92–7)

The response to this multiple crisis is a process of disétatization or state weakening. The corporate interest groups that previously supported the state are beginning to downscale and localize. Trade unions are shrinking and being displaced by enterprise associations, local interest groups and civic initiatives. State intervention by command is reducing but at the same time states are seeking to increase the scope and scale of the market. Many government services are being opened to competitive tendering between the public and private sectors and, as is well known, many state-owned industries are returning to the private sector. Many states have stopped providing welfare in certain areas and others are moving towards demilitarization.

The implications of the crisis of the state and consequent disétatization for globalization have both obvious and less obvious aspects. Clearly any breakdown in the nation-state system leaves an opening for political globalization. So long as the state persists, a sovereign world polity is impossible. The less obvious aspects might be more important however. The crisis of the state makes globalization self-perpetuating. This is because the excuses of politicians for their failures have taken on a global hue: our economy is failing because of the recession in the USA or Europe or Japan or somewhere else, they say; our currency is declining because of the activities of unidentified international speculators, they whine; our air is dirty because someone else has had a nuclear meltdown; we cannot solve the problem of urban crime because it is fed by international drugs syndicates; or, we cannot feed our people because the level of international aid is not adequate. Doubtless there is at least a modicum of truth in these explanations because globalization does reduce state control over vast areas of social life. More importantly, it does establish a widespread globalizing reflexivity within both elites and publics. In so far as politicians deflect blame onto the global arena, collective political actors will focus their attention on that arena and the nation-state will progressively become an irrelevance.

The best and most explicit outline of the path of globalization is given by Held (1991: 207–9). He begins at the level of non-political, inter-societal connections and then takes the argument through a series of steps which see the undermining of the nation-state and its eventual displacement by a world government. The steps in Held's argument are as follows:

- Increasing economic and cultural connections reduce the power and effectiveness of governments at the nation-state level so that they can no longer control the flow of ideas and economic items at their borders and thus their internal policy instruments become ineffective.
- State power is further reduced because transnational processes grow in scale as well as in number: transnational corporations for example are often larger and more powerful than many governments.
- Many traditional areas of state responsibility (e.g. defence, communications, economic management) must therefore be co-ordinated on an international or intergovernmental basis.
- States have thus been obliged to surrender sovereignty within larger political units (e.g. EU, ASEAN), multilateral treaties (e.g. NATO, OPEC), or international organizations (e.g. UN, WTO, IMF).

- A system of 'global governance' is therefore emerging with its own policy development and administrative systems that further curtails state power.
- This provides the basis for the emergence of a supra-national state with dominant coercive and legislative power.

A critical point of debate is how far the world has gone and will go within the last three steps. For many 'realists' (e.g. McGrew 1992) the prevailing territorial sovereignty of nation-states and the meaning they have for their citizens make them the undeniably primary context of political life. For 'modernists' such as Held the sovereignty of the state is already in decline and 'world government', although not taking the same form as contemporary nation-state governments, is a real possibility. We tend towards the second of these possibilities, although the likely outcome is a hierarchy of politico-spatial entities ranging from the local to the global rather than a state writ large.

Our opponents in the debate about class might want to suggest that the decline of the state merely results in its internationalization. Claims are frequently made for the emergence of a global capitalist class (e.g. Sklair 1991) although much more infrequently for a global working class, and even less for an international middle class. The strongest claim that the class struggle has simply moved up a notch from the national to the international level is made by such authors as van der Pijl (1989). Van der Pijl argues that, as globalization proceeds, the capitalist class transforms itself in an international direction in three moments: it develops an international class consciousness; it develops a controlling state-like structure at the international level (the UN); and it socializes labour in order to demarcate an international economic space. These provide the conditions for the development of an informal international capitalist class that consists of a network of big companies linked together by interlocking directorates and cross-shareholdings. These, plus such organizations as the UN, enable this class to manage an international division of labour in such a way as to allow the bourgeoisie to maintain its position in the core societies by exporting poverty.

We would argue that an internationalization of class, at least in so far as it is represented in such vulgar formulations as this, is quite impossible. The following conditions prevent its formation: there cannot be a ruling class without a state and the UN scarcely qualifies as a world state; internal social divisions of labour are tending to dedifferentiate, so that the functions of conceptualization and execution are tending to be reintegrated; firms are downscaling so that core large firms will decreasingly be able to dominate the system; markets are becoming tokenized and decentred, so that they are becoming increasingly difficult to control; and the key means of production are no longer physical plant and machines but human expertise, symbolized information and aesthetic products, each of which is ephemeral, non-accumulable and uncontrollable. This does not mean that the global economy is without its powerful individual movers and shakers. It is impossible to deny the impact of a Rupert Murdoch or George Soros, or that Silvio Berlusconi succeeded, if temporarily, where Ross Perot failed. However, they are powerful precisely because of their individual talents and not because they are the members of a class. Indeed, in a more unpredictable global economy, individual success might be viewed as precarious without class support, *vide* Alan Bond, 'Tiny' Rowland and Donald Trump.

This is not to suggest, however, that economic stratification has disappeared from the face of the earth. Rather, the stratification pattern is now focused on possibilities for consumption rather than production relations. The emerging pattern is indeed an international one, in which members of rich societies, even if they are unemployed, tend to enjoy significantly better consumption possibilities than employees in developing societies. This has been apparent for some time but a significant feature of the current acceleration is the way in which the two worlds are beginning to mingle in global cities. Lash and Urry (1994) identify a new configuration that juxtaposes an affluent, post-industrial service class or middle mass in high-paying relatively autonomous occupations with a disadvantaged *Gastarbeiter* class or underclass that supports its consumption within routine, underpaid and insecure labour situations. Under globalization, migration has brought the Third World back to the global cities where its exploitation becomes ever more apparent.

If community has been eclipsed and the state has collapsed in the face of globalization, then class and family must disappear as reference points for social reproduction because they have no spatial arena in which to operate. Drawing on the ground-breaking work of Beck (1992) and Giddens (1991) we can suggest that the new reference point is the connection between individual biography and the market. For Beck, there are four historical foci for this development. The first is the dissolution of the working-class milieu (see Chapter 6) with its particular domestic arrangements, organization of leisure time, neighbouring patterns, and oral networks. The second is the dissolution of expectations of continuous mutual material support in families and thus the cutting of family ties. The third is the emergence of flexible working hours and the decentralization of the work site, each of which require individual decisions about when and where to work. On these grounds, Beck argues that: 'the family collapses as the "penultimate" synthesis of life situations between the generations and the sexes, and individuals inside and outside the family become the agents of their livelihood mediated by the market, as well as of their biographical planning and organization' (1992: 130). Beck goes further to claim that the process of individualization erodes the boundaries between the public and private spheres. Lifestyle becomes contingent not on familial commitments and relationships but on market success.

Under this process, education is being transformed from its prior close relationship with domestic contexts, in which paths, levels of progression and standards were predictable, into a chaotic mix of glitzy credentials, lifetime education and unpredictable specializations and mixes of subject matter. In other words, education has been itself transformed into a true market in which the players self-consciously trade and bargain. Education involves opportunities for choice and prevents monopolization so that educational values are determined not in relation to hypostatized ultimate standards but in terms of supply and demand. The currency of the educational market is indeed the credential, a symbolic token that attaches to the individual and that is in principle redeemable in the labour market. Paradoxically, credentials had been introduced by professional groups as a means of closure but usurpationary practices by other occupational groups have put such pressure on states and educational institutions to expand the supply of credentials that by the 1960s the system met a crisis (Collins 1979: 191). The currency had hyperinflated and a credential no longer guaranteed a person a decent job; that is, a credential could no longer guarantee reproduction at the class level. Rather the selection of educational courses depended on individual biographical planning and clever market participation, without guarantees.

We would expect this process to be reflected in empirical evidence about the relationship between class background and educational attainment over time, but cohort and panel studies are relatively uncommon.[5] The best information comes from an Australian cohort study by Graetz (1988). He finds that the net advantage of social background halved from 2.8 years of education for the pre-1950 birth cohort to 1.4 years for the post-1970 cohort (1988: 368). On the basis of findings such as these, we would hypothesize that the best indicator of educational performance is now not parental social class but parental education. Indeed, we further suggest that education is becoming a key dimension of social differentiation that constructs both possibilities for consumption and value commitments.

The process of individualization is also eroding systems of patriarchy. Beck (1992: 110–11) sets out five grounds on which a claim can be made that both men and women are being liberated from gender statuses inherited from the pre-modern period. They are: extensions of the female lifespan beyond child-bearing; the technical automation of housework; technological possibilities for contraception and abortion that liberate women from the constraints of child-bearing; a reconceptualization of obligations towards spousal support such that it is no longer regarded as permanent; and the equalization of educational opportunity. Lengermann and Wallace (1985: 195–231) offer a more conventional list: increasing female participation in employment; female entry into professional and technical occupations; increasing female political and educational participation; reduced family size; redistributions of domestic chores; legislation upholding gender equality; 'political correctness' in education and the mass media; and the development of masculine consciousness groups.

We are not announcing a simultaneous 'death of patriarchy' or arguing that equality is achieved but rather proposing that there have been significant moves in this direction. The important conclusion is that, if it ever was, patriarchy can no longer be a structure that reproduces labour power, much less class. The transformation of patriarchy represents not the absorption of women into the class system on an arrangement other than domestic association, but rather the incremental dissolution of both structures in favour of a system of reproduction based on the reflexive individual.

**Conclusion**

Although this chapter is guided by the historical model introduced in Chapter 1, we can now make its salience more explicit. *Economic-class society*, as we have defined it, bore an isomorphic relationship with closed communities operating within the confines of a weak or liberal state. There, class structures stood in a functional relationship with patriarchy in which each served to reproduce the other. Patriarchy was therefore only marginally less effective than in the form it took under feudalism. The family was the sole and effective site for class reproduction.

In *organized-class society*, the nation-state orchestrated national class formation by incorporating its organizational forms into national compacts. Here 'organized classes' were the political expression of occupational groupings but they were far more unstable than their predecessors. This is because education had become a critical vehicle for socioeconomic reproduction. The socioeconomic system was changing and expanding. Positions were expanding to a much wider variety and diversity, especially in what is often called the 'new middle class', and the allocation of persons to positions occurred at least as much in terms of individual ability, good fortune and the capacity of schools to develop talent as they did on family background. Patriarchy was reorganized as women re-entered the public sphere, if only in quasi-domestic roles and subordinated positions.

In the contemporary phase of *status-conventional society* we are seeing the reproductive lineaments of class disappearing. In a globalized world of symbolic currents, the nation-state can no longer orchestrate class groupings, because it has been beaten into submission by irresolvable problems and besieged by entitlement claimants who stand outside the old organized classes. The central site for reproduction is now the mobile, biographically self-composing individual. Moreover, the stress on individual performance and capacity and on individualized selection among lifestyles and value commitments means that there is now a realistic hope that we might, in the not too distant future, dispatch patriarchy to follow class into the trash can of history where they both belong.

**Notes**

1 We need also briefly to address a technical point often raised by class theorists. They often argue that the issue of reproduction is not to do with the allocation of people to positions, which they are often prepared to admit is somewhat egalitarian, but to do with the reproduction of a structure of unequal positions. Our counter-argument would make two points: first, that a system of inequality based on educational credentials is non-economic, and therefore cannot properly or usefully be conceptualized as a class system; second, to the extent that people use educational qualifications to cross class boundaries, those boundaries are without substance.

2 The discussion of disétatization follows the line taken in Crook et al. (1992: 79–105). The material on globalization is drawn from Waters (1995a).

3 Corporatist accommodations were widely accepted as the universal panacea for social pathologies and recipes, if not for social harmony, at least for a lasting truce (Schmitter and Lembruch 1979; Lembruch and Schmitter 1982). Even within the Marxist camp a quietist mood

prevailed. Cataclysmic visions of class war and revolution were displaced by sombre analyses of class domination through state, ideology and culture (e.g. Marcuse 1964; Althusser 1977; Poulantzas 1974).

4 A sense of a crisis as a structural, systemic malady is reflected in a number of social-scientific and ideological figures: 'fiscal crisis'; 'welfare crisis'; 'motivation and legitimacy crisis'; 'governability crisis'; and 'failures of the state' (see e.g. O'Connor 1973; Wilensky 1981; Crouch 1983; Habermas 1976; Birch 1984). The emergence of these epithets marks the beginning of a long 'winter of discontent' triggered by the oil crisis of the mid 1970s.

5 The main findings of these studies, including an American study by Hout (1988), are reviewed in Chapter 7.

# 6

# Cultural Revolutions

Culture is a critical component in the chains of reasoning that guide both class theory and class analysis. As Chapter 1 shows, it links structural class location with consciousness and action. Written in extreme and ideal-typical terms, the class paradigm proposes: that different structural class positions generate different contexts of experience; that these in turn generate internal commonalities of consciousness; that a common consciousness gives rise to systems of shared preferences, norms and symbols that we can call a class culture; that a significant element of the culture of a class society is an ideology that arranges preferences for the maintenance or change of the system of power; that ideology motivates political or industrial action; and that action can succeed in the transformation of the structure of positions. Again, we want to stress that this proposal underlies class analysis as well as class theory. In arguing that class can predict or explain such matters as voting behaviour or educational aspirations, class analysis presupposes a cultural link whether it makes that link explicit or not.

However, one early and influential class-theoretical tradition makes culture paramount. Gramsci, for example, reverses the classic historicist argument of Marxism. Marxism insists that each epoch creates its own specific class cultures and that under capitalism we can therefore expect a division of culture into bourgeois and proletarian segments. Against this, Gramsci (1977) argues that capitalism represses pre-capitalist cultures of primitive communitarian and popular sentiment. The organic intellectuals of the capitalist class control the institutions of culture (state, education, and church) and are thereby able to direct the values and standards by which individuals make judgements, as well as symbolic representations, thus confirming a capitalist hegemony. Similarly, Lukács (1968) argues that capitalist societies are dominated by a common culture of commodification that universally pervades and respecifies human preferences. In each of these modifications of Marxism, the class struggle begins with an effort to alter the consciousness of workers, to re-kindle their primordial commitments and their natural sense of justice, and to turn them away from false knowledge and the materialistic temptations of consumption.

There are two main versions, then, of the class-culture thesis. The first sees culture as a field of class confrontation and struggle. Here, national cultures are split along class lines into separate but coexisting universes or 'nations within nations' in Engels' famous description (1892: 124). Hoggart's classic portrayal (1958) of working-class culture belongs to this tradition. The second version sees national cultures as relatively homogeneous but culturally specific in that they reflect the culturally mediated interests of the dominant class. Examples of this version include the Frankfurt School analyses of popular culture (e.g. Adorno and Horkheimer 1979), Gramscian visions of cultural hegemony (e.g. Connell 1977) and the numerous versions of the so-called 'dominant ideology thesis' (for a review see Abercrombie et al. 1980). Each of these specifies a coincidence between national interests and bourgeois class interests.

We take issue with each of these positions, arguing that so-called class subcultures had by the twentieth century become so divided that one could find more convincing linkages between culture and race, ethnicity, religion and region than between culture and class. This is as true for ruling- as for working-class cultures, so any suggestion that there is a single dominant culture becomes equally spurious.

**Milieu, lifestyle and morality**

We take culture to consist of all the meanings, values, norms, preferences, ideas, customs, beliefs, knowledges, lifestyles and symbolic patterns relevant to a given society or social formation. Following Kant it has become customary to specify it substantively as consisting of three value spheres:[1] the sphere of truth or cognition in which human beings decide what is real and not real; the sphere of beauty or cathexis in which they decide what they love or hate, fear or loathe; and the sphere of morality or judgement in which they establish normative standards by which they can evaluate behaviour. Where culture is class divided we can expect at least serious cleavages within each of these areas according to differential class location. Indeed, class theorists normally expect respective class cultures to be mutually antagonistic.

This tripartite scheme also provides another heuristic. We can trace the development of putative class cultures within each of the three value spheres. However, throughout we must concentrate on the proposal that the working class has a peculiar, distinctive and homogeneous culture because this must be the kernel of any claim that culture is a link in the causal chain connecting class with its own transformation. In so doing we can rely heavily on Hoggart's seminal specification (1958) of working-class culture as the baseline against which we measure the continued salience of class.[2]

*Knowledge*

Hoggart tells us that working-class knowledge is contained in oral traditions, in verbal motifs and proverbs that were brought forward from earlier and pre-capitalist generations. These are used not only as everyday explanations, to locate unforeseen or distressing events in myths and superstitions about fate or luck, but to structure the daily round of activities. Working-class people are expected to talk, to pass the time of day, to confirm their routines in oral terms. As might be expected in an oral tradition the content of conversation

focuses on the immediacies of home, family, neighbourhood and work, particularly on the key and patriarchally differentiated kinship roles of mother
and father. Thus working-class culture rejects the non-immediate, the meta-
physical and the abstract: 'They may appear to have views on general
matters . . . but these views usually prove to be a bundle of largely unexam-
ined and orally-transmitted tags, enshrining generalizations, prejudices, and
half-truths, and elevated by epigrammatic phrasing into the status of maxims'
(1958: 103). Such maxims stress the virtues of the concrete and the material
as against the demands of such abstractions as humanity or the nation or
even the working class. But it also allows working-class people, for example,
to be monarchists, because a royal family is, well, a 'real' family of flesh-and-
blood people.[3]

Such working-class knowledge systems stand in sharp contrast to those
apparent in other class cultures. So-called 'bourgeois knowledge' is, on
Lukács' argument (1968), highly abstracted from human beings and their
activities and relationships. Lukács stresses the scientistic character of bourgeois knowledge, its tendency to desubjectify. Science progressively distances
itself from human experience as the consequence of two processes: first, it differentiates into ever more arcane and localized specialities that deny the
totality of human experience; and second, it is rationalistic, increasingly
restricting its claims only to those supportable by logic and highly technicized
observation. Because such other practices as government and social science
ape the character and success of natural science, they too eliminate human
meaning and emotion, as well as non-empirical constructions, from human
knowledge. If working-class knowledge is characterized by concreteness, a
trust in luck, subjectivity and orality, then bourgeois knowledge is abstract,
rational, impersonal and scripted.

It would be tempting to suggest that bourgeois knowledge began to invade
working-class milieux with extensions of literacy in the late nineteenth century. Certainly primary education offered new means of access to knowledge.
However it is fairly clear that working-class milieux proved highly resilient in
the face of this process of 'internal colonization' (Habermas 1984). Indeed
one of the central problems identified by progressive educationists in the mid
twentieth century, especially in Britain and America, was the resistance that
working-class children put up to the entreaties and enforcements of bourgeois
knowledge by mobilizing their oral knowledge into peer-group defences. So
effective was this resistance that the mass media that sought to exploit newly
found working-class affluence and literacy had to structure their contents in
terms of that prior oral tradition. The 'penny dreadful' and the tabloid have
always reduced complex issues to the immediate, the personal and the prover-
bial, and contemporary soap operas are little different.

Rather, the key development was the extension of secondary education.
This had two effects. First, it gave state education systems an additional
opportunity to ram home the message that bourgeois knowledge is the only
worthwhile kind of knowledge. Althusser (1977: 146), for example, is convinced of the secret effectiveness of an institution that has the obligatory

attention of every member of society for eight hours a day and 200 days a year for ten years. Second, it provided an opportunity for what Hoggart (1958) calls the 'earnest minority', educated and intellectually advantaged members of the working class, to qualify for upward social mobility that would take them away from their class origins. In so far as these intellectual leaders abandoned working-class knowledge they delegitimized it, opening it up to stigmatization, and leaving workers without a vehicle by which publicly to express themselves in a widening state community. Meanwhile, state resources poured into the support and development of scientistic or theoretical knowledge through universities, technical institutes, and government research institutes, expanding its scope and pervasiveness. The so-called 'new middle class' that emerged built the foundations for its claim to high levels of income on its mastery of and its capacity to apply such knowledge. But in so far as 'bourgeois' knowledge has attained exclusivity in modern societies it would be difficult to argue that it remains apposite to a particular class.

However, if the previous statement is contentious, and it may be on a claim that bourgeois knowledge has come to perform the functions of an ideology, it no longer needs to detain us. Scientific knowledge is losing its authoritative status. Within one set of interpretations it is being subjected to processes of postmodernization. For Lyotard (1984), for example, modern knowledge had been organized around legitimating grand or meta-narratives (e.g. 'progress' and 'the Enlightenment'). The current commodification of knowledge, its instrumental stress on performativity as opposed to an emphasis on intrinsic worth, is detaching it from these meta-narratives and thus decreasing credulity. Equally Crook (in Crook et al. 1992: 216–18) envisages the emergence of a 'post-science' in which the qualitative distinctiveness of scientific practice is being eroded. As science is absorbed into society it becomes just one story of reality that must compete with others. By contrast, Beck (1992: 155–82) locates the delegitimation of scientific knowledge in its own substantive failures – its incapacity to offer solutions to environmental risks and its actual generation of such risks through its side effects. These failures also extend to the scientistic administrative practices of governments that appear decreasingly able to orchestrate either economic growth or social consensus or individual welfare.

In summary, contemporary patterns of knowledge no longer originate in or structure class milieux. More importantly, no form of knowledge now has the smack of absolute truth. The worth and validity of knowledge are established by the context of its consumption rather than the context of its production. Consumption patterns are constructed by organizations that find knowledge more or less useful, and by individuals who find it more or less entertaining. It long ago ceased to be the preserve of any class.

*Aesthetics*

Issues of taste and preference appear to energize class theorists more than any other aspect of culture. This is because, in many theories, aesthetic appreciation takes on symbolic significance in marking the boundaries between classes. Members of a given class share common consumption patterns in the aesthetic arena. Indeed, for Bourdieu (1977) cathectic preferences map out the space of class divisions and relationships and actually serve to reproduce them.[4]

However Martin (1981) provides what is perhaps the most useful conceptualization of class aesthetics. She identifies class locations in terms of Douglas' dimensions of 'grid' and 'group'. In a traditional class structure, weak gridness and groupness mark the extremes of the social spectrum. The professional, upper-middle classes and the lumpenproletariat are both characterized by weak boundaries and a low degree of structuring of everyday life: expressive bohemianism and slum disorganization share lifestyle similarities. For the most part, the classes in between all emphasize a rigid framing and organization of behaviour that serve to mark out group boundaries in terms of 'them' and 'us' and to separate the social arena from the liminality of bodily functions and the invasive natural environment. The closer a group is to a critical boundary the more that grid and group are emphasized, especially the former. The boundary between manual and non-manual work is particularly critical, especially in so far as physical labour places people in contact with liminal substances. So the most developed levels of gridness and groupness are found at the centre of the class system, at the interface between the 'respectable' working class, the families of skilled craft workers and direct supervisors, and the lower-middle class, the families of clerical workers. For these groups self-expression is heavily repressed and the individual is subordinated to the normative structure of the group.

Martin shows that in traditional working-class milieux the most apparent representation of gridness can be found in the family home (1981: 53–78). It is divided into areas that provide privacy for the exercise of bodily functions: the front is reserved for formal social occasions, the back for cooking, washing, eating and excretion, and the upper floor for sleeping, sex and illness. The front is furnished as symmetrically as possible using matching items. The front door is always closed to the outside world and the front step is scrubbed and ornaments are placed in windows to provide a 'face' for the house. Household activities are highly organized in time, so that there is a weekly schedule of meals, chores and changes of clothes, a daily schedule of cooking and personal hygiene, and a seasonal schedule of children's games and recreational activity. Strangers are regarded as an intrusion, neighbourliness takes place on the street or over the back fence, only the final and formal stages of youthful courtship are allowed in the house, and cursing is not allowed at all. Pleasure has to be taken at the boundaries: drinking must be done in a public house (a 'pub') rather than a private one and more generalized encounters with the more exciting aspects of liminality can take place in the pleasure periphery of the seaside resort (see Shields 1992; Urry 1987).

Martin characterizes the lower-middle-class milieu as patterned more by grid than group. It carries all the control associated with the exclusion of liminality but also an increased measure of privatization. Whereas working-class people express mutual solidarity, white-collar workers emphasize their individual advancement. By contrast, the commercial middle class is rather more flexible and less defensive. Middle-class homes are more open, both internally and externally, time is less rigidly structured, personal privacy is attenuated, and pleasurable experiences are developed outside the kin group in voluntary associations and friendships that can then be brought back inside.

Martin's explanation for these preferences is as class-theoretical as can be. She is describing the milieux of a class system located at the site of the earliest instance of industrialization, the original bourgeoisie and proletariat, and she frames her explanation in terms of that hard industrial experience. Thus she sources working-class culture in 'the need to create order and meaning in conditions of scarcity and in a context dominated by the nature of the factory' (1981: 61). Working-class culture was created, she argues, both because it was consistent with industrial regulation and because it was a defence against reduction to subhuman status by demeaning material conditions at the level of consumption. She may be overstressing the point about consistency because we would surely expect exploited and dominated workers, unless they were absolute dupes, to build into their domesticity not an extension of the factory but an alternative to it. Indeed, perhaps Martin misses the point that the social construction of patriarchal domesticity is indeed an alternative to the masculine experience of social subordination and of exposure to liminality.

This discussion should indicate that the evidence for the historical existence of particular class tastes and preferences is overwhelming, even if the precise basis for the link between class and culture might be in slight dispute. However, subsequent developments in this arena clearly match the historical sequence outlined in Chapter 1. The principal arguments against the contemporary persistence of class cultures of taste focus on the development of the mass mediation of culture. They propose that milieu class cultures represent a threat to the predominance of capitalist practices both because they offer sites for the development of alternative solidarities, and because they do not provide sufficient attachment to consumption to energize capitalist accumulation. As societies become more organized, in both state and monopoly-capitalist terms, the tastes and preferences of the various classes are homogenized within a mass culture. Adorno and Horkheimer (1979) are iconic figures in this proposal, suggesting that monopoly capital reorganizes culture along industrial lines. Cultural products are packaged as styles that can be marketed as commodities so that culture can fulfil its function as the servant of the capitalist class system:

> By subordinating in the same way and to the same end all areas of intellectual creation, by occupying men's senses from the time they leave the factory in the evening to the time they clock in again the next morning with matter that bears the impress of the labor process they themselves have to sustain throughout the day, this subsumption mockingly satisfies the concept of a unified culture which the philosophers of personality contrasted with mass culture. (1979: 131)

Thus the culture industry has a secret history of 'obedience to the social hierarchy' (1979: 131).

While the substance of Adorno and Horkheimer's proposal might be beyond dispute, an alternative explanation is available. It centres on the claim that the existence of a mass society need not presuppose a class-divided culture. The cultural practices in most twentieth-century capitalist societies approximate a division into 'high' and 'low' or elite and popular cultures, rather than into, say, aristocratic, bourgeois and working-class cultures. This development occurs as what previously had been courtly preferences in music and art trickle down to the *nouveaux riches*. They use their newly established control of state resources to set up public art galleries, museums and libraries, civic symphony orchestras, national opera, ballet and drama companies, and open and secular universities to institutionalize (and socialize the costs of) their newly found sense of taste. As the influence of the European states expanded across the globe, these cultural institutions were carried by colonial and cultural elites, so that no new society and no newly industrialized society, even if state-socialist, could regard itself as having an autonomous national culture without them. By the end of the nineteenth century a global but mainly European cultural tradition had been established in which the same music, the same art and the same literature and science were equally and universally highly regarded. Indeed, new methods of transportation allowed world tours by master practitioners and performers and allowed students to study at international centres of excellence, all of which served to consolidate a homogenized elite culture.

However, popular culture remained nation-state specific until the development of cinematographic and electronic mass mediation. A long-term effect of these media is the democratization of culture. This is because these media refuse to respect the 'specialness' or auratic quality of high-cultural products. They commodify cultural items by allowing them to be replicated at will, and by allowing them to be consumed without effort. Hoggart is in little doubt that they are destroying or have already destroyed the particular culture of working people:

> [T]hey tend towards a view of the world in which progress is conceived as a seeking of material possessions, equality as a moral levelling, and freedom as the grounds for endless irresponsible pleasure. These productions belong to a vicarious spectator's world; they offer nothing which can really grip the brain or heart. They assist a gradual drying-up of the more positive, the fuller, the more co-operative kinds of enjoyment, in which one gains much by giving much. They have intolerable pretensions; and pander to the wish to have things both ways, to do as we want and accept no consequence. (1958: 340)

Hoggart then is a true mass society theorist, insisting, like Adorno and Horkheimer, that popular culture induces at least uniformity if not *con*formity. However, unlike in Adorno and Horkheimer, this uniformity implies the passing of class society and not its persistence.

Given contemporary conditions, however, it would not affect the argument offered here if one were to continue to insist that mass society was a bourgeois construction and thus represented a class culture. If it indeed was the case that the so-called bourgeoisie sought to destroy working-class cultures, then they were in for a shock. In constructing a mass popular culture they created a monster that would eventually turn on and digest the elitist alternative. This development is widely recognized as a contemporary cultural revolution. For Martin (1981) it originates in a cultural segment based on age status rather than socioeconomic status. Within a theoretical framework that privileges the organization of liminality as the primary thematizing point for any culture, Martin proposes that because youth is itself a liminoid status, and because the youthful generation of the 1960s was the first such generation to be affluent, that status group was uniquely placed to mount an assault on the rigid grid/group cultures established by the 'classes'. They fomented what she calls an 'expressive revolution' in which hedonism and chaos increasingly prevailed over standards of abstinence and order. The assault came as a pincer movement between 'working-class' adolescents, the mods, rockers, skinheads and punks, who brought the culture of the slum into the mainstream, and 'middle-class' hippies who established bohemianism as a universal standard rather than a minority delight. While these cultural movements were in many respects antagonistic – liminoid hedonism stands against a sense of anarchical and anti-structural mission – they had the common consequence of attacking and eroding cultural boundaries.

Lash (1990: 18–25) links the process more closely to the familiar stratification processes of social mobility. He attributes the emergence of the culture of postmodernism to its elective affinity for an emerging service class. That class was itself a boundary transgressor: it originated in the 'working class' but, having accomplished some measure of economic and political clout, it sought also to establish its status by seeking to delegitimize the traditional elite culture. The new yuppie culture of postmodernism did this by deliberately mixing cultural products from diverse origins in ironic and playful pastiches. The styles that Adorno and Horkheimer so abhorred were rendered into parodies so that, unlike the succession of styles and avant-gardes associated with modernism, postmodernism is constructed as an absence of style. Under postmodernism there is no absolute standard of taste or opinion, no ground for closure or exclusivity. Martin too, although writing before the rise of postmodernism, sees something of this:

> [T]he riotous market in styles . . . provides a vocabulary, a set of codes, through which we negotiate and display our professional and private identities and achieve a tentative relationship with a complex and impersonal world; the romantic impulse to spontaneity and unmediated experience ends up as irony and self-parody. (1981: 237)

As has been widely canvassed, this new classless culture focuses on consumption rather than production. To identify it as a consumer culture, however, means more than that it simply emphasizes consumption. After all, an interest in consumption is historically and cross-societally universal (Featherstone 1991). Rather, in a consumer culture the items consumed take on a symbolic and not merely a material value so that consumption becomes the main form of self-expression and the chief source of identity. It implies that both material and non-material items, including kinship, affection, art and intellect, become commodified, that is, that their value is assessed by the context of their exchange rather than the context of their production or use. An advanced or postmodernized consumer culture experiences hypercommodification (Crook et al. 1992) in which minute differences between products or minute improvements in them can determine variations in demand, and in which consumption is differentiated on the basis of the signifiers known as 'brand names'. Here consumption, or more precisely a capacity to consume, is itself reflexively consumed. This tendency is captured in such terms as 'taste', 'fashion' and 'lifestyle'. These are the key sources of social differentiation, that displace both class and political affiliation. The consumer culture is created through the advertising and simulatory effects of the mass media. In its original form it was a deliberate creation but under postmodernized conditions it is 'hypersimulated' (Baudrillard 1988) having a life of its own that is beyond the control of any particular class or elite.

Because it is symbolically mediated, consumer culture liberates values and preferences from milieux and invalidates social and political structures more generally. It does so by undermining the cultural classifications of modernity, technically by declassifying or dedifferentiating culture. Bourgeois domination might have been legitimated by its claim to have special knowledge of cultural standards but in a consumer culture these standards merely become some of a range of opinions that can be accepted or rejected at will. Indeed the delegitimation of such standards promotes a more widespread and popular dissemination of what previously would have been regarded as elite cultural products. Perhaps one example can illustrate the point: the 'three tenors' concerts for the World Cups of 1990 and 1994 linked 'bourgeois' operatic music to the 'working-class' sport of soccer, set it up as spectacle as much as a concert, and marketed it by the mass media to a huge global audience.

As late as the mid twentieth century, cultural products and tastes could arguably be mapped against organized classes because they bore some social references and were consistent across similar social locations. The recent shift from organized and standardized cultural production and consumption to diversified niche marketing makes such mapping highly problematic. Such developments as specialized video production, cable and satellite television, regional and specialized presses, and local radio stations are attenuating the cultural-social alignment on a global scale. The key elements of these processes include:

- a differentiation of consumption into individualized tastes, so that not only the community but the family ceases to be the significant consumption unit;
- an aestheticization of consumption combined with an emphasis on distinction and differentiation; and
- a stylization of consumption driven by advertising and focused on the consumption of signs rather than their referents.

*Ethics*

Perhaps the seminal theoretical statement on the ethical commitments of manual workers is Lockwood's (1975) typology of working-class images of society, because it is within such images that evaluations are established. The three types identified by Lockwood are:

- the traditional proletarian worker: associated with bounded and isolated industrial contexts based on work-team production (mining, docking, shipbuilding, timber-getting, fishing); carry over of work-based comradeship into a highly ritualized communal sociability; pronounced consciousness of 'us' and 'them' (bosses, managers, office workers, and the state) (see Hoggart 1958: 72–101); ethical principles often derived from such Nonconformist religions as Methodism that assert individual salvation by election; tendency to form oppositional organizations and supporting ideologies; ethical emphasis on 'wrongness' or 'sinfulness' of society;
- the traditional deferential worker: associated with working relationships inherited from pre-industrial contexts, especially in agriculture (see Newby 1977), low-skilled machine tending (see Blauner 1964: 58–88), highly skilled craft labour, and low-grade clerical labour; highly communal and status conscious; tendency to view authority figures as patrons and as members of a common community; ethical system based in membership of catholic religions; ethical emphasis on divine or traditionalistic ordination of society; and
- the modern privatized worker: associated with mass-production and capital-intensive industrial contexts and with mass clerical work; highly individualized and isolated relationship to task performance; isolated domestic arrangements; tendency to view authority figures as fortunate or able individuals rather than as status unequals; ethical system located in an irreligious instrumental materialism; ethical emphasis on collective material advantage and progress.

Rather than being part of a simultaneous mosaic of ethical systems, these are in fact historically located because of the milieux within which they arise. The two traditional types are associated broadly with nineteenth-century capitalism, deferential ethics being associated with traditional feudally based communities and proletarian ethics with the emerging industrial structures of capitalism. However, by the middle of the twentieth century these communities were becoming minority backwaters within a nationalized community that emphasized the materialistic collectivism of the privatized worker.

Although we would ultimately dispute it, the privatized worker might still be argued to be implicated in a working-class ethical system, if only on an organized-class basis. Williams (1959) insists that the key feature that distinguishes working-class from middle-class culture is its moral basis. Bourgeois morality is based on individualism: 'an idea of society as a neutral area within which each individual is free to pursue his own development and his own

advantage as a natural right' (1959: 325). By contrast, working-class morality asserts that: 'The provision of the means of life will, alike in production
and distribution, be collective and mutual' (1959: 326). Indeed, differences
between the values of the new middle class and those of the instrumentalist
working class precisely turn on the ethics of collectivism:

> [The members of the middle class] endorse the institutional order, celebrate the
> industrial ethic, lay stress on individualism, suspect collectivist tendencies, are
> apprehensive about the growing powers of the state and celebrate through . . .
> socialisation processes, the internalisation of ambition, drive and success in its
> young. (King and Raynor 1981: 58)

From this point of view, the proponents of the embourgoisement thesis
(Goldthorpe et al. 1969) may have overstated their case: the working class
may never have become like the middle class. Nevertheless, if privatized-
instrumental workers were still working class, their ethical system was still
very different from that to which their predecessors were attached.

We have not stopped to debate the issue of whether privatized workers are
déclassés because the issue is immaterial to the argument we are advancing.
Privatization has, since the middle of the century, been overtaken by a
process of individualization such that the values of manual workers have
become indistinguishable from those of the middle class. Beck (1992: 96–102)
perhaps provides the most useful exposition of this view. For him, individualization implies: 'the demand for control of one's own money, time, living
space, and body . . . people demand the right to develop their own perspective on life and to be able to act on it.' Beck attributes individualization to an
anomic process in which individuals are cast adrift to rely on their own
resources in order to survive. The process begins in the education system,
where people are asked to reflect upon themselves and their place in history
(rather than say that of their class), and where they are individually credentialized on the basis of individual performance. The process continues in the
labour market, where endemic occupational and geographical mobility dis-
rupt both communities of deference or of misery and opposition, and
networks of support. As is discussed above, consumption has become
democratized, and Beck points out that labour relations have become juridi-
cal and contractual rather than being based on collective bargaining (1992:
95). Identities are therefore based no longer on location in neighbourhood,
kin or class but on an inward gaze on the self. Material success is the consequence of individual performativity, reflexively established in the competitive
arenas of the educational and occupational markets. Class milieux can no
longer form.

We can therefore propose the emergence of a fourth and a fifth type of
worker to locate alongside Lockwood's typology:

- the postmodern individualized worker: associated with emerging informatic industries and post-industrial service occupations; status based on
  profligate consumption and lifestyle value commitments; denial of the
  possibility of absolute authority; ethical principles hypersimulated from

the mass media; tendency to join temporary associations and ephemeral movements; ethical emphasis on the contingency of society; and

- the marginalized 'underclass' worker: associated with manual service industries and state dependency; status based on postcolonial migration, race, ethnicity, age, gender and family support; authority figures viewed as absolutely powerful and arbitrary in the allocation of employment and welfare; tendency to recruitment to entitlement-claimant blocs manifested in temporary protests rather than enduring organizations; ethical emphasis on an étatist welfarism expressed in terms of human rights to minimum material standards of consumption.

These new types of worker characterize the successors not only of traditional and privatized workers but also of workers who previously might have been described as middle class. The key feature that unites them is that they deny that the worth of any person is defined by their productive contribution to a collectivity and affirm that it is manifested in an individualized capacity to consume.

## Culture and identity

The decline of class cultures is accelerating in the arena of consumption. It is occurring in two phases. The first involves the erosion of hierarchical class cultures owing to the proliferation of what Campbell (1987) calls 'modern hedonism' and taste cultures. Cultural production has been absorbed into mass production and diversified into increasingly individualized tastes. When such individualization reaches the lower echelons of social hierarchies, the process of erosion of class cultures enters a critical phase and boundaries in cultural consumption begin to collapse. The second phase leads from taste culture to style culture, the latter even more radically detached from the social matrix. It coincides with hypercommodification and the spread of symbolic consumption. Stylized consumption is radically detaching from family, community and class and is becoming self-referential and driven by the dynamics of advertising. In McCracken's (1988) words, it forms 'culturally constituted worlds'. When styles congeal into lifestyles, and when such lifestyles form identities, the process of cultural decoupling reaches its apex. Stylized consumption not only is autonomous in relation to social divisions, but also loses its internal consistency and its links with cultural values, moral judgements and cognitive structures. Such a fragmented 'postculture' of stylized consumption has no clear social referent.

The explosion of class cultures does not leave an anomic vacuum at the level of meaning. The realm of collective beliefs and meaning systems, as Abercrombie, Hill and Turner (1980) indicate, was never fully colonized by class ideologies. As economic class has decomposed, these non-class collective idea systems have expanded. However, they are more autonomous and more decoupled from the sphere of productive relations than their predecessors. They are also global in their scope, and they are spreading rapidly through the electronic media.

The emergence of this classless culture has provoked a debate about whether class still forms a central component of personal identities. Indeed the issue of personal identity is often regarded as a critical test of class-cultural claims. Marshall, Newby, Rose and Vogler (1988: 145) are convinced that 'social identities are widely and easily constructed in class terms.' They make this claim on the basis of a finding that 60 per cent of their British sample thought of themselves as belonging to a particular social class and over 90 per cent could place themselves in a class if prompted by a list. Two things need to be said about their argument, only one of which has been said before. First, what respondents usually mean by 'class' is what a sociologist would call an occupational or socioeconomic status group. Marshall et al.'s respondents used such terms as 'professional people', 'office workers', and 'the unemployed' to describe the classes with which they identified, and not such terms as 'working class', let alone 'proletariat'. For the upper class, perhaps uniquely in Britain, they used feudal-estate rather than capitalist-class concepts, referring to the 'aristocracy' rather than the 'bourgeoisie' (1988: 146). Quite simply, occupations are not classes and nor indeed are feudal estates. Secondly, and as has been said elsewhere, Marshall et al. did not seek to establish the *relative* identificational salience of class because class was all they asked about. As Saunders witheringly asks:

> Are we seriously to believe that in their everyday lives people think of themselves as members of a class rather than say as British, as parents, or as white or black, or as male or female, young or old, married or single, drinkers, smokers, football supporters . . . ? . . . On holiday in Spain we feel British, waiting for a child outside the school gates we know we are a parent, shopping in Marks and Spencer we are a consumer – and answering questions, framed by sociologists with class on the brain, we are working class. (*Network* May 1989: 4–5)

Identity is probably not quite as situational as Saunders suggests, but the leading nature of the questions asked by social researchers is certainly an issue. The Australian sociologists Emmison and Western (1990; also in Baxter et al. 1991: 279–305) find, first, that unlike many notable sociologists, individuals are clearly able to differentiate between occupation and class as sources of identity. More importantly, they find that out of fifteen possible sources of identity, class ranks a distant ninth. Occupation, family role and Australian citizenship are far and away the most important, and gender, ethnicity, age, region of residence, and, Saunders would be gratified to know, being a supporter of a sports team all beat social class. Moreover, respondents link class not to the sphere of production or the market, but rather to more primordial and ascriptive status characteristics: it is held to be akin to gender or ethnicity.[1] The latter point would tend to support Beck's argument that, within the popular consciousness, class and its cultures function as traditionalistic remnants rather than as truly modern phenomena. Emmison and Western reach a similar conclusion: 'the discursive salience of class for identity is almost minimal' (1990: 241).

## Fragmented ideology

The ideological developments that connect with these cultural ones are probably best described in Bell's (1976) cultural sociology.[6] The Weberian reference point for his analysis of contemporary culture is the bourgeois morality that arose in early capitalist society and that was underpinned by Protestantism (1976: 54–61). The latter encompassed two phenomena: a Protestant ethic, a commitment to work as an end in itself; and a puritan temper, a commitment to an orderly and ascetic lifestyle. They emphasized, then, 'work, sobriety, frugality, sexual restraint, and a forbidding attitude towards life' (1976: 55). In their American manifestation they were associated with the institutions established by the New England pilgrims – farms, mercantilism, artisanship, the nuclear family and, above all, the small town. The growth of the boisterous immigrant cities and the feudalism of the antebellum South notwithstanding, Bell insists that: 'The life and character of American society were shaped by the small town, and its religions' (1976: 56). Small towns were highly effective social settings in shaping value commitments because community sanctions could enforce codes of behaviour.[7]

This Protestant ethic was undermined by internal developments. It had restrained not only bourgeois profligacy, but also any proletarian quest for freedom from the disciplines of work and production. However, capitalist enterprises remade themselves not only to constrain the aspirations to individual freedom of their workers, but to expand production in the Fordist direction of massification. While workers were expected to be restrained while on the job, capitalist expansionism also required that they should be unrestrained consumers in their domestic contexts. The masses had to be puritans at work and hedonists at home, or as Bell puts it: 'a corporation finds its people being straight by day and swingers by night' (1976: xxv). So during the middle 50 years of the twentieth century capitalism was rejigged to produce 'the life styles paraded by the culture' (1976: xxv) in the form of consumption goods produced to meet wants rather than needs and of mass-mediated images.

Within this transition, the distribution of economic power changed markedly. Bell often describes early capitalism as 'family capitalism' under which private property was the source of individual power. Society was run by an elite group of ruling families. The mass expansion of capitalism was marked by a separation of ownership and control so that property became corporate rather than private. In a formulation that might owe something to Burnham, access to managerial positions is now based on technical skill rather than ownership and is therefore non-heritable. This becomes the source of an attenuation of managerial power. It loses the legitimations that derive from a conception that it has a natural right to rule.

Bell's view thus runs counter to a belief fashionable in Marxist circles in the 1970s known as 'the dominant ideology thesis' (DIT). It suggests that each societal type, including contemporary capitalism, contains a relatively consistent set of popular beliefs, that are functional to the dominant class by incorporating the subordinate classes, stifling dissent and cementing the status quo (see Althusser 1977 for a statement of the position; Abercrombie et al. 1980 for a critique). Abercrombie, Hill and Turner (1980; 1990; Abercrombie and Turner 1978) set out the theoretical and empirical problems that face the thesis and support Bell's interpretation. First the DIT incorporates circular reasoning. It argues that as long as capitalism persists, whatever people believe in must be conducive to its persistence and *ergo* functional to the benefiting class. Second, there are problems with evidence. Despite the existence of well-developed 'agencies of ideological transmission', there is no sign of a widespread and coherent belief system underlying social practices in contemporary Western capitalism analogous to the Christian *Weltanschauung* in the feudal period. Popular beliefs are 'inconsistent and contradictory' (Abercrombie et al. 1980: 140). This reflects the fragmentation of the ruling class and the declining importance of ideological bonds for the functioning of the socioeconomic system. Nor is there evidence of the ideological incorporation of 'subordinate' classes. The dominant classes were the principal consumers of their own ideologies. Societal domination, Abercrombie, Hill and Turner conclude, is exercised through mechanisms of socioeconomic, rather than ideological, incorporation, through what Marx describes as the 'dull compulsion of economic relations'. So: 'Late capitalism operates largely without ideology' (1980: 185).

We need to remind ourselves of these conclusions because some veiled forms of the DIT are creeping back. This time the leading candidate for the status of 'dominant ideology' is not traditionalism, managerialism and welfarism, but an equally vaguely defined 'economic rationalism' (Pusey 1991). Ironically, economic rationalism developed as a counter-ideology to welfarism, the latter having been identified by many class analysts in the 1970s and 1980s as a key mechanism of ideological incorporation. If rationalism is indeed more consistent with the logic of capital accumulation, and hence with capitalist class interests, it is obviously much less effective than its predecessors. While fashionable among managers and economic bureaucrats, it can scarcely be attributed with a capacity to permeate the social structure and to generate quiescence among the 'subordinate classes'.

The critique of the DIT by Abercrombie, Hill and Turner (1990) can be expanded. The increasingly global scope of contemporary capitalism makes it much more diverse and inclusive as far as beliefs and ideas are concerned. The range of *Weltanschauungen*, religious creeds and popular outlooks is increasing. American capitalism prospers in the context of individualistic and liberal-democratic beliefs, while the capitalist revolution in South East Asia has taken place within the context of much more collectivist and often non-liberal orientations (see Berger 1987). Étatist welfarism and its ideological nemesis, market rationalism, equally fit happily into the capitalist framework. If one endorses the DIT, one must be forced to admit either that the ruling class is highly fragmented, or that it varies widely across the capitalist world, or that the correspondence between popular beliefs, the social structure and the socioeconomic system has become highly contingent. The last of these views is the most plausible.

We hasten to say that we do not endorse the end-of-ideology thesis (Bell 1988) in so far as this means the end of doctrinal belief systems. Ideological belief systems, both religious and secular, are proliferating in advanced societies. As is discussed in Chapter 7, the moral creeds of the new right, religious fundamentalisms of various sorts, as well as such emerging secular world views as ecologism and feminism, are energizing powerful new social movements. But such belief systems can hardly be linked to class positions that are derived from production relations and linked with economic interests. They cut across the remnants of class identification, and evade, if not directly oppose, traditional class issues.

Nor does a rejection of the DIT imply a denial of ideological conflict. However, it does imply that the cleavages that have emerged since the end of the Cold War differ from the old class-ideological conflict pattern. They are less organized, more multilateral, and more clearly linked to ideal rather than material interests than in the past. Nascent nationalisms in Eastern Europe, conflicts about pan-Europeanism, and confrontations within and between religious fundamentalisms clearly defy the class-ideological model. Even the clearest candidate for a class-ideological conflict, that of étatist welfarism against market rationalism, is difficult to trim to the procrustean bed of class analysis. As Papadakis (1994) shows, attitudes to welfarism simply do not correlate with supposed class locations.

**Conclusion**

The theory that contemporary cultures are 'reflections' of class is highly questionable. Such theory not only implies an unacceptable economic-productivist reductionism, but also fails to recognise the salient links between cultures and non-class aspects of social location. It exaggerates the symmetry between values, norms and tastes, on one hand, and the social matrix, on the other. Class subcultures should be viewed rather as historically specific products of early industrialization. They are the emanations of local communities of fate. They survive only in the isolated enclaves of 'company towns', mining settlements and rural communities. The organization of national classes cannot re-create these cohesive communal class cultures. National classes have always been culturally heterogeneous and fragmented. Their cultural correlates are increasingly diverse taste cultures that are vaguely aligned with occupational hierarchies via the mechanisms of fashion and tradition. However, national classes do have in common, as is argued in Chapters 5 and 7, a degree of political-ideological cohesion imposed by class-mobilizing organizations and their ideologues. These meta-narratives, the grand visions of socialist, liberal and traditional society, do not penetrate popular meaning systems, social norms, consumption patterns and images very deeply. Their impact on lifeworlds is limited to a handful of committed and ideologically conscious activists and intellectuals. Class ideologies function mainly as elite political formulas. They are organizationally elaborated and maintained, but largely detached from socioeconomic milieux and ineffective at the level of popular consciousness. With the diremption of meta-narratives, and the corresponding decline of class organizations, the last vestiges of class ideology are disappearing.

The historical shifts can now, once again, be confirmed. Economic-class societies were characterized by bounded subcultures. Capitalist-class families legitimated their capital accumulation and its inheritance by reference to a dominant ideology of Protestant thrift, divine election and puritan temperament. They were entitled to their privileges, they believed, because they had earned them in the pursuit of their calling, and God recognized that fact. Working-class cultures absorbed such cultural imposts in expressions of deference, although radicalization was possible. Organized-class societies, especially in their corporatized and welfare versions, transformed these cultural orientations. Class cultures became more differentiated, profligate and indulgent at the top and the bottom but regulative and privatized in the middle. Nationally organized political ideologies matched this development: social democracy favoured a redistribution of consumption possibilities to the bottom; liberalism favoured rewards for hard work in the middle; and conservatism the maintenance of privilege at the top. Status-conventional societies are experiencing simultaneous cultural homogenization and fragmentation. They are homogenizing at the level of material culture and milieu by emphasizing a symbolically mediated consumption, but fragmenting at the level of lifestyles and value commitments as the latter become redefined as matters of election and choice. Each of these developments spells the demise of class subcultures and class ideologies.

If collective action presupposes commonality of orientation then we should expect politics to follow a pattern similar to the one specified here. If we can find no identifiable class cultures, it is unlikely that we will find a class politics. The next chapter explores this issue.

### Notes

1 This Kantian division between value spheres is mentioned by Weber (1948: 147) and is reflected in Parsons' nested usage of the cognitive, cathectic and evaluative aspects of action (Parsons et al. 1951).

2 There is a small danger that this analysis will be regarded as unrepresentative because it is based on studies by Hoggart and Martin that focus on class cultures in the north of England. The analysis is defensible because this region was the earliest site of capitalist industrialization in the world and the class cultures based on capitalism were most deeply entrenched there. Indeed working-class culture has persisted in that area to a remarkable degree. The discussion here is consistent with other British studies by Dennis et al. (1969), Jackson (1968), and Young and Wilmott (1962), and with the American community studies of Lynd and Lynd (1959) and Stein (1964). Alt (1976: 80), while subscribing to mass society theory, describes the situation in the USA in similar terms: 'the transition to monopoly capitalism tends to shift the source of social relations, culture, and ideology from a class culture of work to a mass culture of consumerism . . . This trend is facilitated by the fragmentation of traditional bonds of social interdependence (those of class). In cultural terms, this trend has been interpreted as a shift from a daily class experience, rooted in occupational communities and functionally related to the labor fetishism of early capitalism, to a relative social privatization of daily existence rooted in the family and mediated by a mass consumer culture provided by corporate institutions. Through this process, the

working class has lost its culture-defining character as wage labor: the dialectical reproduction of their labor in the free space of unreified leisure. The world of class, and all that it meant in terms of labor experience, leisure, and political action, has been eclipsed.'

3 Like many class theorists, we take the view that working-class culture is not at all conducive to class mobilization. Indeed trade-union and political mobilization becomes more possible precisely at those points at which traditional working-class culture breaks down. Reform and revolution are only possible where knowledge consists of abstractions.

4 Although Bourdieu's work has become highly influential in class-cultural analysis it can be regarded as a *class* theory only if one stretches the concept to extremes. First his 'objective division into classes' includes age groups and genders as well as social classes (1984: 468). Second, the maps he draws of preferences (e.g. 1984: 128–9) are actually mappings of the locations of multiple occupational groups rather than classes. Third, his dimension of cultural capital is independent of and intersects with the dimension of economic capital, whereas a normal baseline in the sociological definition of class is that it is primarily an economic phenomenon.

5 Emmison and Western, unlike ourselves, are clear supporters of the class paradigm. However, they are rigorous empiricists and are prepared to report results as they find them.

6 This material on Bell's theory of contemporary culture is drawn from Waters (1995c).

7 Although Bell's thesis appears to be restricted to America it can be generalized much further. It is applicable, for example, to the religious Nonconformist cultures of the industrial and mining towns of Scotland, Wales and northern England, to the Protestant mining regions of north-western France, to Lutheran Germany, and perhaps above all to the Calvinistic regions of Switzerland and the Low Countries.

# 7

# Choice Politics

Politics is the most hotly contested territory in the current debates about class. These debates centre on the disparity between the original promise of class theory to explain conflict and change, as expressed in the 'rules of motion' of modern capitalism, and an apparent decline in the centrality of class identification, class consciousness and class action in the contemporary polity. The particular empirical problem for class analysis specifically is that since the peak of class effects during the middle of the twentieth century, the significance of class as a basis for political identification and behaviour and as a force for change has been declining.[1] European liberal corporatism was the highest point in the historical life cycle of class. Class-oriented milieu parties and trade unions acquired a central role within the configuration that became known as 'democratic class struggle' (Lipset 1960; Korpi 1983; Hout et al. 1994), 'institutionalized class conflict' (Dahrendorf 1959) or 'cleavage politics' (Lipset and Rokkan 1967). Even when they were condemned as divisive, class issues of wages, working conditions and welfare entitlements dominated political agendas. Class identification even became popular outside working-class milieux as the concept of the 'middle class' entered the vocabulary. With it, class discourse became the legitimate language of politics.

As Chapter 5 indicates, social classes gained a new political lease on life at that critical period when their economic foundations were decaying owing to market fragmentation and an elaborating division of labour. The political-organizational superstructures of class, trade unions and parties now took on the dominant structuring role. Class issues and interests were articulated, elaborated and disseminated within their platforms and policies. So were class ideologies, global packages combining specific social values with general strategies of implementation. Socialism, liberalism and conservatism became associated with broad class interests precisely because of their deployment as the political formula of the major parties. They organized popular identifications and outlooks and created a context within which 'class interests' could be defined. The working class was closely identified with social-democratic party support and an allegiance to a socialist-left ideological position. Liberal-conservative parties and ideologies defined the middle classes as the beneficiaries of their programmes. Even the rightist extremism of the inter-war period acquired class overtones in so far as fascist parties appealed to the anti-modernist and anti-industrial sentiments of the petty bourgeoisie (Lipset 1960; 1981). Thus while, as communities and subcultures, classes exhibited signs of morbidity, they were being born again as the social referents of the main actors in national politics.

The reconstitution of classes in the corporatist welfare state (discussed in Chapter 5) is analogous to the process of reconstitution of nations by the modern state. Like nations before them, classes became 'imagined communities' (Anderson 1983), powerful abstractions occupying a central place in individual and collective identifications. This reconstitution of classes involved not only the political articulation of class organizations to become real class actors, but also the development of uniform class symbols and icons, and of capacities to disseminate class identities and discourses. It coincided with a glorification of class parties, especially on the left of the political spectrum. Parties took over the heroic mantle of economic classes, just as states had monopolized national sentiments. In extreme cases, this identification was enforced by authoritarian means. For socialist revolutionaries, like Lenin, as for intellectuals, like Lukács, the party was the only true expression of class. Social democrats also affirmed the equation of class with party, although they mitigated the claim by increasingly vocal warnings about the dangers of party bureaucratization and oligarchic decay (e.g. Michels 1958).

A reversal in this trend took shape between 1960 and 1990. It was manifested in such phenomena as class and partisan dealignment, declining partisanship and party trust, the appearance and growth of 'third parties', especially of the left-libertarian type, and a growing tide of 'new politics', 'issue politics' and 'life politics' (Baker et al. 1981; Dalton 1988; Giddens 1990; Kitchelt 1989). This political disorganization of class marks the final phase in its dissolution. Without institutionalized means of social reproduction, classes cannot survive. The process primarily affects the most advanced societies of Western Europe, North America, East Asia and Australasia. Some aspects can also be observed in post-communist Eastern Europe.

We can now analyse the main features of this process, beginning with the conventional political arena, where dealignment marks the decline of class politics, and then moving on to examine the rise of a new politics that takes no account of class.

### The waning of class politics

The central feature of the declining influence of class on politics is party–class dealignment. The term refers to three parallel processes:

- a decline of class voting and of class-based allegiance to political parties;
- a decline of class-based organizations; and
- a decline of the use of class imagery and consciousness in politics.

The dealignment process, and the concomitant collapse of corporatist arrangements, occurs within the context of a devolution of state powers (see Chapter 5; Crook et al. 1992: 79–105). After a century of growth and expansion, the powers of the state are now contracting. This trend includes several component developments: a decentralizing 'horizontal' shift of powers and responsibilities to sub-state territorial and functionally specialized organizations; a vertical redistribution to civic activism and social movements; a decline in the scope of state intervention manifested in processes of privatization and marketization; and a shift of some state powers 'upwards' to supra-state bodies and agencies. These processes are undermining the corporatist frameworks within which national classes thrived. The cleavage politics of corporatist class compromises, and the highly institutionalized and organized forms of the 'democratic class struggle' (Lipset 1960; Korpi 1983; Hout et al. 1994), cannot be maintained under conditions of declining control by nation-states of their economic, political and legal environments. Dealignment can be seen both as an aspect and as a consequence of this general process. It affects class divisions precisely because these divisions were so closely linked with corporatist–partisan divisions, and so dependent on political reproduction by means of party appeals and loyalties. Just as the weakening state undermines national unity and identity, so class organizations, progressively weakened by dealignment, are increasingly unable to support and reproduce their class referents in civil society.

### Cleavage politics

The most widely employed measure of dealignment is the Alford index (AI) of party–class voting (Alford 1963: 79–80). It is constructed by taking the percentage of voters in manual occupations who cast votes for leftist parties and subtracting from it the percentage of voters in non-manual occupations voting for such parties. The AI has been declining since the 1960s in almost all advanced societies for which longitudinal data on voting behaviour are available (see Saarlvik and Crewe 1983; Rose and McAllister 1985; Clark et al. 1993). Although the decline varies in its pace and intensity it appears nevertheless to be universal (Table 7.1).

Critics of the index focus on its alleged crudeness and inappropriateness. However the three main bases on which they make this allegation cannot withstand careful examination.

First, Hout, Brooks and Manza (1993: 265–6) argue that the index is so

Table 7.1   *The Alford index of class voting, and proportion of variance in left voting explained by 'social structure', 1960s and 1980s.*

| Country | Alford index | | Variance explained (%) | |
|---------|------|-------|-------|-------|
|         | 1964 | 1980s | 1960s | 1980s |
| Britain | 42 | 21 | 19 | 10 |
| France | 20 | 14 | 19 | 6 |
| Germany (FR) | 26 | 10 | 15 | 16 |
| Sweden | 46 | 34 | 28 | 18 |
| USA | 18 | 8 | 10 | 11 |

*Sources*: Lipset 1981: 505; Franklin et al. 1992: 387; Clark et al. 1993: 312

empirically crude and oversimplistic that it exaggerates the effects of dealignment. This criticism is unconvincing. While simple in its construction, the AI is extremely useful in international and historical comparisons, because of the clarity and universality of the manual/non-manual division on which it relies. The division corresponds very closely to the *major* industrial classes as defined by class theory, a fact that is recognized even by the most trenchant critics of the index. After all, dealignment is significant only if it affects the major classes and their political representatives, and only if it can be confirmed in many societies. Moreover, none of the critics appear to have produced evidence that more refined measures of class–party alignment reveal trends that are inconsistent with those indicated by the AI. In fact, studies using standard regression techniques confirm the dealignment trend (e.g. Franklin et al. 1992; Clark et al. 1993; see below for details).

Second, Hout, Brooks and Manza (1993) and Marshall, Newby, Rose and Vogler (1988) also argue that the AI is theoretically crude because it assumes both a simplistic two-class model, and an 'unmediated' connection between class and voting. As to the former, it is not clear that a more complex conceptualization of class would reveal different historical trends than that indicated by the AI. The criticism about the unmediated nature of the relationship appears to be equally spurious. We agree with Przeworski and Sprague (1986), Marshall, Newby, Rose and Vogler (1988) and Hout, Brooks and Manza (1993) that class effects are organizationally and politically mediated, and that the declining Index may indicate an attenuation of this mediation. However, the claim that such weakening does not impinge on the social reality of class and the effectivity of class politics is quite bizarre. If sociopolitical 'mediation' is the main means for class reproduction, a relaxation of the links between political organizations and their class constituencies will cause a failure in the sociopolitical reproduction of classes. Hout, Brooks and Manza (1993: 266) remain resolutely fideistic, arguing that, despite a severely reduced politicization of classes, they still exist as important social forces: they are there even if they appear not to be there. 'Class interests', and therefore the objective classes that mobilize them, they insist, 'may remain latent in the political arena.' On such a formulation, latent classes and their interests must be the secular equivalent of the Holy Ghost.

Third, Marshall, Newby, Rose and Vogler (1988: 230–6) claim, in addition, that the AI distorts the facts because it focuses on absolute rather than relative rates of class defection voting. For example, the relative rates, it is claimed, show that defections occur 'across the board' and are not specific to the working class. The bases for this criticism are particularly dubious. Surely, wholesale defections from ostensibly class parties, as Marshall and his colleagues acknowledge the British Labour and Conservative Parties to be, to such non-class parties as the (Liberal/Social-Democratic) Alliance, must be interpreted as evidence of dealignment rather than its absence. In fact, relative rates of class–party allegiance do not offer a privileged measure of class effects but simply allow the charting of class-specific trends in (de)alignment.

If Marshall and his colleagues want to claim that only evidence of working-class-specific defection would constitute acceptable evidence of the declining political relevance of class, they can be accused of fencing their position behind unreasonably restrictive conditions of counter-factual evidence.

However, if the AI is indeed unacceptable, perhaps a convincing alternative investigation of voting trends can be found in Franklin, Mackie and Valen's (1992) study of electoral behaviour in sixteen industrialized societies between 1960 and 1990. Their key research question concerns the impact of social-structural factors, especially class position, on party support and voting patterns. The importance of this study rests not only on its impressive comparative scope, but also on a sophisticated methodology that uses regression techniques to reveal electoral trends. The results of the study relate to three topics: the decline of cleavage politics, the particularization of the voting choice, and the rise of new political divisions.

Franklin, Mackie and Valen confirm that contemporary electoral choice is decreasingly influenced by social cleavages, most importantly class cleavages, that formed the social bases of electoral politics in the past:

> While social structure does appear to have been an important determinant of partisanship in most countries in the 1960s (explaining more than 16 per cent of variance in left voting in eleven countries) by the 1980s there were only five countries left where this was still true. Even more telling, while in the 1960s there were eight countries in which more than 20 per cent of variance was explained by social structure (Norway, Belgium, Denmark, Netherlands, Sweden, Italy, France and Britain), by the 1980s only Norway and Italy were left in this position. (1992: 388)

Their theoretical interpretation of these results confirms the dealignment thesis:

> [W]e are now able to see the cross-national commonality of the process which involves the breakdown of linkages between particular social groups and political parties which used to represent the interests of those groups electorally. This breakdown of traditional linkages involves nothing less than the disintegration of cleavage politics, which in turn, makes it possible for other factors to play an increasing role in influencing voter choice. (1992: 408)

They argue this process to be universal but developmental. It affects all advanced societies but with differing speed and intensity. It began in the USA in the period preceding the historical scope of the study and has subsequently affected most other advanced societies during the last three decades. Class dealignment is thus an aspect of the broader process of autonomization of politics and of the declining importance of social-structural location for electoral choice.

On this argument, political choice is less and less constrained by membership in such large social aggregates as classes. This shift is a function of two processes: 'de-massification' (Toffler 1980), the declining influence of such large organizational structures as parties, unions and corporations on people's identifications and lifestyles; and the 'particularization' of political choice in a 'post-collectivist' era. Under the latter process:

> [T]he social categories describing traditional social cleavages are no longer at the

appropriate level of aggregation for explaining current political preferences and orientations . . . [T]he transformation of objective into subjective reality is increasingly mediated by social characteristics additional to the simple categorizations which are so popular in political sociology. (Franklin et al. 1992: 413)

Obviously, the key object of this critical comment is the 'simple categorizations' of class. The particularization process indicates a progressive decoupling of politics from the social structure and the ascendancy of a complex and unpredictable issue and preference politics.

The symptoms of these changes can be found in the rise of new political agendas and new issue sets:

Some of these (the introduction of new technology, the disposal of toxic and radioactive waste, and the effects of industrial production on the environment) create insecurities and even hardships that cut across class lines. These problems, along with others mentioned in earlier sections [women's rights, civil liberties], may be seen by many as more salient than the problems of social justice that were the bread and butter of socialist party platforms in earlier years. (1992: 425)

These new agendas, issues and public concerns cannot easily be accommodated within the left–right political spectrum. They also defy standard political-ideological packages and the policy lines of the major class parties. The dealignment process undermines the political role of these cleavage organizers, and results in the blooming of new parties, political groups and social movements.

## Organizational fragmentation

The parties of the left, especially those employing the class idiom in their appeals, were destabilized by these processes. After electoral victories in the 1970s that were based on a significant dilution of socialist programmes and shifts to the middle ground, support has nevertheless declined quite rapidly. In 1981 in Belgium, for example, and a year later in the Netherlands, the social-democratic parties were replaced by pragmatic pro-market coalitions. The British Labour government was defeated in 1979, and in 1983 Labour's electoral support sunk to its lowest level since the Second World War. Its leadership had failed to erase class referents and socialist commitments from its programme, and it remains in opposition well towards the end of the century despite the incoherence of its Conservative opponents. Even the seemingly unassailable Scandinavian social-democratic parties have fallen victim to the disease. In 1991 the Swedish Social Democratic Party was defeated, and, although it subsequently returned to power, it was forced to govern in coalition and to alter drastically its political programme and rhetoric. Similarly: the German SPD that had presided over the consolidation of the *Wirtschaftswunder* has been out of power throughout the 1980s and 1990s; in France, the PSF that provided the Mitterrand presidency was by the mid 1990s at its lowest parliamentary ebb in thirty years, while the PCF had virtually disappeared; and in Italy the PSI literally decomposed in the early 1990s, along with the Christian Democrats and the PCI, as the consequence of the judicial discovery of widespread political corruption. By the mid 1990s, among the large Western European democracies, only in Spain did a social-democratic party, the PSOE, cling to government, and then only by its fingertips.

Clearly, decline in support for the social-democratic left is contingent and periodical. However, this decline is part of a long-term syndrome in which electoral support is decreasingly attached to forces that ally themselves closely with class idioms, issues, programmes and rhetoric. The electoral feats of the Labo(u)r Parties of Australia and New Zealand during the 1980s are instructive in this respect because they are founded on an intentional desertion of class appeals in favour of such issues as civil liberties, the environment and marketizing reforms. Similarly, the relatively successful Danish Social Democrats rapidly abandoned commitments to egalitarian redistribution, support for nationalization and state ownership, and an emphasis on corporate co-determination in management. The British Labour Party began to institute similar policy reforms in the mid 1990s and almost instantly appeared to be an excellent prospect for electoral success. Leftist parties that continued to cultivate class agendas, such as the PSF, looked increasingly like long-term losers. Success relies on adjusting appeals to embrace non-class issues of citizen autonomy, privacy, women's rights, self-organization, environment, community and market efficiency.

Another important aspect of this process is the rapid rise of various 'third' and non-aligned political forces, including single-issue parties, and an increasing number of 'independents'. While they formed only marginal residues in the immediate post-War period, since the 1970s they have moved into the political mainstream. The bipartisan understandings that were the foundation of corporatist arrangements have been crumbling under pressure from these new political bodies. Their rise to prominence mirrors the decline of class-based parties.

The organizations that are perhaps the most affected by the decline of class are the archetypal 'representatives of the working class', the trade unions. As is indicated in Chapter 4, their decline has been both universal and very rapid throughout the industrialized world (Western 1995; Golden and Pontusson 1992; Regini 1992).[2] Class universalism appears to be least attractive to young and highly skilled workers in the competitive sectors of the economy. The symptoms of this crisis include not only declining membership, but also the multiple fragmentation of union organizations. The latter involves the autonomization of individual unions relative to peak organizations, the ascendancy of local unions relative to centrals, and splits between private- and public-sector unionism. Class unions appear to be afflicted by the same post-Fordist logic that afflicts class parties. They are unable to cater for the increasingly diverse demands and interests of their constituencies (see Kern and Sabel 1992; Streek 1992). As Golden and Pontusson (1992) suggest, this is a crisis of *large* unions, those that attempt to represent major sections of employees within a general and indiscriminate idiom of sectional class interests. By contrast, more successful small unions are breaking with the idiom of class conflict and joining what Kern and Sabel (1992) call a 'productive coalition' with management that is necessary for implementing a programme of flexible specialization (also see Streek 1992).

The crisis of class politics is affecting not only the working-class organizations of the left, but also the traditional right-of-centre class parties. In the early 1970s an entire family of new, right-wing 'progress', 'populist', 'protest' and 'tax-revolt' parties appeared, mainly in Northern Europe, especially in Scandinavia. They proved to be more than a flash in the pan, consolidating their electoral support and becoming a permanent feature of the political landscape. Moreover, any suggestion that they were another petty-bourgeois development to parallel fascism proved to be inaccurate, because they were also able to attract the support of manual and new white-collar workers. Like left-libertarian parties, these 'progress' parties do not correspond with the class model. Their programmes bear no relation to material class interests, even those petty-bourgeois stalwarts of anti-liberalism and anti-industrialism. Rather, they are articulating a new sectoral cleavage in production, consumption and lifestyle. They are opposed not so much to the welfare state *per se* as to the 'excesses' of welfarism, to 'uncontrolled immigration' and, more recently, to the 'foreign diktats' of the European Union. These issues represent a perception of threat to one's status, lifestyle and values rather than to material interests. This 'post-industrial materialism' (Minkenberg 1994: 54; Andersen and Bjørklund 1990; Minkenberg and Inglehart 1989) embraces, then, a *Wohlstandchauvinismus* (lifestyle chauvinism) combined with a developed tribal consciousness.

This new dimensionality in contemporary politics is also affecting the mainstream parties of the right. The traditional parties of business and property seem to be losing support to political third forces. The British Conservative Party has not fared well in terms of electoral support, despite retaining government because of an unrepresentative first-past-the-post electoral system.[3] The real electoral winners in the most recent elections in Britain have been third parties, the Liberal Democrats and the Greens. A similar pattern can be found throughout Western Europe. In Germany, for example, in 1994 there was a proportional decline in support for the CPD-CSU-FPD (but no success for the SPD). In Italy, 1994 saw the total collapse of the traditional right-of-centre forces, and their realignment on a non-class basis.

Although American politics might be regarded as exceptional because the main parties have long since ceased to be class parties, if they ever were, there is considerable evidence that the main processes there parallel those in Western Europe (see Franklin et al. 1992). The Democrats lost their predominantly populist Dixiecrat and blue-collar support under assault from an effective Republican campaign mounted by that most populist of Presidents, Ronald Reagan, during the 1980s. During the 1990s the Democrats have moved closer to policies combining post-materialism and minority rights under the baby-boomer President, Bill Clinton. Meanwhile, under the influence of the new Christian right movement, the Republican Party moves ever closer to a *Wohlstandchauvinismus* that emphasizes communal morality, rights to life, opposition to affirmative action, economic rationalism, aggressive mercantilism in trade, lower taxes, and law and order.

In summary, class determination of voting behaviour is declining towards insignificance, as measured both by the traditional Alford index and by more sophisticated measures of the social-structural base. Political surveys reveal a decline in traditional voting patterns, including a decline in class-specific political loyalties and patterns, especially among younger respondents (see Franklin et al. 1992). This shift in attitudes and voting behaviour has now been documented in some fifteen advanced societies in Europe, America and Australasia. Even such convinced supporters of class as Marshall, Newby, Rose and Vogler (1988: 230) acknowledge that class can predict, at best, only 10–12 per cent of the variance in voting preference. This must be counted a rather modest result for a candidate for the role of 'key independent variable' in the analysis of politics.

The explanations that are offered for the new non-class configuration in voting preference vary very widely: Dunleavy (1980) attributes dealignment to de-traditionalization; Baker et al. (1981) and Dalton (1988) argue that the new cleavages represent new political dimensions; Toffler (1980) sees it as an aspect of de-massification; Inglehart (1990) links it to the decline of materialist values; Franklin (1985) attributes it to increasing party appeals to non-class audiences and to the breakdown of class–party socialization; Rose and McAllister (1985) concentrate on the growth of non-class-specific and marginal electorates; Franklin, Mackie and Valen (1992) identify a process of particularization that undermines the old class-specific repertoires of concern; and Clark, Lipset and Rempel (1993) say that it is due to increased affluence, privatism and rapid mobility. Whatever combination of factors is responsible, they agree that the old pattern of class voting is disappearing.

*Images and consciousness*

This shift has also affected sociopolitical imagery. Popular images of social structure may still be expressed in terms of class but the concept has taken on a variety of meanings that are often contradictory. Ossowski's (1963) foundational formulation suggests a basic typology of four such images: a polar dichotomy between exploiters and exploited; a gradational hierarchy running from upper to lower classes; a functional system of complementary classes; and a synthesis of the others. Empirical research on class imagery in fact reveals 'complex, diverse, fragmentary, ambiguous and even contradictory class conceptions' (Graetz and McAllister 1994: 238). Within this complexity, however, the gradational model is overwhelmingly popular and is typically interpreted as associated with income (see Lockwood 1966; Davies 1967; Blackburn and Mann 1975; Graetz 1986). Moreover, there is little correspondence between class images and actual class locations. Equally, there is only a small relationship between imagery and what Graetz (1983: 80) calls 'class sentiments', and little evidence of a relationship to class consciousness (Mann 1973: 13).[4] Indeed the concept of 'class consciousness' now seems to be extinct, in so far as it seldom figures in the repertoire of empirical research on class.

Research fragmentation, differences in the conceptualization of class and class consciousness, and methodological differences all make it difficult to draw any clear conclusion as to trends in class imagery, identification and consciousness. However, if we follow a suggestion made by Wright (1985) that class consciousness should be analysed through both sentiments and *action,* there can be little doubt of a decline during the last quarter of the twentieth century. The waves of class conflict that washed across Western societies in the 1950s and 1960s have since diminished to a ripple. The popularity of class idiom is also in decline, in popular speech, in political rhetoric and even in sociological analysis. The compulsive fixation on class analysis that afflicted the collective psyche of Western academia throughout the 1960s and 1970s has largely been put to rest.

The disparity between economic positions, political attitudes and political activism is widening. Graetz's Australian studies (1983; 1986; 1992) of the relationship between inequalities, images, attitudes and political activism confirm that popular beliefs are seldom dissentious in the way that class models would suggest. Rather, beliefs about inequality and political opinions depend primarily on political values and cut across class and status divisions. He concludes that class-based beliefs and opinions 'exert no more than a marginal impact upon the propensity for political action' (1992:172–3).

## The waxing of new politics

There is a wide-ranging consensus on the view that old political divisions, especially those based on class, are eroding, but there is much less agreement as to the nature and shape of new political divisions. In a pioneering analysis of political change in Germany, Baker et al. (1981) coin the term 'new politics' to typify the new political configuration, and this concept has now become widely influential. Conceptualizations of this new politics vary widely, to include: new value preferences (Inglehart 1990); new issues and concerns (Dalton 1988); a new political culture, especially new norms of direct involvement (Gibbins 1989); new institutional forms, including new social movements (Scott 1990); and new social bases (e.g. Offe 1985). However, the new politics is invariably contrasted with the 'old', party-controlled, organized, bureaucratized and class-based politics.

For Baker et al., a key feature of new politics is its generational base:

A new generation has developed in the postwar years in Germany that is more involved in the democratic political system. In part, this has resulted from the accumulation of experience in the role of a participatory citizen, but it may also involve the inculcation of democratic norms of participation. Thus one source of increasing political involvement must be the growing size of the young participatory segment of the electorate, and the acceptance of their example by older generations. (1981: 57)

By contrast, the importance of class factors in directing political allegiances and behaviour has been declining. In a claim that is elaborated in Franklin et al.'s (1992) subsequent study, Baker et al. declare that: 'The declining importance of class appears to be the major factor in accounting for the decline in the explanatory power of social characteristics as a whole' (1981: 192).

Inglehart develops a similar argument (1977; 1990). Here, new political configurations reflect new value preferences brought about by post-war generations. These new value priorities are 'post-materialist' in so far as they transcend former concerns with material well-being and security. Post-material value hierarchies prioritize quality of life, self-actualization and civil liberties. This view is based both on a Maslowian theory of a need hierarchy, and on a much less controversial Mannheimian view that political orientations are carried by particular generations. This means that generations, and not classes, are now the major social referents in political sociology. The carrier of new values in the developed West is the post-war generation that shares the formative experience of the 'long boom'.

Kitchelt (1994) perhaps provides the most useful account of the detachment of Western European party politics from class, and the emergence of new political divisions that cut across the traditional ideological spectrum. According to him, the class-related master cleavage between left and right is ceasing to be an adequate conceptual guide to contemporary politics. Increasingly, voter preferences and party choices are based on such non-class factors as market and organizational location, production sector, generation and life cycle, gender, and consumption style, including home ownership. Support for new political forces reflects the increasing salience of these new divisions. Skilled blue-collar workers, for example, especially the younger ones working in internationally competitive economic sectors, are turning against traditional working-class packages of protection and welfare. Their unskilled colleagues, especially the older ones working in domestic services and manufacturing, together with low-skilled white-collar workers, tend to support authoritarian-communitarian appeals. Highly educated 'symbol processors' working in the public sector and human services, especially women, prefer libertarian policies with a socialist bent. Kitchelt concludes:

> Socialist appeals to class politics thus do not unite the working class, but divide it in different ways than a moderate pro-capitalist programme. On the socialist-capitalist axis then, social democrats choose . . . between mobilising different segments of the working class. As a consequence, class politics is no longer a foundation of a broadly successful social democratic electoral coalition. (1994: 33)

Politics, most contemporary critics agree, is ceasing to be a distributive game monopolized by corporate actors. Its institutional boundaries have been challenged (Offe 1985) and its agendas expanded (Dalton 1988). This 'post-Fordist politics', like post-Fordist production, is a politics of highly specialized, issue-centred, niche consumption. It responds to the specific demands of progressively smaller segments of the population, differentiated by education level, skill level, gender, type of work, government employment, production sector, exposure to international markets, generation, religion, and family and sexual lifestyle. These divisions do not cleave uniformly but vary from region to region and by both social location and career trajectory. Importantly they are subject to significant conjectural variation. Some of them are detached from social locations to an extent that suggests that a general decoupling of political orientations and preferences from the social is under way (see Crook et al. 1992).

### New actors

Many 'action' sociologists and Gramscian Marxists take classes to be the major political actors within modern capitalism. Such an interpretation would suggest that the political significance of class cannot be reduced to partisan alignment, political identification or voting behaviour. Rather political involvement is an *essential* feature of classes regardless of the particular social composition of their membership. A class, according to Touraine (1981; 1985), is any collective actor capable of challenging the central normative structure of society. This view, then, seeks to reverse the normal propositions of class theory outlined in Chapter 1. There classes are the basis for political formations, but on this view, any effective political collectivity can become the basis for class formation. It is a view, as we indicate in Chapter 3, that has been challenged on both theoretical and empirical grounds. For Hindess (1987; 1992), for example, broad socioeconomic categories cannot be understood to 'act' in any meaningful sense. Collective political action can only be an aggregation of individual action. He also questions the associated notion that class interests are objectively given to persons occupying class positions, thus providing common grounds for collective action. Both such notions, he argues, must figure in an allegorical rather than a genuinely theoretical model of politics.

There have also been empirical challenges to this view of class actors that focus on the declining importance of labour movements and 'working-class action' in advanced societies. The contributors to Maheu (1994) outline the increasing salience of new collective actors that are transfunctional, attracting support from diffuse social categories based on locality, gender, ethnicity and lifestyle. Their membership is transient and fluid, and their organizational structure is decentralized, informal and polymorphous (also see Feher and Heller 1983; Cohen 1985; Offe 1985; Pakulski 1993a). These collectivities experience a tension between expanding spheres of human autonomy in civil society and growing administrative regulation inherent in the logic of late capitalist developments. Such tension cannot be reduced to economically based class conflict. Rather, it is generated by malintegration at the interface between the economic, political-administrative and normative subsystems.

For Dalton, Kuechler and Burklin (1990) the central actors animating the new politics are 'new social movements'.[5] These new movements may be understood as being constituted by generational divisions (Inglehart 1990; Abramson and Inglehart 1992), status blocs and 'life politics' (Turner 1988; Giddens 1991) and 'civil society' (Cohen 1985; Cohen and Arato 1992). They include movements focusing on such issues as ecology, peace, civil rights and racial equality, feminism, gay rights, indigenous land rights, democratic participation, rights to life, ethnic and national independence, and opposition to postcolonial immigration. None of these issues can successfully be linked to class repertoires that focus on working conditions, welfare provision and market relations.

One defensive response to the disparity between class schemes and new politics is the old trick of theorizing new classes (see Chapter 3). Eder (1993; 1994), for example, sees new politics, including the new social movements, as an attempt by the 'new middle classes' to displace the industrial proletariat as the main source of challenges to the *status quo*. He admits that the conflict which this new class articulates is quite different from industrial class conflict because it focuses on the tension between economy and ecology, and the legitimacy of cultural identities. However, he insists that such conflict has a class character not only because it engages class-specific constituencies, but also because it cannot be resolved other than by general systemic change, 'because there is no other solution to this antagonism than by structural changes in the distribution of power' (1994: 42).

The problematic nature of such theoretical constructs should be clear in the light of both Hindess' critique (1987; see above) and the received wisdom of the sociology of knowledge. The contradiction between the assumed social coherence of the 'class actor' and its capacity to act in a consistent class-related manner is highly problematic. It is only movement organizations and their elites that can be considered as political actors. The relationship between such actors and broader social entities, such as classes, is entirely problematic, especially in so far as the non-productive, non-economic focus of the new political issues makes class attributions of any type highly dubious. In fact, the members of all classes must share an interest in environmental prudence. The proposition about the allegedly insoluble nature of the new conflicts over ecology and identity is equally problematic. The successful absorption of ecological principles within capitalist productive practices (see Papadakis 1994) contradicts Eder's view. So also does the apparent proliferation of identities in liberal-democratic societies. The latter do not generate the level of tension and volatility that the notion of class conflict would seem to imply. Lastly, 'new-class' arguments that theorize new-class actors verge on circularity. If we were to accept that classes must be articulated through collective action, then almost any type of collective political endeavour must, *ipso facto*, have a class character. This brings the class interpretation of politics dangerously close to a tautology.

### Post-ideological values

Liberalism, conservatism and socialism crystallized in the nineteenth century. Socialism, in particular, was the ideological child of industrial class conflict, but liberalism and conservatism were also reformulated in response to the socialist challenge. Although national politics relied heavily on ideological constructs, imagined communities of class were even more reliant on them, because of their increasing internal heterogeneity. The appropriation of the major political ideologies by national classes occurred, as is indicated above, via the class parties. Parties and unions defined class issues and formulated general strategies that were then used in political appeals. Supporters of these ideological packages could thus define themselves in class terms. They were now constituted as social classes not so much by working conditions and commonalities of fate, but by shared organizational loyalties and ideological commitments.[6] This also resulted in the articulation of popular class discourses, class identities and the strengthening of a left–right polarity in political attitudes (Parkin 1972).

This ideological articulation of classes is now crumbling, especially on the left. A survey of the socialist parties by Lipset (1991) reveals a 'consistent abandonment of social welfare state/distributive issues' and of traditional socialist strategies. As *The Economist* (11 June 1994) notes: 'Today's socialist parties have all but abandoned many of their old policies. By the end of the 1980s, most of Europe's left-of-centre parties already advocated (albeit grudgingly) slimmer government, lower taxes and privatization – measures to which they were once bitterly opposed. Where parties called "socialist" are doing better, it is partly because they no longer espouse socialism.' This is doubtless much to do with the collapse of Soviet communism and a concomitant global shift to marketized strategies of economic growth. Throughout the early 1990s the egalitarian-étatist principles and strategies that formed the backbone of socialism have been abandoned by most parties of the left. The most ideologically committed organizations, such as the communist parties of Italy and France, collapsed and could be revived only by employing pseudonyms and by reining in ideological commitments. Such developments are confirmed by surveys of social-democratic parties in Europe by Kitchelt and Hellmans (1990) and Kitchelt (1994).

However, it is not merely socialism that is decomposing but the fundamental and underlying ideological polarities of left and right, socialism and liberalism, that we have come to associate with industrial capitalism. The consistency of these polarities has been undermined by the emergence of unaligned issues, new dimensions of politics, and the mobilization of ideological *mélanges*, such as those of American new fiscal populists, the Western European left libertarians and the Northern European progressivists. The emergence of civil rights concerns, lifestyle politics, consumer choice, ecological prudence, and feminist concerns has outdistanced the inclusive capacities of the old ideologies. Despite such desperate attempts at accommodation as the 'green left', the new concerns are splitting and overshadowing the old class allegiances. The old left–right continuum is differentiating into a multidimensional ideological-political space. Inglehart (1991), Offe (1985), Dalton et al. (1990) and Poguntke (1993) each argue that left–right is now transsected by an old–new dimension. Kitchelt (1990; 1994) describes it as a libertarian–authoritarian dimension. In a more elaborate version (1994: 27), he charts ideological-political orientations along three axes: socialist–capitalist, libertarian–authoritarian and left–right, to yield six major clusters. The social referents of these clusters, it must be stressed again, can no longer be described in class terms (see also Offe 1985; Dalton et al. 1990; Poguntke 1993).

Such mixed ideologies as new fiscal populism that embrace liberal-leftist social attitudes but oppose economic egalitarianism, collectivism and heavy welfare spending, present a major difficulty for class analysis.[7] Such analysis normally resorts either to linking the new configurations with yet another version of the usefully nebulous middle class or to theorizing an altogether new class, which comes out of nowhere but can promptly be customized to fit the newly discovered ideological syndrome (see e.g. Eder 1994; Eckersley 1990).

The ideological decomposition of the left can be viewed as part of a general 'crisis of socialism' (Held 1992) whose moral implications transcend the party-political dimension. Socialism is in a crisis because it suffers from a fatal flaw. It allies itself too closely with class and with non-democratic politics, thus embracing an ultimately fatal étatist egalitarianism that is insensitive to libertarian concerns.[8] The revival of democratic aspirations associated with the 'third wave of democratization' (Huntington 1991) has placed socialist ideology in a politically ambiguous position *vis-à-vis* global democratic and libertarian trends. The upsurge in libertarianism and the rediscovery of market efficiency put socialism on the defensive. It must retreat from a commitment to progress to a conservative stance that alienates it from the new ideological streams of libertarianism, ecologism, feminism, and neo-communitarianism.

## Post-communist politics

These processes are not confined to Western Europe and North America. The post-communist societies of Eastern Europe and Russia offer no evidence of the revival of class politics that was expected by many political observers. The reintroduction of the market and private property failed to generate a class consciousness anything like that encountered in industrial Europe at the turn of the century. With the single exception of the Polish Peasant Party (PSL), the class credentials of which must anyway be in doubt,[9] no major party in post-communist Europe is connecting itself with class constituencies or embracing typical class issues. In particular, there is no sign of a revival of the 'working-class politics' typical of the industrial era.

We can try to explain this as a peculiarity of post-communism that reflects the discreditation of the class idiom under communist rule and the overpowering strength of nationalist revivalism. Whatever the reason, post-communist politics cannot be usefully analysed using the class paradigm. Class location has little impact on political preferences and these preferences do not express either class issue repertoires or class ideological packages. The major political forces, especially the organized parties, do not embrace class identities, issues or discourses. The politics of Eastern Europe is dominated by national and ethnic cleavages, religious and regional divisions, issues related to strategies of economic reform, and relationships with the West, especially the European Union (see Zagorski and Kelley 1994).[10]

## Conclusion

Nearly a decade ago, Hindess asked: 'How far . . . does class analysis take us in the understanding of political institutions, ideologies and conflicts?' (1987: 20). The answer for him, even then, was 'not very far'. Today, that answer must be even more circumscribed. Class analysis offers remarkably little by way of intellectual returns that can unlock the secrets of politics and explain the dynamics of change. As we might expect, practitioners of politics are realizing this more quickly than are academic analysts. No serious political organization in any advanced society, including post-communist societies, espouses class-oriented programmes and ideologies. Class appeals and class rhetoric are on the wane even among the true believers of the far left.

Class analysis, even in its most open and humble articulation, cannot cope with the diversity of new politics and the variety of new social actors. The most damning evidence of the declining relevance of class comes from recent, historically influential, political events: the ascendancy of the Asian tiger economies, the East European revolutions and European unification. None of these involves class groupings, class identities, class conflicts or class ideologies. Class theory and analysis are proving impotent in undertaking the very task for which they were originally constructed: discovering the 'rules of motion' of society and manipulating them to improve the human condition.

With the decline of class politics and the withering away of class ideologies the last vestiges of class society are disappearing. It completes the radical dissolution of class, a process that we have now charted through its socioeconomic, social-reproductive, sociocultural and sociopolitical dimensions. We are witnessing the death of class society as a historical formation. However, the dissolution of class is by no means the 'end of history' (cf. Fukuyama 1992). Social divisions will persist even if social conflicts follow different patterns and polarities. Nor is this the end of capitalism as a system of generalized commodity production guided by rationalized capital accounting. But emerging post-class capitalism defies all the predictions of class theory, socialist criticism and liberal apologia. It is neither class divided nor egalitarian and harmonious. Since it is too early to discern its shape with any degree of certainty, we can only speculate about post-class society and take the risk that our own vision of the future will share the fate of its much more illustrious predecessors. Our remaining task is to communicate that vision.

## Notes

1 Hindess distinguishes in political analysis between classes as aspects of the social structure 'that may have some bearing on the political attitudes or values of voters and the behaviour of political parties' (1987: 1) and as 'major social forces that arise out of fundamental structural

features of society and . . . are supposed to have significant and wide-ranging social and political consequences' (1987: 2).

2 The decline varies in its speed of development, but is most rapid in countries with traditionally high unionism. For example, in Australia, the proportion of unionized employees fell from over 50 per cent in the mid 1970s to 35 per cent in the mid 1990s (data from Australian Bureau of Statistics 1995). Among OECD countries only Sweden and Finland did not experience de-unionization in the 1980s (Western 1995).

3 By the mid 1990s the British Conservative Party appeared to be fractionalizing between moderates of the middle ground, on one hand, and economic rationalists and 'Eurosceptics' whose ideology was similar to that of the progress parties of continental Europe, on the other. The prospect of electoral defeat at the hands of a revitalized, libertarian/post-materialist Labour Party may well drive the Tories entirely towards a post-materialism of the right.

4 Mann identifies four elements of class consciousness: identity, opposition, totality and alternative (see 1993: 27–35). For the broader 'class-consciousness debate' see Graetz (1983; 1986), Gorz (1982), Robertson (1984), Franklin (1985), Marshall et al. (1988) and Evans (1992).

5 Neither new forms of activism nor new issues can be trimmed into the old class schemes. Attempts to construct new-class schemes capable of containing these aspects of new politics are unconvincing and *ad hoc* (e.g. Eckersley 1989; Eder 1993). They are arbitrary in tailoring new classes to fit the new concerns and ignore evidence on the social heterogeneity of new-issue supporters. See also Dalton (1988), Gibbins (1989) and Pakulski (1993a).

6 The best known versions of this class-party/ideology alignment can be found in Lipset (1960) and Parkin (1972). The latter places the issue of inequality and state redistribution at the centre of class politics. Lipset adds that smaller and less consistent packages were developed for agrarian classes, as well as for sections of the population mobilized in non-class terms (religious, regional, ethnic, etc.). He also interprets mass social movements (fascist, communist, Peronist, etc.) in class terms.

7 Unaligned issues primarily include green, anti-nuclear, feminist and civil-libertarian concerns. One of the key such issues in Britain is the European Union. It became the key political issue in the political debates of the mid 1990s. The new fiscal populism is analysed by Clark and Ferguson (1983), Dalton (1988) and Clark et al. (1993).

8 By implication, in Eastern Europe, the terms 'socialism', 'class ideology' and 'class analysis' have acquired some dark connotations. They evoke images of Stalinist and Maoist political persecution. In the West, socialism connotes an étatism that is often insensitive to libertarian concerns and an egalitarianism that is often insensitive to meritocratic principles and considerations of efficiency.

9 Peasants in Poland, it can be argued, approximate an estate rather than a class. The key elements of the PSL's programme include traditionalism, nationalism and Catholicism.

10 The only class schemes that can find some applicability in East European political analysis are those derived from Bourdieu's analyses of cultural capital (e.g. Szelenyi and Szelenyi 1993).

# 8

# Life after Class

To conclude, we begin with a parable. In the early nineteenth century a scholar observes the emergence and consolidation of industrial capitalism. She has spent a lifetime seeking to understand the quasi-feudal relationships between lord and peasant, merchant and artisan. She is devoted to, even occasionally ideologically fixated on, old concepts and categories. After all, she thinks, anyone who believes that inequality is divinely ordained needs to be set straight. So she has no choice but to conceptualize capitalists and workers as 'new estates'. Indeed, she will argue that there is a considerable continuity in social forms, that the bourgeoisie is really the continuation of the feudal aristocracy.[1] She can be comforted by her theoretical brilliance in multiplying these 'new estates' on an ever more complex 'estate map' until she has created perhaps a dozen of them. Her view is confirmed empirically because estates, old and new, can explain small proportions of behaviours and attitudes. The concept of class never enters the social-scientific vocabulary.

Although they fell victim to some errors, those brilliant theorists of class, Marx and Weber, did not insist on such retrospection. They recognized that within the continuous flow of history an acute social observer could detect fundamental shifts in social arrangements. They understood that they were the inhabitants of an entirely new order of stratification that had succeeded feudalism, and they were hungry to conceptualize the new forms of social inequality that were emerging. Fortunately, a concept was readily to hand because the term 'class' had already entered popular discourse:

> Development of *class* in its modern social sense, with relatively fixed names for particular classes . . . belongs essentially to the period between 1720 and 1840, which is also the period of the Industrial Revolution and its decisive reorganization of society . . . The crucial context for this development is the alternative vocabulary for social divisions, and it is a fact that until [the early eighteenth century] and residually well into [the nineteenth] and even [the twentieth century], the most common words were *rank* and *order*, while *estate* and *degree* were still more common than *class*. In virtually all contexts where we would now say *class* these other words were standard . . . The essential history of the introduction of *class* as a word which would supersede older names for social divisions, relates to the increasing consciousness that social position is made rather than merely inherited. (Williams 1983: 61, original emphases, some punctuation deleted)

Although we have already done so from time to time in this book, especially towards the end of each of the preceding four chapters, this conclusion begins to consolidate our conceptualization of new patterns of social inequality, division and conflict. In one sense this possibility is beyond the scope of a book that seeks primarily to indicate the end of a historical and theoretical era rather than to outline a new one. We do not aspire to fill the shoes of Weber or Marx, but even if we did, our difficulties would be compounded by the fact that the popular lexicon contains no handy term that we can happily appropriate and refine. Perhaps this is why the concept of class drags on, wearily seeking to cloak new formations in its ancient and tattered garments. So the alternative possibility of conceptual adaptation needs to be addressed one last time before we make our proposal.

### Old concepts and new tricks

We are often tempted to stretch old concepts in order to baptize new social forms. We tend intellectually to domesticate the new and 'foreign' as a sub-category of the old and familiar. New-class schemes are a primary example of attempts to recycle conceptual packaging in this way. In repackaging, however, we pay the price of declining precision in our conceptual tools and a theoretical incapacity to explain. 'Class', like 'bureaucracy' or 'ideology', ends up meaning everything and nothing. Conceptual stretch, as Sartori (1970) says, paralyses research and stifles theorizing, preventing us from appreciating the new.

The recycled version of class resembles the cars in a well-known 'Radio Erevan' joke:

Q:   Is it true that they give away cars on Red Square in Moscow?
A:   Yes, in principle. However, not Red Square in Moscow but Red Square in Pskov . . . and not cars but bicycles . . . and, well, they do not exactly give them away, they actually steal them.

So, if one asks whether there are classes in contemporary society, the class analyst's answer is:

Yes, in principle there are two or three classes. Well, not actually two but somewhere between seven and twelve, and the number is increasing. And they are generated not by production or property relations, but mainly by working conditions, authority relations, credentials, income and skills. Of course, if you follow Bourdieu, they can be based on any form of cultural, social, symbolic, or biological difference, in fact, almost anything you fancy. Naturally, they are not realized in social action or closure or conflict or exploitation. Fluid boundaries, weakening inheritance of position, and growing career mobility are merely evidence of a shift in the structure and configuration of classes and not of their disappearance. Of course, classes are not actually important to people, and they are not the basis for their self-conception. And class parties, class-based worker and employer groups, class issues and class struggle have all mainly disappeared as well. But there are certainly classes, and we should certainly analyse their effects.

There is a second, even more self-delusional, possible answer. It is reminiscent of the shopkeeper's lines in the famous 'dead parrot' comedy sketch from 'Monty Python's Flying Circus'. Here a customer goes into a pet shop to complain that the 'Norwegian Blue' parrot that he has been sold is dead. 'Ah no!', explains the pet shop owner, 'it's only asleep.' The customer tries to indicate the obvious, pointing out that 'this parrot has passed away, it has gone to meet its maker, it is deceased, extinct, stuffed' etc. 'No', says the shopkeeper, 'if you look carefully, you'll see that it's just resting.' 'Resting!', screeches the customer, 'Resting! The bloody thing's been nailed to its perch!' Similarly the class theorist says: 'You can't be looking hard enough. You must look past appearances. What you see as non-class actors, issues and conflicts, are *really* class phenomena in disguise or new classes in embryonic form. If you look carefully, you will see that although class appears to be dead it is actually just resting. It is only a matter of hammering away at the theory and then we can nail it down.'

This 'look harder' response is most common among neo-Marxists. By comparison, neo-Weberians tend to limit their aspirations for the concept. For them 'social class' is scarcely distinguishable from an occupational category. So the number of social classes swells, and class maps converge with maps of the occupational hierarchy. Links with culture, identity and politics are relaxed, and class is not expected to explain exploitation and poverty, social distance, community formation or political conflict. This soft or *gesellschaftlich* version of class (Holton and Turner 1994) is much easier to defend, but we might want to ask how much intellectual return an investment in such an approach can yield. A 'class theory' stripped of all its classical elements can scarcely be worth calling a theory of class. Likewise, a minimalist class analysis that is hesitant about granting class a privileged status might more happily be called a stratification analysis. Even then we might want to ask whether what such an analysis can offer is worth knowing. If it can explain only, say, 17 per cent of income variation, 10 per cent of voting behaviour, and almost nothing else of interest, it is hardly doing enough to be regarded as central. If the proof of the class pudding is in the explanatory eating, perhaps the chef needs to be fired.

However, the key incapacity of class in turning new tricks is its failure to account for configurations and developments that have emerged at the end of the twentieth century. A short list can show where this explanatory deficiency is particularly apparent:

- changes in the structure of work and employment, especially post-Fordist forms of flexible specialization;
- the globalization of market relations and the rapid rise of Asian tiger economies and dragon societies;
- the original growth and the current decomposition of the welfare state;
- partisan dealignment and the demise of corporatist politics; and
- changing forms of identification and political action, in particular the rising tide of new politics.

If further confirmation of our thesis is required, it can be noted that the class paradigm has remarkably little to offer in explaining the key social and political events of the century, including:

- the rise and the subsequent collapse of fascist regimes;
- the formation of Soviet-type societies;

- decolonization and postcolonial formations;
- the 'velvet revolutions' and the collapse of communism; and
- widespread democratization and marketization.

Class is even less capable of explaining immediate conflicts and global patterns of change. Class simply does not fit the wars and conflicts of the Middle East, the rise of Islamic fundamentalism, the Bosnian conflict, or the religious and ethnic conflicts on the Indian subcontinent. National, religious, local, regional, ethnic, gender, racial and sexual-preference identities are much more important. It is true that these non-class identities have always been present, and were occasionally dominant in the past. But during the nineteenth and early twentieth centuries the social question of class was at the centre of the political agenda, class imagery was strong and clear, and class identification was firm, especially among the workers. None of these is true today. The intellectual armoury of class theory is about as useful for the contemporary social and political scene as a cavalry brigade in a tank battle.

Our argument might be viewed as both confused and unfair: confused because it mixes levels of analysis, and questions of heuristic value, theoretical utility, empirical validity and political usefulness that are normally considered separately; unfair, because it compounds a range of class constructs that vary in their sophistication and accuracy. This accusation of unfairness can easily be dispatched by reference to the range of class concepts and positions covered in this book. We deliberately seek to expose the vacuity of even the most tentative of class claims, on the view that the grandiose claims of class theory must be even less supportable.

An accusation of confusion can be answered by reference to the classical tradition. We are making a global assessment of intellectual returns, of the fit of the class paradigm with contemporary developments in social structure, culture and politics. The validity of class theory for Marx and Weber did not hinge upon it explaining a small fraction of income or voting variation. It is merely fideistic, to use Gramsci's term, to take the view that the class structure forms the dominant power grid, and is the key mechanism in structuring life chances, but that we cannot see it clearly because class formation or structuration is impaired. If structures do not manifest themselves and if there is no evidence that they are operational, then there is little point in clinging to the concepts that reference them. Most sociologists will accept that structures are historical, that they are formed and then they inevitably expire. Let class also rest in peace, respected and honoured, but mainly relevant to history.

## Post-class society

An immediate expectation might be that we will now propose that history is phasing into a utopian classless society that is egalitarian and harmonious. In fact, we want to propose a version of Ossowski's notion (1963) of non-egalitarian classlessness. However, the Ossowski proposal was developed to describe the steep but continuous non-discrete social hierarchies in the

American and Soviet societies of the 1950s, and the emerging formation clearly is not taking on this shape. An alternative temptation is to describe the emerging formation simply as 'non-class' or 'post-class' in order to avoid the confusing interference of the semantic halos that such popular concepts as classlessness carry. Such a society might be theorized as neither egalitarian, nor harmonious. Its structure would be complex and its hierarchies discrete, yet in a different way from the structure and hierarchies of the typical class societies of the industrial era. But such a formulation would be an easy fix, lacking both courage and specificity. It would leave us in the position of arguing that there was nothing after class. We would rather insist that social inequality and conflict will remain a central issue in any future society.

Instead, we return to the historical model that we introduced in Chapter 1, which proposes that the stratification system is moving into a culturalist or *status-conventional* phase. Figure 8.1 is a kind of master diagram that summarizes the substantive argument of this book. It shows that the historical transformation from economic-class society to organized-class society to status-conventional society is not merely an issue of stratification but one of wide-ranging societal transformation. The argument offered here is therefore part of the general theoretical effort that focuses on post-industrialization (Bell 1976), detraditionalization (Beck 1992; Giddens 1991), postmodernization (Crook et al. 1992; Harvey 1989; Lyotard 1984) societal disorganization (Lash and Urry 1987; 1994; Offe 1985) and globalization (Featherstone 1990; Robertson 1992; Waters 1995a).

The emerging stratificational picture is represented in such work as that of Kornblum (1974) on Chicago steelworkers that reveals anything but structural and cultural homogeneity. He shows that dense social networks of primary groups cross-cut old class boundaries and establish salient non-class divisions along regional-residential, ethnic, racial and status lines. These are the main focuses for identity formation and local politics. A similiar picture is emerging from British studies of communities (e.g. Pahl and Wallace 1985; Williams 1975), political behaviour (e.g. Rose and McAllister 1985; Dunleavy and Husbands 1985) and consumption (Saunders 1990; Featherstone 1991). Here, gender divisions, market fragmentation, housing and consumption-sector cleavages, and state dependency are the main influences on political identities and voting patterns.

Equally Phizacklea's study (1990) of the fashion industry in Britain reveals deep divisions created by combinations of economic inequality, race, gender and locality. She argues that a dual labour market is generated in the garment industry by an intersection between organizational factors (relations between large corporations and small subcontractors), racial and ethnic divisions and a gendered-labour pattern exerted by domestic norms and relations. Recession and cheap imports have pushed 'ethnic entrepreneurs', mainly of Asian extraction, into family businesses that rely on low-paid female labour. These women workers are vulnerable to exploitative conditions by dint of gendered social norms, i.e. notions of 'women's work', modes of migration that often subject female dependants to indebtedness,

**System level**

| Axial principle | World | Society | Politics | Economy | Community | Domesticity | Gender | Individual |
|---|---|---|---|---|---|---|---|---|
| Economic class | Colonialism | *Laissez-faire* state | Plutocratic and revolutionary parties | Owner capitalism | Property order | Reproduction site | Patriarchy | Worker |
| Organized class | Imperialism | Corporatism | Mass parties | Fordism | Occupational order | Consumption sphere | Reorganized patriarchy (viriarchy) | Citizen |
| Conventional status | Globalization | Nation | Niche parties | Flexible specialization | Value order | Significant lifeworld | Hyperdiff-erentiation | Human |

Figure 8.1 *The registration of stratification orders through system levels*

and social discrimination that restricts their employment options. Such studies of multiple segmentation at the local level are becoming increasingly common.

This multiple socioeconomic and sociocultural fragmentation is very distant from the kind of class differentiation identified by Lockwood (1958) or Goldthorpe et al. (1969) a generation earlier. They proposed differentiated sub-types of working-class and lower-middle-class orientation that created locally concentrated and culturally homogeneous class communities. By contrast contemporary studies emphasize cultural diversity, especially among younger people. According to Willis (1990), this is the consequence not only of the decline in class-communal ties, but also of a drift away from the institutions that have engendered class identities in the past including community associations, trade unions, and schools. The mass unemployment of the 1980s that placed many young people beyond the class-formational impact of work situation and increasingly under the individualizing effects of commercialized consumer culture also contributed to the process.

We can now theorize this transformation more formally. Chapter 1 disaggregates class theory into four propositions and these propositions can then be used to explain the substantive aspects of class (see Figure 1.1). We can follow a similar procedure in theorizing status-conventional society. The four propositions that class theory makes are: economism; groupness; behavioural linkage; and transformative capacity. A status-conventional theory would offer the following parallel propositions:

- The proposition of *culturalism*. Status-conventional stratification is primarily a cultural phenomenon. It is based on subscription to lifestyles that form around consumption patterns, information flows, cognitive agreements, aesthetic preferences and value commitments. Material and power phenomena are reducible to these symbolically manifested lifestyle and value phenomena.

- The proposition of *fragmentation*. Conventional statuses, like classes, are real phenomena. However they consist of a virtually infinite overlap of associations and identifications that are shifting and unstable. Status-conventional society is a fluid matrix of fragile formations that cycle and multiply within a globalized field.

- The proposition of *autonomization*. The subjective orientation and behaviour of any individual or aggregate of individuals are very difficult to predict by virtue of stratificational location. There is no central cleavage or single dimension along which preferences can be ordered. Such attributes as political preference, access to educational opportunity, patterns of marriage and income are self-referential rather than externally constrained.

- The proposition of *resignification* based on subjective interests. The stratification process is continuously fluid. Its openness allows a constant respecification and invention of preferences and symbolic dimensions that provide for continuous regeneration. The source of novelty is a process of restless subjective choice that seeks to gratify churning and unrepressed emotions that include anxiety and aggression as well as desire.

Figure 8.2 outlines the substantive status-conventional parallels to Figure 1.1. It shows that the propositions can specify the possible phenomena that sociologists might seek to theorize and analyse in the emerging configuration. The starting point is the top left cell, which indicates that the objective-generative phenomena in which we should be interested are 'symbolic dimensions'. By these we mean socially subscribed scales or networks of symbols that can provide focuses for identification and preference. They are broadly similar to the phenomena that Appadurai (1990) refers to as 'scapes' (ethnoscapes, theoscapes, financescapes etc.) in his analysis of cultural globalization. These symbolic dimensions include some of the 'economic' phenomena traditionally associated with class, including socioeconomic status, but in a symbolicized form. So 'occupation' is now critical not in terms of its capacity to put one in a relationship of exploitation but because it is a badge of status, an indicator of one's importance and of one's capacity to consume. Alongside these we can place dimensions of ascribed status membership that have now become value infused, symbolicized and reflexive (ethnicity, religion, education, race, gender and sexual preference), plus consumption statuses (yuppie, trekkie, hacker, clothes-horse, punk, gothic, jogger, opera buff etc.) and value-commitment statuses (feminist, environmentalist, Zionist, redneck, right-to-lifer etc.). Identity is thus not linked either to property or to organizational position. Under conditions of advanced affluence, styles of consumption and commitment become socially salient as markers and delimiters.

The proposition of culturalism specifies that these symbolic dimensions will compete with each other in the field of social structure. This will produce the phenomenon of multiple status cleavages. The stratificational categories

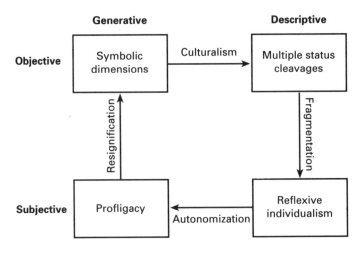

Figure 8.2 *Aspects of a sociology of status-conventional society*

of status-conventional society constitute a complex mosaic of taste subcultures, 'new associations', civic initiatives, ethnic and religious revolutionary groups, generational cohorts, community action groups, new social movements, gangs, alternative lifestyle colonies, alternative production organizations, educational alumni, racial brotherhoods, gender sisterhoods, tax rebels, fundamentalist and revivalist religious movements, internet discussion groups, purchasing co-ops, professional associations, and so on. Many are ephemeral, some are continuous and stable.

A key feature of these multiple status cleavages is that because they are specialized and intersecting, membership in any one does not necessarily contradict membership in any other. From the subjective point of view the proposition of fragmentation ensures that individuals apprehend the stratification system as a status bazaar. Individuals can operate simultaneously as members of several status groups and have the potential to be members of any others. Their identities are reflexively self-composed as they move between status adherences. However, the fact of a status market does not imply an absolute voluntarism, and indeed the freedoms in most cases are relevant to exit from status groups rather than entry. Closure processes remain effective in status-conventional society.

The proposition of autonomization nevertheless allows individuals to be profligate in their behaviour. They will tend to spend their resources of time, energy, money, influence, and power in the pursuit of symbolic attachments that tend to advance the interests, identities, values and commitments to which they subscribe and aspire. The very act of doing this will, by the proposition of resignification, tend to redefine and reorder the symbolic dimensions that reference the system. Indeed, a particular effect is the redefinition of some traditional status-membership dimensions, especially education, religion, and ethnicity, into a more ephemeral and conventional regime. So education becomes a marketplace for credentials, religion becomes a vehicle for handling this week's anxieties as one is born again and again and again, and ethnicity is something one rediscovers through community action and involvement.

We must stress one last time that we are not arguing for a decline in inequality and conflict but for a decline in *class* inequality and conflict. One last illustration can confirm the point. Chapter 4 shows that, even allowing for recent reversals, during the twentieth century household wealth has become more widely distributed. This is an indicator of the decomposition of class, as normally defined in relation to property. However, at the present time there is also an increasing inequality of income (*The Economist* 5 November 1994). This is not evidence of increasing class inequality but it is evidence of increasing inequality of sumptuary capacity and this links directly with the kind of status-conventional stratification that is theorized here. The income-poor so-called 'underclass' is not class defined but is rather status defined by the symbolizations attached to postcolonial migration, race, ethnicity, gender, age and pattern of family support. Exclusionary closure based on these status attributes consigns people to an 'underclass'. The stigmatization that attaches to the 'underclass' is a function not of its members' exploitation but of their incapacity to consume. An earlier generation of social scientists wrote of poverty as a culture (Lewis 1961; 1966; Valentine 1968). Perhaps it is time to do so once again.

All of this means that complexity is likely to increase. This calls for a theoretical stance that rejects any notion that there is a single conceptual or theoretical crowbar or even a magic word that can open the treasure cave of stratification, inequality and conflict. Contemporary sociology needs to be sensitive to and appreciative of diversity. It must be humble in the face of complexity and ready to accept contingency in relation to social attitudes and behaviours. It must not force a lively, engaging and ethically fraught reality into an inherited and stultifying conceptual strait-jacket. If it continues on its procrustean path it will lose its audience.

## Notes

1 For works that argue just such a case see Anderson (1964: 30), Mayer (1981), Moore (1973: 29–39) and Waters (1995b).

# References

Abercrombie N, S Hill and B Turner (1980) *The Dominant Ideology Thesis* London: Allen & Unwin.

Abercrombie N, S Hill and B Turner (1990) *Dominant Ideologies* London: Unwin Hyman.

Abercrombie N and B Turner (1978) 'The Dominant Ideology Thesis' *British Journal of Sociology* 29(2): 149–70; and in A Giddens and D Held (eds) *Classes, Power and Conflict* (1982) Berkeley: California UP: 396–414.

Abercrombie N and J Urry (1983) *Capital, Labour and the Middle Classes* London: Allen & Unwin.

Abramson P and R Inglehart (1992) 'Generational Replacement and Value Change in Eight West European Societies' *British Journal of Political Science* 22(2): 183–228.

Adamski W (1982) 'Structural and Generational Aspects of a Social Conflict' *Sisiphus* 3: 49–57.

Adorno T and M Horkheimer (1979) *The Dialectic of Enlightenment* (1944) London: Verso

Alford R (1963) *Party and Society: The Anglo-American Democracies* Chicago: Rand McNally.

Alt J (1976) 'Beyond Class: The Decline of Industrial Labor and Leisure' *Telos* 28: 55–80.

Althusser L (1977) *Lenin and Philosophy and Other Essays* London: New Left.

Amin S (1980) *Class and Nation* New York: Monthly Review.

Amsden A (1985) 'The State and Taiwan's Economic Development' in P Evans, D Rueschemeyer and T Skocpol (eds) *Bringing the State Back In* Cambridge: CUP: 78–106.

Anderson B (1983) *Imagined Communities* London: Verso.

Anderson P (1964) 'The Origins of the Present Crisis' *New Left Review* (23): 26–54.

Appadurai A (1990) 'Disjuncture and Difference in the Global Cultural Economy' in M Featherstone (ed.) *Global Culture* London: Sage: 295–310.

Arato A and E Gebhardt (1978) *The Essential Frankfurt School Reader* New York: Urizon.

Aron R (1968) *Progress and Disillusion* London: Pall Mall.

Aron R (1988) *Power, Modernity and Sociology* London: Edward Elgar.

Bachrach P and M Baratz (1963) 'Decisions and Non-Decisions' *American Political Science Review* 23: 632–42.

Baker K, R Dalton and K Hildebrandt (1981) *Germany Transformed: Political Culture and the New Politics* Cambridge: Harvard UP.

Baltzell D (1962) *An American Business Aristocracy* New York: Collier.

Baran P and P Sweezy (1966) *Monopoly Capital* New York: Monthly Review.

Barbalet J (1986) 'Limitations of Class Theory and the Disappearance of Status' *Sociology* 20(4): 557–75.

Barbalet J (1988) *Citizenship* Milton Keynes: Open UP.

Barber B (1959) 'Discussion of Papers' *Pacific Sociological Review* 2(1): 25–7.

Barker D and S Allen (1976) *Dependence and Exploitation in Work and Marriage* London: Longman.

Barrett M (1980) *Women's Oppression Today* London: Verso.

Baudrillard J (1988) *Selected Writings* Stanford: Stanford UP.

Bauman Z (1982) *Memories of Class* London: Routledge.

Baxter J (1991) 'The Class Location of Women' in J Baxter, M Emmison, J Western and M Western (eds) *Class Analysis and Contemporary Australia* Melbourne: Macmillan: 202–22.

Baxter J, M Emmison, J Western and M Western (eds) (1991) *Class Analysis and Contemporary Australia* Melbourne: Macmillan.

Beck U (1992) *Risk Society* London: Sage.

Bell C and H Newby (1971) *Conmmunity Studies* London: Allen & Unwin.

Bell D (1976) *The Coming of Post-Industrial Society* New York: Basic/Harper Torchbook (first published 1973).

Bell D (1979a) *The Cultural Contradictions of Capitalism* London: Heinemann.

Bell D (1979b) 'The New Class: A Muddled Concept' *Society* 25: 15–23.

Bell D (1988) *The End of Ideology* New York/Cambridge: Free Press/Harvard UP (first published 1960).

Berger P (1987) *The Capitalist Revolution* Aldershot: Wildwood.

Berle A and G Means (1967) *The Modern Corporation and Private Property* New York: Harcourt (first published 1932).

Birch A (1984) 'Overload, Ungovernability and De-Legitimation' *British Journal of Political Science* 14: 135–60.

Bishop M (1994) 'Corporate Governance' *The Economist* 29 January (supplement).

Blackburn R and M Mann (1975) 'Ideology in the Non-Skilled Working Class' in M Bulmer (ed.) *Working-Class Images of Society* London: Routledge: 131–60.

Blackburn R and M Mann (1979) *The Working Class in the Labour Market* London: Macmillan.

Blau P and O Duncan (1967) *The American Occupational Structure* New York: Wiley.

Blauner R (1964) *Alienation and Freedom* Chicago: Chicago UP.

Bottomore T (1994) *Elites and Society* London: Routledge (first published 1964).

Bourdieu P (1977) 'Cultural Reproduction and Social Reproduction' in J Karabel and A Halsey (eds) *Power and Ideology in Education* Oxford: OUP: 487–510.

Bourdieu P (1980) *Distinction: A Social Critique of the Judgement of Taste* London: Routledge.

Bourdieu P (1984) *Distinction* London: Routledge.

Bourdieu P (1994) *Language and Symbolic Power* Cambridge: Polity.

Bowles S and H Gintis (1976) *Schooling in Capitalist America* London: Routledge.

Braverman H (1974) *Labor and Monopoly Capital* New York: Monthly Review.

Brenner J and M Ramas (1984) 'Rethinking Women's Oppression' *New Left Review* 144: 33–71.

Britten N and A Heath (1983) 'Women, Men and Social Class' in E Gamarnikow (ed.) *Gender, Class and Work* London: Heinemann.

Broom L, F Jones, P McDonnell and T Williams (1980) *The Inheritance of Inequality* London: Routledge.

Burnham J (1941) *The Managerial Revolution* New York: Doubleday.

Campbell C (1987) *The Romantic Ethic and the Spirit of Modern Consumerism* Oxford: Blackwell.

Carchedi G (1975) 'On the Economic Identification of the New Middle Class' *Economy and Society* 4(1): 2–26.

Carr E (1964) *The Twenty Years' Crisis, 1919–1939* New York: Harper & Row (first published 1946).

Clark T and L Ferguson (1983) *City Money* New York: Columbia UP.

Clark T and S Lipset (1991) 'Are Social Classes Dying?' *International Sociology* 6(4): 397–410.

Clark T, S Lipset and M Rempel (1993) 'The Declining Political Significance of Social Class' *International Sociology* 8(3): 279–93.

Clegg S, P Boreham and G Dow (1986) *Class, Politics and the Economy* London: Routledge.

Cohen J (1982) *Class and Civil Society: The Limits of Marxian Critical Theory* Oxford: OUP.

Cohen J (1985) 'Strategy or Identity: New Theoretical Paradigms and Contemporary Social Movements' *Social Research* 52(4): 663–716.

Cohen J and A Arato (1992) *Civil Society and Political Theory* Cambridge: MITP.

Collins R (1979) *The Credential Society* Orlando: Academic.

Collins R (1986) *Weberian Sociological Theory* Cambridge: CUP.

Connell R (1977) *Ruling Class, Ruling Culture* Sydney: CUP.

Crompton R (1991) 'Three Varieties of Class Analysis: Comment on R.E. Pahl' *International Journal of Urban and Regional Research* 15: 108–13.

Crompton R (1993) *Class and Stratification* Cambridge: Polity.

Crompton R and G Jones (1984) *White-Collar Proletariat: Deskilling and Gender in the Clerical Labour Process* London: Macmillan.

Crook S, J Pakulski and M Waters (1992) *Postmodernization* London: Sage.

Crouch C (1983) 'The State, Capital and Liberal Democracy' in D Held (ed.) *States and Societies* New York: New York UP: 320–9.

Crouch C and A Pissorno (eds) (1978) *The Resurgence of Class Conflict in Western Europe since 1968* London: Macmillan.

Dahrendorf R (1959) *Class and Class Conflict in Industrial Society* Stanford: Stanford UP.

Dahrendorf R (1988) *The Modern Social Conflict* London: Weidenfeld.

Dalton R (1988) *Citizen Politics in Western Democracies* Chatham: Chatham.

Dalton R, M Kuechler and W Burklin (1990) 'The Challenge of New Movements' in R Dalton and M Kuechler (eds) *Challenging the Political Order: New Social and Political Movements in Western Democracies* Cambridge: Polity.

Davies A (1967) *Images of Class* Sydney: Sydney UP.

Davis K and W Moore (1945) 'Some Principles of Stratification' *American Sociological Review* 10: 242–9.

Delphy C (1984) *Close to Home* London: Hutchinson.

Dennis N, F Henriques and C Slaughter (1969) *Coal is our Life* London: Tavistock.

Djilas M (1957) *The New Class* London: Thames & Hudson.

Domhoff G (1967) *Who Rules America?* Englewood Cliffs: Prentice-Hall.

Duncan O (1959) 'Discussion of Paper' *Pacific Sociological Review* 2(1): 27–9.

Dunleavy P (1980) 'The Urban Basis of Political Alignment' *British Journal of Political Science* 9: 409–44.

Dunleavy P and C Husbands (1985) *British Democracy at the Crossroads* London: Allen & Unwin.

Eckersley R (1989) 'Green Politics and the New Class' *Political Studies* 37(2): 205–23.

Eckersley R (1990) *Environmentalism and Political Theory* London: UCLP.

Eckland B (1970) 'Theories of Mate Selection' *Eugenics Quarterly* 15: 62–83.

Eder K (1993) *The New Politics of Class* London: Sage.

Eder K (1994) 'The Middle Class Movements' in L Maheu and J Urry (eds) *Social Movements and Social Classes: The Future of Collective Action* London: Sage.

Edgell S (1980) *Middle Class Couples* London: Allen & Unwin.

Edgell S (1993) *Class* London: Routledge.

Ehrenreich B and J Ehrenreich (1979) 'The Professional-Managerial Class' in P. Walker (ed.) *Between Labor and Capital* Boston: South End: 5–45.

Eisenstein Z (ed.) (1979) *Capitalist Patriarchy and the Case for Socialist Feminism* New York: Monthly Review.

Eisenstein Z (1981) *The Radical Future of Liberal Feminism* Boston: Northeastern UP.

Elliott B and D McCrone (1982) *The City* London: Macmillan.

Emmison M and M Western (1990) 'Social Class and Social Identity: A Comment on Marshall et al.' *Sociology* 24(2): 241–53.

Engels F (1892) *The Condition of the Working Class in England in 1844* London: Hamden.

Ericksen E (1988) 'Estimating the Concentration of Wealth in America' *Public Opinion Quarterly* 52(2): 243–53.

Erikson R and J Goldthorpe (1992) *The Constant Flux* Oxford: Clarendon.

Erikson R, J Goldthorpe and L Portacarero (1982) 'Social Fluidity in Industrial Nations: England, France and Sweden' *British Journal of Sociology* 33(1): 1–34.

Esping-Andersen G (ed.) (1993) *Changing Classes* London: Sage.

Etzioni-Halévy E (1993) *The Elite Connection* London: Polity.

Evans G (1992) 'Is Britain a Class-Divided Society?' *Sociology* 26(2): 233–58.

Evans P, D Rueschemeyer and T Skocpol (eds) (1985) *Bringing the State Back In* Cambridge: CUP.

Featherman D, F Jones and R Hauser (1975) 'Assumptions of Mobility Research in the US: the Case of Occupational Status' *Social Science Research* 4: 329–60.

Featherman D and R Hauser (1978) *Opportunity and Change* New York: Academic Press.

Featherstone M (1990) *Global Culture* London: Sage.

Featherstone M (ed.) (1991) *Consumer Culture and Postmodernism* London: Sage.

Feher F and A Heller (1983) 'From Red to Green' *Telos* 4: 35–45.

Field L and J Higley (1980) *Elitism* London: Routledge.

Frank A (1971) *Capitalism and Underdevelopment in Latin America* Harmondsworth: Penguin.

Franklin M (1985) *The Decline of Class Voting in Britain* Oxford: OUP.

Franklin M, T Mackie and H Valen (1992) *Electoral Change: Responses to Evolving Social and Attitudinal Structures in Western Countries* Cambridge: CUP.

Frenkel B (1982) 'On the State of the State' in A Giddens and D Held (eds) *Classes, Power and Conflict* Berkeley: California UP: 257–73.

Fröbel F, J Heinrichs and O Kreye (1980) *The New International Division of Labour* Cambridge: CUP.

Fukuyama F (1992) *The End of History and the Last Man* London: Hamish Hamilton.

Galbraith J (1958) *The Affluent Society* Cambridge: Riverside.

Galbraith J (1967) *The New Industrial State* Harmondsworth: Penguin.

Gans H (1962) *The Urban Villagers* New York: Free Press.

Gibbins J (1989) 'Contemporary Political Culture: An Introduction' in J Gibbins (ed.) *Contemporary Political Culture* London: Sage: 1–30.

Giddens A (1973) *The Class Structure of Advanced Societies* London: Hutchinson.

Giddens A (1981) *A Contemporary Critique of Historical Materialism* London: Macmillan.

Giddens A (1985) *The Nation State and Violence* Cambridge: Polity.

Giddens A (1990) *The Consequences of Modernity* Cambridge: Polity.

Giddens A (1991) *Modernity and Self-Identity* Cambridge: Polity.

Glazer and Moynihan (1975)

Gold H (1982) *The Sociology of Urban Life* Englewood Cliffs: Prentice-Hall.

Golden M and J Pontusson (eds) (1992) *Bargaining for Change: Union Politics in North America and Europe* Ithaca: Cornell UP.

Goldfield M (1987) *The Decline of Organized Labor in the United States* Chicago: Chicago UP.

Goldthorpe J (1980) 'On the Service Class: Its Formation and Future' in A Giddens and G Mackenzie (eds) *Social Class and the Division of Labour* Cambridge: CUP: 162–85.

Goldthorpe J (1983) 'Women and Class Analysis' *Sociology* 17(4): 465–88.

Goldthorpe J (1987) *Social Mobility and Class Structure in Modern Britain* (1980) Oxford: Clarendon.

Goldthorpe J and K Hope (1974) *The Social Grading of Occupations: A New Approach and Scale* Oxford: Clarendon.

Goldthorpe J, D Lockwood, F Bechhofer and J Platt (1969) *The Affluent Worker in the Class Structure* Cambridge: CUP.

Goldthorpe J and G Marshall (1992) 'The Promising Future of Class Analysis: A Response to Recent Critiques' *Sociology* 26(3): 381–400.

Gordon D, R Edwards and M Reich (1982) *Segmented Work, Divided Workers* Cambridge: CUP.

Gorz A (1982) *Farewell to the Working Class* London: Pluto.

Gouldner A (1979) *The Future of the Intellectuals and the Rise of the New Class* New York: Seabury.

Graetz B (1983) 'Images of Class in Modern Society' *Sociology* 17(1): 79–96.

Graetz B (1986) 'Social Structure and Class Consciousness' *Australian and New Zealand Journal of Sociology* 22(1): 46–64.

Graetz B (1988) 'The Reproduction of Privilege in Australian Education' *British Journal of Sociology* 39(3): 358–76.

Graetz B (1992) 'Inequality and Political Activism in Australia' *Research in Inequality and Social Conflict* 2: 157–77.

Graetz B and I McAllister (1994) *Dimensions of Australian Society* (2nd edn) Melbourne: Macmillan.

Gramsci A (1977) *Selections from Political Writings (1910–20)* New York: International.

Grew R (1984) 'The 19th Century European State' in C Bright and S Harding (eds) *Statemaking and Social Movements* Ann Arbor: Michigan UP: 83–120.

Habermas J (1976) *Legitimation Crisis* Boston: Beacon.

Habermas J (1984) *The Theory of Communicative Action* (vol. 1) Boston: Beacon.

Habermas J (1987) *The Theory of Communicative Action* (vol. 2) Cambridge: Polity.

Hakim C (1988a) 'Self-Employment in Britain' *Work, Employment and Society* 2(4): 421–50.

Hakim C (1988b) 'Homeworking in Britain' in R Pahl (ed.) *On Work* Oxford: Blackwell: 609–32.

Halaby C (1993) 'Reply to Wright' *American Sociological Review* 58(1): 35–6.

Halaby C and D Weakliem (1993) 'Ownership and Authority in the Earnings Function' *American Sociological Review* 58(1): 16–30.

Halsey A, A Heath and J Ridge (1980) *Origins and Destinations* Oxford: Clarendon.

Hartmann H (1982) 'Capitalism, Patriarchy, and Job Segregation by Sex' in A Giddens and D Held (eds) *Classes, Power and Conflict* Berkeley: California UP: 446–69.

Harvey D (1989) *The Condition of Postmodernity* Oxford: Blackwell.

Hauser R (1978) 'A Structural Model of the Mobility Table' *Social Forces* 56: 919–53.

Heath A (1981) *Social Mobility* London: Fontana.

Heberle R (1959) 'Recovery of Class Theory' *Pacific Sociological Review* 2(1): 18–24.

Hechter M (1975) *Internal Colonialism* London Routledge.

Held D (1991) 'Democracy and the Global System' in D Held (ed.) *Political Theory Today* Cambridge: Polity: 197–235.

Held D (1992) *Political Theory and the Modern State* Cambridge: Polity.

Hibbs D (1978) 'On the Political Economy of Long-Run Trends in Strike Activity' *British Journal of Political Science* 8: 153–75.

Hindess B (1987) *Politics and Class Analysis* Oxford: Blackwell.

Hindess B (1992) 'Class and Politics' in M Hawkesworth and M Kogan (eds) *Encyclopedia of Government and Politics*: London: Routledge: 555–67.

Hoggart R (1958) *The Uses of Literacy* Harmondsworth: Penguin.

Holmwood J and A Stewart (1983) 'The Role of Contradictions in Modern Theories of Stratification' *Sociology* 17(2): 234–54.

Holmwood J and A Stewart (1991) *Explanation and Social Theory* Basingstoke: Macmillan.

Holter H (1984) 'Women's Research and Social Theory' in H Holter (ed.) *Patriarchy in a Welfare State* Oslo: Universitetsforlaget: 9–25.

Holton R and B Turner (1989) *Max Weber on Economy and Society* London: Routledge.

Holton R and B Turner (1994) 'Debate and Pseudo-Debate in Class Analysis: Some Unpromising Aspects of Goldthorpe and Marshall's Defence' *Sociology* 28(3): 799–804.

Hout M (1983) *Mobility Tables* Beverly Hills: Sage.

Hout M (1988) 'More Universalism, Less Structural Mobility' *American Journal of Sociology* 93: 1358–400.

Hout M, C Brooks and J Manza (1993) 'The Persistence of Classes in Post-Industrial Societies' *International Sociology* 8(3): 259–78.

Hout M, C Brooks and J Manza (1994) 'The Democratic Class Struggle in the United States, 1948–92' Bielefeld: XVII World Congress of Sociology (unpublished).

Huntington S (1991) *The Third Wave* Norman: Oklahoma UP.

Inglehart R (1977) *The Silent Revolution: Changing Values and Political Styles among Western Publics* Princeton: Princeton UP.

Inglehart R (1990) 'Values Ideology and Cognitive Mobilization in New Social Movements' in R Dalton and M Kuechler (eds) *Challenging the Political Order: New Social and Political Movements in Western Democracies* Cambridge: Polity: 43–66.

Inglehart R (1991) *Culture Shift in Advanced Industrial Society* Princeton: Princeton UP.

Jackson B (1968) *Working Class Community* London: Routledge.

Jencks C (1972) *Inequality* New York: Basic.

Jones F and P Davis (1986) *Models of Society: Class, Gender and Stratification in Australia and New Zealand* Sydney: Croom Helm.

Jones F and P Davis (1988) 'Class Structuration and Patterns of Social Closure in Australia and New Zealand' *Sociology* 22: 271–91.

Katzenstein P (1984) *Corporatism and Change: Austria, Switzerland and the Politics of Industry* Ithaca: Cornell UP.

Katzenstein P (1985) *Small States in World Markets: Industrial Policy in Europe* Ithaca: Cornell UP.

Keane J (ed.) (1988) *Civil Society and the State* London: Verso.

Kerckhoff A, R Campbell and I Winfield-Laird (1985) 'Social Mobility in Great Britain and the United States' *American Journal of Sociology* 91: 281–308.

Kern H and C Sabel (1992) 'Trade Unions and Decentralized Production' in M Regini (ed.) *The Future of Labour Movements* London: Sage: 217–49.

King R and J Raynor (1981) *The Middle Class* (2nd edn) London: Longman.

Kitchelt H (1989) *The Logic of Party Formation* Ithaca: Cornell UP.

Kitchelt H (1990) 'New Social Movements and the Decline in Party Organization' in R Dalton and M Kuechler (eds) *Challenging the Political Order: New Social and Political Movements in Western Democracies* Cambridge: Polity: 179–209.

Kitchelt H (1994) *The Transformation of European Social Democracy* Cambridge: CUP.

Kitchelt H and S Hellmans (1990) *Beyond the European Left: Political Action in Left-Libertarian Parties* Durham: Duke UP.

Konrad G and I Szelenyi (1979) *Intellectuals on the Road to Class Power* Brighton: Harvester.

Kornblum W (1974) *Blue Collar Community* Chicago: Chicago UP.

Korpi W (1983) *The Democratic Class Struggle* London: Routledge.

Kristol I (1979) *Two Cheers for Capitalism* New York: Basic.

Kurz K and W Müller (1987) 'Class Mobility in the Industrial World' *Annual Review of Sociology* 13: 417–42.

Larson M (1977) *The Rise of Professionalism* Berkeley: California UP.

Lash S (1990) *The Sociology of Postmodernity* London: Routledge.

Lash S and J Urry (1987) *The End of Organised Capitalism* Cambridge: Polity.

Lash S and J Urry (1994) *Economies of Signs and Space* London: Sage.

Lee D (1994) 'Class as a Social Fact' *Sociology* 28(2): 397–415.

Lembruch G and P Schmitter (eds) (1982) *Patterns of Corporatist Policy-Making* London: Sage.

Lengermann P and R Wallace (1985) *Gender in America* Englewood Cliffs: Prentice-Hall.

Lenin V (1939) *Imperialism* New York: International.

Lewis O (1961) *The Children of Sanchez* New York: Random House.

Lewis O (1966) *La Vida: A Puerto Rican Family in the Culture of Poverty* New York: Random House.

Lipset S (1960) *Political Man* New York: Doubleday.

Lipset S (1964) 'The Changing Class Structure of Contemporary European Politics' *Daedalus* 63: 26–78.

Lipset S (1981) *Political Man* (2nd edn) Baltimore: Johns Hopkins UP.

Lipset S (1991) 'No Third Way: A Comparative Perspective on the Left' in D Chirot (ed.) *The Crisis of Leninism and the Decline of the Left* London: Washington UP.

Lipset S and R Bendix (1959) *Social Mobility in Industrial Society* Berkeley: California UP.

Lipset S and S Rokkan (eds) (1967) *Party Systems and Voter Alignments* New York: Free.

Lipset S and H Zetterberg (1956) 'A Theory of Social Mobility' *Transactions of the Vth World Congress of Sociology*: 155–77.

Lockwood D (1958) *The Blackcoated Worker* London: Allen & Unwin.

Lockwood D (1966) 'Sources of Variation in Working Class Images of Society' *Sociological Review* 14(3): 244–67.

Lockwood D (1975) 'Sources of Variation in Working-Class Images of Society' in M Bulmer (ed.) *Working-Class Images of Society* London: Routledge: 16–31.

Lukács G (1968) *History and Class Consciousness* London: Merlin.

Lukes S (1974) *Power: A Radical View* London: Macmillan.

Lynd R and H Lynd (1959) *Middletown* New York: Harcourt & Brace.

Lyotard J (1984) *The Postmodern Condition* Manchester: Manchester UP.

McAdam D (1988) *Freedom Summer* Oxford: OUP.

McCracken G (1988) *Culture and Consumption* Bloomington: Indiana UP.

McGrew A (1992) 'Conceptualizing Global Politics' in A McGrew, P Lewis et al. *Global Politics* Cambridge: Polity: 1–29.

Maheu L (ed.) (1994) *Social Movements and Social Classes: The Future of Collective Action* London: Sage.

Mallet S (1975) *The New Working Class* Nottingham: Spokesman.

Mann M (1973) *Consciousness and Action among the Western Working Class* London: Macmillan.

Mann M (1986a) 'A Crisis in Stratification Theory' in R Crompton and M Mann (eds) *Gender and Stratification* Cambridge: Polity: 40–56.

Mann M (1986b) *The Sources of Social Power* (vol. 1) Cambridge: CUP.

Mann M (1987) 'Ruling Class Strategies and Citizenship' *Sociology* 21(3): 339–54.

Mann M (1993) *The Sources of Social Power* (vol. 2) Cambridge: CUP.

Mannheim K (1952) *Essays on the Sociology of Knowledge* London: Routledge.

Marcuse H (1964) *One-Dimensional Man* London: Routledge.

Marshall G (1991) 'In Defence of Class Analysis: A Comment on R E Pahl' *International Journal of Urban and Regional Research* 15: 114–18.

Marshall G, H Newby, D Rose and C Vogler (1988) *Social Class in Modern Britain* London: Hutchinson.

Marshall T (1950) *Citizenship and Social Class* Cambridge: CUP.

Martin B (1981) *A Sociology of Contemporary Cultural Change* Oxford: Blackwell.

Marx K (1962) 'Selections' in A Giddens and D Held (eds) *Classes, Power and Conflict* Berkeley: California UP.

Marx K (1977) *Karl Marx: Selected Writings* Oxford: OUP.

Marx K (1982) 'Selections' in A Giddens and D Held (eds) *Classes, Power and Conflict* Berkeley: UCP: 12–39.

Marx K and F Engels (1964) *The German Ideology* Moscow: International.

Mayer A (1981) *The Persistence of the Old Regime* New York: Pantheon.

Melucci A (1988) 'Social Movements and the Democratization of Everyday Life' in J Keane (ed.) *Civil Society and the State* London: Verso.

Merkl P (1980) 'The Nazis of the Abel Collection: Why They Joined the NSDAP' in S Larsen, B Hagtvet and J Myklebust (eds) *Who Were the Fascists?* Bergen: Universitetsforlaget: 268–82.

Michels R (1958) *Political Parties* Glencoe: Free Press (first published 1911).

Miliband R (1977) *Marxism and Politics* Oxford: OUP.

Miliband R (1989) *Divided Societies* Oxford: Clarendon.

Mills C (1956) *The Power Elite* Oxford: OUP.

Minkenberg M (1994) 'The New Right in France and Germany: A Comparative Analysis of Changing Cleavage Structures and New Configurations in European Politics' Berlin: XVI IPSA Conference (unpublished).

Minkenberg M and R Inglehart (1989) 'Neoconservatism and Value Change in the United States: Tendencies in the Mass Public of a Postindustrial Society' in J Gibbins (ed.) *Contemporary Political Culture* London: Sage: 81–109.

Moore B (1973) *The Social Origins of Dictatorship and Democracy* Harmondsworth: Penguin.

Mosca G (1939) *The Ruling Class* (1923) New York: McGraw-Hill.

Mullins P (1991) 'The Identification of Social Forces in Development as a General Problem in Sociology' *International Journal of Urban and Regional Research* 15:119–29.

Murray F (1988) 'The Decentralization of Production' in R Pahl (ed.) *On Work* Oxford: Blackwell: 258–78.

Naisbitt J (1993) *Global Paradox* London: Sidgwick & Jackson.

Newby H (1977) *The Deferential Worker* London: Allen Lane.

Nisbet R (1959) 'The Decline and Fall of Social Class' *Pacific Sociological Review* 2(1): 11–28.

O'Connor J (1973) *The Fiscal Crisis of the State* New York: St Martin's.

O'Connor J (1984) *Accumulation Crisis* Oxford: Blackwell.

OECD (1992) *Labour Force Statistics 1970–90* Paris: OECD.

Offe C (1984) *Contradictions of the Welfare State* London/Cambridge: Hutchinson/MITP.

Offe C (1985) 'New Social Movements: Challenging the Boundaries of Institutional Politics' *Social Research* 52(4): 817–68.

Offe C (1987) *Disorganised Capitalism* Cambridge: Polity/MITP.

Ossowski S (1963) *Class Structure in the Social Consciousness* London: Routledge (first published 1958).

Pahl R (1965) *Urbs in Rure* London: LSE.

Pahl R (1988) 'Historical Aspects of Work, Employment, Unemployment and the Sexual Division of Labour' in R Pahl (ed.) *On Work* Oxford: Blackwell: 7–20.

Pahl R (1989) 'Is the Emperor Naked?' *International Journal of Urban and Regional Research* 13: 709–20.

Pahl R (1991) 'R.E. Pahl Replies' *International Journal of Urban and Regional Research* 15: 127–9.

Pahl R and C Wallace (1985) 'Household Work Strategies in Economic Recession' in N Redclift and E Mingione (eds) *Beyond Employment* Oxford: Blackwell.

Pakulski J (1986) 'Leaders of the Solidarity Movement' *Sociology* 20(1): 64–81.

Pakulski J (1993a) 'Mass Social Movements and Social Class' *International Sociology* 8(2): 131–58.

Pakulski J (1993b) 'The Dying of Class or of Marxist Class Theory' *International Sociology* 8(3): 279–92.

Papadakis E (1994) *Politics and the Environment* Sydney: Allen & Unwin.

Pareto V (1935) *The Mind and Society* New York: Harcourt & Brace.

Parkin F (1968) *Middle Class Radicalism* Manchester: Manchester UP.

Parkin F (1972) *Class Inequality and Political Order* London: Paladin.

Parkin F (1979) *Marxism and Class Theory: A Bourgeois Critique* London: Tavistock.

Parry G (1969) *Political Elites* London: Allen & Unwin.

Parsons T (1954) *Essays in Sociological Theory* Glencoe: Free Press.

Parsons T (1959) 'The School Class as a Social System' *Harvard Educational Review* 29: 297–318.

Parsons T, E Shils, H Tolman, G Allport, C Kluckhohn, H Murray, R Sears, R Sheldon and S Stouffer (1951) *Toward a General Theory of Action* New York: Harper.

Perkin H (1989) *The Rise of Professional Society* London: Routledge.

Phizacklea A (1990) *Unpacking the Fashion Industry: Gender, Racism and Class in Production* London: Routledge.

Piore M and C Sabel (1984) *The Second Industrial Divide* New York: Basic.

Poguntke T (1993) *Alternative Politics: The German Green Party* Edinburgh: Edinburgh UP.

Pollert A (1988) 'The "Flexible Firm"' *Work, Employment and Society* 2(3): 281–316.

Poulantzas N (1974) *Classes in Contemporary Capitalism* London: Verso.

Poulantzas N (1978) *State, Power, Socialism* London: Verso.

Poulantzas N (1982) 'On Social Classes' in A Giddens and D Held (eds) *Classes, Power and Conflict* Berkeley: California UP: 101–12.

Prandy K (1990) 'The Revised Cambridge Scale of Occupations' *Sociology* 24(4): 629–55.

Przeworski A and J Sprague (1986) *Paper Stones: A History of Electoral Socialism* Chicago: Chicago UP.

Pusey M (1991) *Economic Rationalism in Canberra* Melbourne: CUP.

Raynor J (1969) *The Middle Class* London: Longman.

Regini M (ed.) (1992) *The Future of Labour Movements* London: Sage.

Rex J and S Tomlinson (1979) *Colonial Immigrants in a British City* London: Routledge.

Robertson R (1984) 'The Sociological Significance of Culture' *Theory, Culture and Society* 5: 3–23.

Robertson R (1992) *Globalization* London: Sage.

Roche M (1992) *Rethinking Citizenship* Cambridge: Polity.

Rockwell R (1976) 'Historical Trends and Variation in Educational Homogamy' *Journal of Marriage and the Family* 38: 83–95.

Rootes C (1990) 'A New Class? The Higher Educated and the New Politics' Madrid: XII World Congress of Sociology (unpublished).

Rose R and I McAllister (1985) *Voters Begin to Choose* London: Sage.

Saarlvik B, and I Crewe (1983) *Decade of Dealignment* Cambridge: CUP.

Sartori G (1970) 'Concept Misformation in Comparative Politics' *The American Political Science Review* 64 (4): 1033–53.

Saunders P (1978) 'Domestic Property and Social Class' *International Journal of Urban and Regional Research* 2: 233–51.

Saunders P (1989) 'Left Write in Sociology' *Network* (May): 4–5.

Saunders P (1990) *A Nation of Home Owners* London: Unwin Hyman.

Saunders P (1995) 'Might Britain be a Meritocracy?' *Sociology* 29(1): 23–41.

Schmitter P and G Lembruch (eds) (1979) *Trends towards Corporatist Inter-Mediation* London: Sage.

Schumpeter J (1951) *Imperialism and Social Classes* New York: Kelley.

Scott A (1990) *Ideology and the New Social Movements* London: Unwin Hyman.

Scott J (1986) *Capitalist Property and Financial Power* Brighton: Wheatsheaf.

Scott J (1991) *Who Rules Britain?* Cambridge: Polity.

Scott J (1994) 'Class Analysis: Back to the Future' *Sociology* 28(4): 933–42.

Shields R (1992) *Places on the Margin* London: Routledge.

Simmel G (1964) 'The Metropolis and Mental Life' in K Wolff (ed.) *The Sociology of Georg Simmel* Glencoe: Free Press: 409–24.

Sklair L (1991) *Sociology of the Global System* Hemel Hempstead: Harvester Wheatsheaf.

Skocpol T (1985) 'Bringing the State Back In: Strategies of Analysis in Current Research' in P Evans, D Rueschemeyer and T Skocpol (eds) *Bringing the State Back In* Cambridge: CUP: 3–43.

Sørensen A (1991) 'On the Usefulness of Class Analysis in Research on Social Mobility and Socioeconomic Inequality' *Acta Sociologica* 34: 71–87.

Sorokin P (1964) *Social and Cultural Mobility* New York: Free Press.

Stacey M (1960) *Tradition and Change* London: OUP.

Stein M (1967) *The Eclipse of Community* New York: Harper Torchbook.

Steinmetz G and E Wright (1989) 'The Fall and Rise of the Petty Bourgeoisie' *American Journal of Sociology* 94(5): 973–1018.

Stewart A, K Prandy and R Blackburn (1980) *Social Stratification and Occupations* Basingstoke: Macmillan.

Streek W (1992) 'Training and the New Industrial Relations' in M Regini (ed.) *The Future of Labour Movements* London: Sage: 250–69.

Sweezy P (1942) *The Theory of Capitalist Development* New York: Monthly Review.

Szelenyi I and S Szelenyi (1993) 'Changing Patterns of Elite Recruitment in Post-Communist Transformations' Palo Alto: Stanford University (unpublished).

Thompson E (1980) *The Making of the English Working Class* (2nd edn) Harmondsworth: Penguin (first edn 1968).

Toffler A (1980) *The Third Wave* New York: Basic Books.

Touraine A (1981) *The Voice and the Eye: An Analysis of Social Movements* Cambridge: CUP.

Touraine A (1985) 'An Introduction to the Study of Social Movements' *Social Research* 52(4): 749–88.

Trimberger E (1978) *Revolution from Above* New Brunswick: Transaction.

Turner B (1986) *Citizenship and Capitalism: The Debate over Reformism* London: Allen & Unwin.

Turner B (1988) *Status* Milton Keynes: Open UP.

Turner B (1990) 'An Outline of a Theory of Citizenship' *Sociology* 24(2): 189–217.

Turner B (ed.) (1993) *Citizenship and Social Theory* London: Sage.

Tyree A and J Treas (1974) 'The Occupational and Marital Mobility of Women' *American Sociological Review* 39: 293–302.

Urry J (1981) *The Anatomy of Capitalist Societies* London: Macmillan.

US Bureau of the Census (1986) *Statistical Abstract of the United States* Washington: Bureau of Census.

Useem M (1984) *The Inner Circle* Oxford: OUP.

Valentine C (1968) *Culture and Poverty* Chicago: Chicago UP.

Van der Pijl K (1989) 'The International Level' in T Bottomore and R Brym (eds) *The Capitalist Class* Hemel Hempstead: Harvester: 237–66.

Van Liere K and R Dunlap (1980) 'The Social Bases of Environmental Concern' *Public Opinion Quarterly* 44: 181–97.

Visser J (1992) 'Trends in Trade Union Membership' in OECD *Employment Outlook* Paris: OECD: 97–134.

Voslensky M (1984) *Nomenklatura: Anatomy of the Soviet Ruling Class* London: Bodley Head.

Walby S (1990) *Theorizing Patriarchy* Oxford: Blackwell.

Wallerstein I (1974) *The Modern World-System* New York: Academic.

Wallerstein I (1980) *The Modern World-System (vol. II)* New York: Academic.

Warner W (1949) *Democracy in Jonesville* New York: Harper & Row.

Warner W and P Lundt (1941) *The Social Life of a Modern Community* New Haven: Yale UP.

Waters M (1989) 'Patriarchy and Viriarchy' *Sociology* 32(2): 193–211.

Waters M (1990) *Class and Stratification* Melbourne: Longman Cheshire.

Waters M (1991) 'Collapse and Convergence in Class Theory' *Theory and Society* 20: 141–72.

Waters M (1994a) 'Succession in the Stratification Order: a Contribution to the "Death of Class" Debate' *International Sociology* 9(3): 295–312.

Waters M (1994b) *Modern Sociological Theory* London: Sage.

Waters M (1995a) *Globalization* London: Routledge.

Waters M (1995b) 'The Thesis of the Loss of the Perfect Market' *British Journal of Sociology* 46(3): 409–28.

Waters M (1995c) *Daniel Bell* London: Routledge.

Weber M (1948) *From Max Weber* London: Routledge.

Weber M (1978) *Economy and Society* Berkeley: California UP (first published 1922).

Weber M (1982) 'Selections from *Economy and Society*, vols 1 and 2, and *General Economic History*' in A Giddens and D Held (eds) *Classes, Power and Conflict* Berkeley: California UP: 120–32.

Wesolowski W (1979) *Classes, Strata and Power* London: Routledge (first published 1966).

Westergaard J (1972) 'Sociology: The Myth of Classlessness' in R Blackburn (ed.) *Ideology in Social Science* Glasgow: Collins: 119–63.

Westergaard J and H Resler (1975) *Class in a Capitalist Society* London: Heinemann.

Western B (1995) 'A Comparative Study of Working-Class Disorganization: Union Decline in Eighteen Advanced Capitalist Countries' *American Sociological Review* 60(2): 179–201.

Wild R (1974) *Bradstow* Sydney: Angus & Robertson.

Wilensky H (1981) 'Democratic Corporatism, Consensus and Social Policy' in *Welfare State in Crisis* Paris: OECD.

Williams C (1981) *Open Cut* Sydney: Allen & Unwin.

Williams R (1959) *Culture and Society 1780–1950* London: Chatto.

Williams R (1975) *The Country and the City* London: Paladin.

Williams R (1983) *Keywords* London: Fontana.

Willis P (1990) *Common Culture* Milton Keynes: Open UP.

Wilson W (1987) *The Truly Disadvantaged* Chicago: Chicago UP.

Wolff E (1987) *International Comparisons of the Distribution of Household Wealth* Oxford: OUP.

Wolff E (1991) 'The Distribution of Household Wealth' in L Osberg (ed.) *Economic Inequality and Poverty* Armonk: Sharpe: 92–133.

Wolff E (1992) 'Changing Inequality of Wealth' *American Economic Review* 82(2): 552–8.

Wright E (1978) *Class, Crisis and the State* London: New Left.

Wright E (1985) *Classes* London: Verso.

Wright E (1989) 'A General Framework for the Analysis of Class Structure' in E Wright (ed.) *The Debate on Classes* London: Verso: 3–43.

Wright E and B Martin (1987) 'The Transformation of the American Class Structure 1960–1980' *American Journal of Sociology* 93:1–29.

Young M and P Willmott (1962) *Family and Kinship in East London* Harmondsworth: Penguin.

Zagorski K (1976) *Zmiany struktury i ruchliwosc spoleczna w Polsce* [Changes of structure and social mobility in Poland] Warsaw: GUS.

Zagorski K (1984) *Social Mobility into Post-Industrial Society: Socio-Economic Structure and Fluidity of the Australian Workforce* Canberra: RSSS ANU.

Zagorski K and J Kelley (1994) 'Changes in Egalitarian-Inegalitarian Attitudes and their Consequences' Sydney: Post-Communism Conference (unpublished).

# Index